1.00

THE AMERICAN RED CROSS
IN THE GREAT WAR

THE MACMILLAN COMPANY
NEW YORK · BOSTON · CHICAGO · DALLAS
ATLANTA · SAN FRANCISCO

MACMILLAN & CO., LIMITED
LONDON · BOMBAY · CALCUTTA
MELBOURNE

THE MACMILLAN CO. OF CANADA, LTD.
TORONTO

NATIONAL HEADQUARTERS OF THE
AMERICAN RED CROSS

THE AMERICAN RED CROSS
IN THE GREAT WAR

BY

HENRY P. DAVISON
CHAIRMAN OF THE WAR COUNCIL
OF THE AMERICAN RED CROSS

New York
THE MACMILLAN COMPANY
1919

Copyright, 1919,
By THE AMERICAN NATIONAL RED CROSS.

Set up and electrotyped. Published October, 1919.

Norwood Press
J. S. Cushing Co. — Berwick & Smith Co.
Norwood, Mass., U.S.A.

Dedicated

TO

THE MILLIONS OF WOMEN

CHILDREN AND MEN

WHO

THROUGH

THE AMERICAN RED CROSS

WORKED AND SACRIFICED

THAT THE MISERY OF

WAR MIGHT BE

ALLEVIATED

FOREWORD

It is the effort of this book to set forth the scope, character and effect of the work of the American Red Cross during the Great War. When the war closed more than thirty million Americans were enrolled in the organization. Some of these were in foreign fields; most of them were at home. But, in one way or another, they were all helping. All of them working together made up the American Red Cross.

Stories of special sacrifice or devotion cannot be given here and yet few organizations have so closely touched the great currents of human life. Detailed narratives will accordingly follow this book. I have sought here to summarize the work of the thirty millions as a whole. To characterize the Red Cross work of any man or woman, or to attempt to describe it with any regard to proper perspective, would be invidious if not impossible. I have therefore omitted the mention of names. The highest satisfaction any worker in the Red Cross can derive from his work is from the fact that the work itself was well done.

The files of the War Council have been freely drawn upon in the preparation of this book. And I want to make special acknowledgment to every member of the force at headquarters, and to the special correspondents and staffs of our foreign commissions, who seemingly have vied with one another in supplying me, either orally or in writing, with material without which the scope of this book could not be what it is. Indeed it may accurately be said that the book itself is a product of the American Red Cross.

H. P. Davison.

New York,
September 20, 1919.

CONTENTS

PART I

ILLUSTRATIONS

THE AMERICAN RED CROSS
IN THE GREAT WAR

THE AMERICAN RED CROSS IN THE GREAT WAR

PART I

CHAPTER I

WHEN THE STORM BURST

Nationalization — President Wilson Becomes President of the Red Cross — Red Cross Mercy Ship — Increase in Membership — American Relief Clearing House in Paris — Departure of the German Ambassador from Washington — President Declares War — Appointment of the War Council — The First Drive for $100,000,000.

IN the year 1905 the American National Red Cross, profiting, perhaps, not a little by the lessons of the Spanish War, was finally and permanently incorporated and nationalized; the President of the United States became its president; and the War Department its auditor. It had behind it the full sponsorship of the United States Government; its books were open; it was the property of the people and in their hands. In that sense, and in almost no other, it was ready for the frightful thing that Germany was preparing for the world.

It is, of course, not my intention to do more than refer to the activities of the Red Cross of that day. Save for prompt and effective relief to sufferers from fire and flood and every other form of calamity, no matter where occurring, it pursued a helpful but on the whole rather a pacific and uneventful course. The Red Cross of the first three years of the Great War may, likewise, be told briefly. All the effort of the organization at that time — and there was earnest effort, however stereotyped, in many directions — may be said to have centered around the conscription of funds, the enlistment of personnel, and the gathering of supplies to meet an infinitely greater demand for help than ever before. Factories were driven to top speed in the production of materials. Warehouses were filled to bursting with incoming gifts. Yet, in the face of so great a necessity, the leaders of the Red Cross were hampered by the laggard movement of monetary contributions. The psychology of this unwillingness to loosen the purse-strings is clear now. The truth was that America was still cased in its shell; it resented a war that it did not understand.

None the less, a month after the German troops crossed the Belgium border, a Red Cross ship sailed away, — a German keel, painted with the authorized red strake which, by agreement of the nations, marked the mercy ship, — and distributed her hospital units and medical supplies, her gauze and anæsthetics, her hospital garments, cigarettes, and camp comforts for the fighting men of countries whose prayers had not availed to save them from this stroke of manifest destiny. Into France and England, into Russia and Serbia, into every place where the blight of war had fallen, even into Germany, these well-chosen benefactions found their way. To be sure it was a very small incident, this sailing of that stout little ship, and in the shadow of a year or more of vast accomplishment no wonder that it seems indistinct and ineffably far away.

But it is all an old story now —even that pregnant time when surely, if slowly, the picture on our moral retina was changing; when one after another the studied German insults, the revelation of guile, the wanton destruction of peaceful vessels, the brutal violations of neutrality, in short, the whole train of deliberate offenses against decency, were preparing the inevitable result.

. . . .

Nothing could be more dramatic than the change that came over the United States in the first three months of the year 1917. It was almost magical in its swiftness. The war was at the summit of its intensity; the tortured Allies, armies and populace alike, had come almost to the extremity of effort; conditions in France were as ominous as they were heartbreaking. This supreme moment found many people without the bare necessities of life. The roads were full of the homeless, the hungry, and the half clad. The cities were clogged with them! Simultaneously, in the United States, the weary period of inaction was drawing to its end. The signs were no longer to be misread. Honor had been stretched to its last shred of endurance and continued peace, it was plain, could only be had at the price of shame. During all this wretched time the conduct of the American Red Cross was, to say the least, most creditable. Crippled by public inertia, by the popular inclination to keep out of war at all hazards, those who guided the destinies of the organization nevertheless strained every nerve, utilized every resource, to prepare for the storm which they knew was bound to come. They were held back by the ancient habit of the people — of waiting to give to the Red Cross until some great catastrophe had shocked the world and newspaper pictures from the zone of disaster furnished ocular proof of ruin, disease, and starvation. Day and night, however, they labored, formulating plans, creating a nucleus which proved of inexpressible value when the day of trial arrived, and saved months of slow and retarding toil. By dint of the most industrious and carefully organized effort they increased the membership

in a few months from 22,000 to 280,000, and the number of
Chapters by more than a hundred.

At this period President Wilson penned an appeal to the
American people on behalf of this sorely tried organization,
in which he said : "It is for you to decide whether the most
prosperous nation in the world will allow its national relief
organization to keep up with its work or withdraw from a
field where there exists the greatest need ever recorded in
history."

And even the President's summons failed to arouse the
people from their lethargy.

Dissecting the military and civilian needs, incident to the
creation of an army, the Red Cross organized and equipped
base hospitals as rapidly as they could accumulate the
money. The service to our forces on the Mexican border
had given some opportunity for practical training, which
they improved to the uttermost. They directed their relief
work for the Allied armies — such as they were able to
perform — through the American Relief Clearing House in
Paris, which had been organized early in the war to cen-
tralize and promote all American activities. By so doing
they fortified and insured the efficacy of that institution
which, afterwards, was classed as one of the greatest relief
organizations in Europe. What that alliance meant is
shown by the fact that from that time on all members of the
Clearing House wore the uniform of the American Red
Cross.

From February, 1917, events moved with a rapidity
that, in retrospect, leaves one almost breathless, though at
the time it seemed painfully slow. On the second of February Count Von Bernstorff, the German Ambassador, was
handed his papers and, on the following day, the Red Cross
moved its scanty belongings into the New Memorial building, as yet without heat and equipment, and still littered
with the débris of construction. The vice-chairman sent

out to the 267 Chapters a telegram which deserves to be immortalized in the history of the Red Cross, and in the history of humanity, as a master-work of preparedness : —

"If not already active appoint following committees : finance, hospital garments and surgical supplies, comfort bags (see Circular 126), packing and shipping, publicity and information, motor service; appoint committee on coöperation with outside organizations. . . . If not already done appoint committee on education (outlined in Circular 144). . . . Possibility of organizing sanitary training detachments should be taken up at once. (See Circular 136.)"

That was on a Saturday. On Sunday and for many long days afterward the answers by wire and mail came pouring into the great building. The marble halls were crowded with stenographers, who worked from dawn till dark and long after in a temperature far below freezing, answering the thousands of letters that came from all corners of the country asking for orders or instructions how to form Chapters.

Then March came with its swift making of history: the Zimmermann note stripped off Germany's mask; and the House upheld the bill for the arming of American merchant-men. Inauguration Day, usually a pompous ceremonial, passed like a mere incident in the Washington routine. Two days later the last Romanoff abandoned in terror the throne of all the Russias and the German annihilation of the Eastern front had begun. The German plot for a Hindu uprising in India startled England. Three American ships in a day went down before the German submarines. Berlin was "bitterly surprised" at America's resentment, and fifteen thousand people crowded in Madison Square Garden and cheered for war. The pacifists were pleading for delay with a thousand tongues, and the "willful men" in the Senate still struggled to keep the muzzle on the dogs of war.

And then, decently and in order, the thing was done. On

April 6th Congress, called by the President, in special session, voted war. Twenty thousand militia were called out, and then four thousand more; enlistment in the Navy was ordered for immediate service overseas; money was placed at the disposal of the President, and the selective draft system was adopted. Men in khaki, forerunners of millions that were to follow, began to appear in the city streets. English and French Commissions hurried to America. The United States was launched on the greatest and most perilous conflict in history.

Meanwhile, the Red Cross, like the Army, to the utmost limit of its means had mapped out the work of the "crowded hour" that was at hand. Base hospital units for the Army had been multiplied with all possible speed, and were steadily increasing throughout the country. Twenty-five were already organized and equipped ready for service, and four more were in progress. Three field columns had been formed, and three additional bases for navy hospitals organized. Through the Chapters and other organizations, surgical dressings, garments, and other supplies to the value of eight thousand dollars for each unit had been made and contributed, in addition to all the offerings that had already been sent abroad. The Red Cross had enrolled more than seven thousand graduate nurses, and plans for the training of another regiment of nurses were under way. Even the little knowledge that we had at hand of Europe in the throes of war was sufficient to teach us that every doctor and every nurse should prepare; that every city and town should be ready on the instant to get under its burden; and that voluntary service and coördination of relief agencies, under the Red Cross, was a crying necessity.

Naturally, the country had no understanding of all this. It did not know that the Red Cross was not in shape to take care of an Army, although neither the army nor the Red Cross was blind to this fact. From studious investigations

in Europe the Red Cross knew in detail the most effective
methods of organizing base hospitals, medical supply bases,
ambulance sections, civilian relief centers, and all other
way-stations of mercy and restoration.

"I spent a year and a half," wrote one of the organizers of that early
Red Cross, "in the heart of the war in Europe — one year of it as the
American Delegate of the Commission for Relief in Belgium, in charge
of the Belgium Province at Antwerp. I saw how refugees must be fed
and clothed, sheltered and administered to, how those dependent on the
soldiers at the front must be assisted, and how the civilian population
must be organized and energized, if it is to survive where the waves of
war have passed over it. To do such work adequately means the loyal
support of every man, woman and child in the land. We have this in
Belgium. To do the work which the Red Cross should do, and must do,
in America, requires the support of far more members than the American
Red Cross has to-day. The work should touch all humanity, alien or
friendly, rich or poor, high or low."

But while the membership under active urging was increasing with great rapidity, the money lagged. It was
clear enough now that the task facing the Red Cross was
no longer a matter of sending a Red Cross ship to scatter its
hastily collected supplies around the globe. Red Cross
shipments, if its work was to be competent and nearly equal
to the needs, would be measured in fleets; and such a
Red Cross required a wider horizon, a longer arm, and a
deeper pocket. It had been computed on the basis of the
old condition that the organization must have at least five
millions of dollars to meet the needs of the war.

.   .   .   .

On the 10th of May, 1917, President Wilson appointed a
War Council for the American National Red Cross, and I
was asked to take the chairmanship.

It was not long before it became very apparent that our
mission, at least in the narrow aspect of it, would be to
look after the men of our own Army and to assist the

War Department in doing the things it could not do alone or that did not fall wholly within its province. That was indeed our duty, but the bitter sacrifices of the other nations for three long years had brought into the equation the vital and imperative question, however illuminating the answer later, whether there was in the world — or in America — any such thing as national gratitude and appreciation; whether plain, simple humanity had been utterly submerged in an ocean of commercialism.

In this whole development the War Council held firmly to two things: first, a vision of our bounden duty as a people; and, second, an abiding faith that our national heart, when we found it, would prove to be in the right place. Nobody could fail to discern the need: Thousands of old men, women, and children were homeless and starving, fleeing before a relentless enemy; whole towns and cities were crumbling into dust under the increasing pounding of the guns; food, clothing, and medicine were lacking; and disease was raising its ugly head in the wake of death and desolation. If ever the brotherhood of man was to be demonstrated and proved, the hour had surely come.

But while emphasis gradually was laid upon the necessity of money, if we were to do our part, nevertheless we of the War Council did not lose sight of the fact that money would be the smallest part of it — merely the bridge by which we must cross to the land where our duty called us and where our opportunity lay. You might, we agreed, pack the building with dollars and still fail to do the thing we ought to do. Our concentration here was about the amount of money we should ask for. In working out this problem we discussed at length about a request for twenty-five millions of dollars. The essential thing, if the Red Cross was to accomplish its maximum of good, was to have everybody share in it; to be able to go now, at the very climax of need, to the suffering people of Europe, carrying the message of good-will from all the people of America, — the poor, the rich, the young, and the old, all asking the privilege of helping them in their distress.

And so the appeal went out to the country for a hundred million dollars. It was a neat sum but, as time has shown, small for the magnitude of the work involved. In taking account of stock we found that the Red Cross statement showed one liability. True, it was a moral one, making it all the more binding, viz., the obligation to meet and relieve suffering caused by the world tragedy. But it also showed one asset — an asset that overbalanced all : the good-will of the American people. In sum total the statement seemed an excellent one to me. I believed that the American people would see far more in the Red Cross effort than simply taking care of our own men and that they would look upon it, as I did, as an opportunity to do the great big human thing; nor did I have the smallest doubt but that the campaign to raise that money would start a spirit of giving and of sacrifice that would mean a great deal more than the money itself.

There were obstacles in the way : summer was coming on and the people were preparing to go away; moreover, the first Liberty Loan drive had the right of way and nothing must interfere with that. We were all bound to take off our coats and help it. It was finally and definitely decided that we should fix June 18–25 — three days after the closing of the loan drive — as Red Cross week. From that time on it was like a military campaign. The gentleman who had been chosen to head the Executive Committee for the campaign went at the task like a veritable Foch. Like Foch he certainly proved to be a great offensive commander, and his staff were of the same dynamic character.

We had one month, to be exact, in which to prepare for this task. A New York friend of the Red Cross set a keynote for the undertaking by an initial gift of a million dollars.

It is my belief that it was this inspirational act that gave to the whole undertaking an almost decisive influence. An interesting feature was the calling to Washington of some 450 leading men from all parts of the country for the purpose of laying before them the foundation of our plans. The conference, strictly speaking, developed into a great patriotic gathering and resulted in enlisting the services of a group of men with large experience in financial matters and in the raising of funds.

The next step was to extend the organization. The country was mapped out into four divisions, each with a director in charge, and under these were 114 field agents and an office force that grew to more than 300 members. Presently, and while the whole country was organizing, we were flooded with letters and telegrams, all of which must be answered. It seemed as if all the brains and energy in the world were concentrated on delivering the message to the people, awakening their interest, and getting results.

The whole country was humming with activity long before the drive started. Men left important positions to come and ask what they could do. They were given a desk and a job and went at it. And when the local workers wanted "ammunition," it was provided in the form of advertising copy, placards, street-car signs, banners, slogans for electric-signs, pictures for lantern slides, material for speeches, sermons and lectures, newspaper features, and advice without end. And, curiously enough, the public never realized that all through that fevered time when city, town, and country were at white heat over the drive, the Red Cross organization was busier than it had ever been in its life, planning and putting into action the work of relief which the money was to do.

With the team leaders it was a game, and they played it with all the sporting joy in the world. Everywhere people vied with one another in giving. Rival cities strove with one another to be first in raising their allotment, and then started a new contest to see which should go farthest beyond the mark.

But why recount now the story of that week! It is still fresh in everybody's memory. It was a typical American accomplishment, and when at the close of the campaign it was known that the country had given $115,000,000, there was rejoicing like that which follows a great political victory. Better far than that, for it was the rejoicing of a great people in that they had demonstrated a vast capacity for unselfishness. And there was still more good news to come, at least to the managers of the campaign: it was found that the collecting of this great fund, thanks to the willingness of everybody to help, had cost only a little over one half of one per cent.

CHAPTER II

MASSING THE FORCES OF MERCY

Plans of the War Council — Appointment of Foreign Commission — Muster Roll of Volunteers — Word from General Pershing — Decentralization — The Working Machine at National Headquarters.

AGAINST the dark background of that eventful year few things, naturally, stand out more luminous to me than the arrival of the Red Cross at a commanding financial position. Obviously, such an increase in money power meant that we could do for our soldiers and sailors all that we should do; it meant that our people indorsed our purpose to go to the peoples of Europe in the way that we should go; and, finally, it meant nothing more nor less than a resolve on the part of the Nation that liberty should triumph at any cost. . . .

There was no time, however, to dream over the great mission of the future. In the numberless informal conferences which it held prior to its first formal meeting on the 21st of May, 1917, the Red Cross War Council had taken the measure of its task and proceeded with the work of massing the forces of mercy side by side with the raising of the great army which America, now awake and full of purpose, was creating in record time, and for the doing of which we had the faith, the credit, and the women — the problem of the moment being how to capitalize them all.

In general our plan divided itself into two problems: first, to get the necessary relief to Europe in the shortest possible time, and so avert what we now know would have developed before long into a colossal catastrophe; second, to organize ample means of caring for all the various needs of our own army. For the solution of this problem we had three possessions of value : the first was the machine which our predecessors in control of the Red Cross had worked to build up ; the second was a now rapidly growing membership and Chapter organization; the third, — and of inestimable importance in the work of expanding the machine and of putting it on a war footing, — was the volunteer service of an army of some of the most competent, aggressive, and experienced men in the country, and of women who had brains, initiative, and the inborn quality of leadership. Indeed, the day was an exceptional one which did not reveal new Red Cross assets of superlative value. It began to be borne in upon us that we had not more than half read the Red Cross balance sheet.

It was not a matter of sentiment alone that brought the War Council, at its very first meeting, to a realization that our duty was to get help to France; on the contrary, it was a clear business proposition to ascertain without a minute's delay just what was needed there first and to start it on its way there as early as possible. We had a sufficiently clear picture of the situation ; what we needed was to measure it up, even if only tentatively, in the terms of necessary dollars.

Then it was that the Red Cross asked General Pershing what it could do for him, and almost immediately came his answering cable : —

"If you want to do something for me for God's sake 'buck up the French.' They have been fighting for three years and are getting ready for their fourth winter. They have borne a tremendous burden, and whatever assistance we can lend them promptly will be of the greatest possible value."

It must not, however, for a moment be supposed that the spirit of the *poilu* was broken or that he was not fighting with the dash and unflinching courage of his race; but there were sectors where the conditions of war and the long continuation of service were beyond the endurance of body and soul and, added to which, there was the consuming anxiety which preyed upon the soldier from the devastated regions concerning the whereabouts and welfare of his family.

To this end a commission of eighteen men, bent on clearing away a mountain of misery, was dispatched to Europe, and landed in France on the 13th of June.

Meantime, the American Ambulance in Paris needed new cars; and the Civilian Relief in France, trying to cope with the tremendous problem of the soldiers, the refugees, and the numberless pitiful children, called by cable for women's and children's clothing, preserved milk, seeds, farm tools, and money for the mayors of villages to distribute among the starving refugees that had been quartered upon them. Further funds were needed for the purchase of hospital supplies and hospital garments, rubber goods, and surgical instruments — all matters of life and death.

Unquestionably, those early days were full days. Headquarters was on the tiptoe of expectancy and perilously near chaos. The whole world, it seemed to me, was writing to Red Cross Headquarters at Washington upon a thousand-and-one different subjects.

Through the end of May and into June, while the Commission to France was hurrying across the Atlantic and the War Fund drive was going on, we were trying with one hand to handle the incoming business, and with the other to frame up an organization that should be broad and strong enough in all directions to "carry on" as long as the war would last. The success or failure of this whole undertaking hung upon it. In due time we chose legal counsel, and selected a great New York trust company to handle the money end of the business; we formally appointed the

DECEMBER 16th '23

WHERE
COLVMBIA
SETS
HER NAME
LET
EVERYONE
OF YOU
FOLLOW
HER

AN AMERICAN RED CROSS SUMMONS.

Secretary of the Treasury of the United States as treasurer of the war fund, and the trust company provided from its office force a corps of forty trained men to look after the finances. And while we were seeking everywhere for experienced men to fill important positions, it was a ray of encouragement to receive this message from a former United States Minister : "You will find men everywhere are ready to coöperate enthusiastically with you to a greater extent than you are perhaps aware."

One by one, as the expansion progressed, we found them. All through the hot summer months we kept on building up the machine. During the day the War Council held meetings at Headquarters, and in the evening, to change the scene and put new life into our work, we continued them at my house in Washington. There was no let-up to the volume of correspondence from all over the country; nor was there any cessation of the cries for help which kept the cables continuously busy.

But while the work of foreign relief was imperative, it involved, perhaps, less of difficulty than did the solving of the problem of selecting the right men for the Commissions, which were being formed to represent and to do the work of the American Red Cross in foreign countries. What we required was to get men who, although sympathetic and human in their appreciation, had expert knowledge, unbounded energy, initiative, cold judgment, keen perception of the point of attack, and the faculty of instant decision and consummate skill in organization; we needed men who could cut red tape, men who could rise to emergencies; we needed men of tact and diplomacy for the handling of what, unquestionably, was a most difficult mission. For there are in all the world no more sensitive peoples than the Latin races, and to have gone to them in such a crisis with anything that bore the faintest tinge of charity or condescension would have been fatal to the intent and purpose of the Red Cross. Our money would have been given its value as money but nothing more. Here, again, the future and the cause of humanity hung in a fine balance. The story of what was achieved in France and Italy will show with what delicacy this critical phase of the work was carried through. But while the task of planning for the relief of Europe and determining what was best to do first was put squarely upon the shoulders of the Commissions which, one after another, were rapidly dispatched to the various countries, nothing was enacted, whether military, diplomatic, or financial, which had not received thorough consideration from every angle and with confirmative advice from those within whose special province it fell.

From the very beginning it was the controlling principle of the War Council that nothing, however small, should be done which could not bear careful scrutiny and which was not fully warranted by existing conditions. The Red Cross forever maintains a scrupulous regard for the fact that it is the people's servant and is spending the people's money; its books and its transactions at all times have been open to public inspection. All of which, nevertheless, increased materially the burden of the work. At a very early stage of the proceedings, therefore, it became apparent that the Headquarters' force, augmented though it had been, was soon coming to the point where it would be submerged unless some means of simplifying its duties could be found.

In appointing a general manager the Red Cross found a man who was versed in the handling of big problems and knew how to reduce them to little ones. He solved the difficulty with the word "decentralization" which, in this case, resolved itself into the partitioning of the United States into thirteen divisions, each division a smaller Red Cross, with all its departments and bureaus under a divisional chief and a force complete in every detail with the various lines of endeavor firmly and clearly outlined. It cleared the sky in a day — it saved the situation. When once the foundation was complete, the War Council had no more to do with the Chapters or any of their activities, save in the way of judging the needs, devising methods, and fixing standards. The Chapter's business was regulated in the department to which it belonged by the divisional officers. The division manager was the general and supreme in his division. He was to his division what the general manager in Washington was to the entire organization. Washington Headquarters was now free to proceed with the handling of the larger problems which, with the widening of the sphere of effort and the progress in army-building, were growing daily to greater magnitude and importance. It was simply taking a leaf from the book of armies and of big business, and it multiplied the efficiency of the whole Red Cross organization at a time when efficiency, or the lack of it, spelled victory or defeat. The main problem of the division arrangement lay, as it did in the Commissions to Europe, in selecting with the most studious care the men to head the divisions. It was not until September that this important matter was finally settled and the roster of division chiefs and their forces brought to completion.

In order to secure the maximum result from all lines of effort, it was necessary to expand and reform in many points the work of the several departments. The Chapters and the membership, which in the preceding year had been substantially extended, now increased automatically and with a speed which told clearly enough that the human force throughout the country was aroused and at work. In January, 1917, the Red Cross managers had started a campaign for a million members before the following year. By September there were six millions, and the Chapters, numbering six hundred when war was declared, now ran into the thousands. At the end of the membership drive in Decem-

c

ber there were 22,000,000 names on the lists. All through the summer singers, actors, and people of every trade and calling taxed their wits to devise entertainments for the benefit of the Red Cross. To enumerate the sources of contribution is impossible. The stimulation of interest, which in earlier days had been one of our vital concerns, had ceased to bother us. Interest had stimulated itself.

Meanwhile the Chapter organization had done its work well. Production was going forward in a wave. It was the age of wool; everybody was knitting! In the large cities, particularly the division centers, model workrooms were established; to the last little auxiliary in the farthest town everybody was doing something for the Red Cross.

The divisional plan, distributing as it did the burden of details, had enabled Headquarters to do effective things in standardizing and perfecting the system of production, collection, and shipment. So that before the summer was far advanced a great volume of earnest, but misdirected effort had been turned into established channels, its effectiveness doubled, and confusions and waste of strength and nervous tissue greatly reduced.

Millions of circulars were sent out to the Chapters through the divisional offices, giving diagrams and explicit directions for the making of knitted goods and other requirements, not only for equipment of our Army but for the hospital work of the units which were hurried to war, and to supply the urgent needs of Allied hospital service now so sorely taxed. With an eye to future requirements the educational work of the Chapter organization was vigorously expanded. The Red Cross, like the Government, was making its preparations for a long war. With this in mind, training classes were established and the Junior Red Cross, so long looked upon as "child's play," was converted into a large contributive factor, both for the present and the future.

Throughout the country there was a multitude of willing

souls, bursting with patriotism, eager to help in some way, but debarred by sex, age, or physical infirmity from going into the trenches. The Red Cross was their lodestar. It was the work of the Department of Development to concentrate, to organize, to direct this mass of energy. Much of it also was absorbed by what had previously borne the stilled and unconvincing name of "Civilian Relief," but which, now that its day of supreme usefulness had come, was made over into a practical instrument under the expressive title of "Home Service."

In the schedule which the Red Cross was perfecting, Home Service was the ultimate power behind the man behind the gun, the force that never slept, and that must know, from day to day, the condition, the needs, and the worries of the families left behind. As the building of the Army progressed, no branch of Red Cross effort gave more substantial proof of its value than this. It was the guardian and the surety of national morals. What Home Service did towards helping to better the condition of the *poilu* it likewise did for the American soldier at the front and the reserve army of waiting folks at home.

The vital factor in Home Service is neighborly feeling, sympathy, appreciation, personal approach. For that reason its work had to be correlated with the Chapters; and so in every Chapter there was a Home Service section, not bothered with knitting, paying no heed to bandages or hospital garments, but concentrating on the personal needs, the strictly private troubles of the soldier's family. It soon became apparent that the field of Home Service would grow wider with every fresh detachment of men sent overseas. An educational system was devised centering in the colleges and summer schools, but extending in less elaborate form down to the Chapter branches, to teach both theory and practice to fit people for what was bound to be a necessary and in more respects than one a delicate mission. In a few months an immense work of organization was done in the field.

The selective draft was now in full swing. The tramp, tramp, tramp of the men of twenty-one to thirty-one of every state, city, and township was ringing in our ears. This was no mere memory of '61! In the Red Cross we lived from day to day in the consciousness of the fact that the Army's manifold needs was hard upon our heels. The Army was only one item in our duty, but it was our first charge under the terms of our charter and, besides, it was America — our home folks. Moreover, in the War and Navy Departments whose servants, primarily, the Red Cross was, we had superiors who wanted quick delivery.

The equipment of soldiers with sweaters, helmets, wristlets, socks, comfort kits, and all the other manifold things necessary to keep them comfortable was, to say the least, a substantial order, yet it was merely an incident in the program. For the training of its multitudes the Government, at that moment, was building thirty-four camps and cantonments in various parts of the country, and the Red Cross must be on hand in them all prepared to do everything and more than it was created to do. There would be sick soldiers and cases of accidents, for which we must furnish hospital units, nurses, and medical supplies; also, we must have competent people there to look after our work, for this was not a case where a casual clerk or shiftless office boy would do. We must provide housing for a Red Cross "lighthouse" in every camp to which the soldier, worried or in need, could find his way; and when he left training and moved from one camp to another or to the ship which was to bear him away on the great adventure, we must break the journey with a little food, a little cheer, and medical attendance if necessary. There was welfare work around the camp, too, and care, both material and moral, of the adjacent communities. There was the maintenance of the

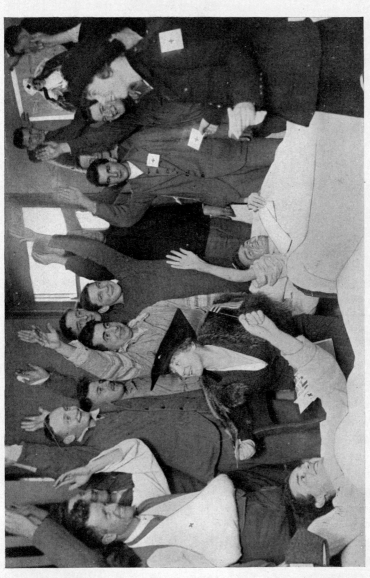

ENROLLMENT OF THE MEN OF WARD A AT DARTFORD HOSPITAL IN THE AMERICAN RED CROSS FOR THE CHRISTMAS DRIVE.

Red Cross Motor Corps, not alone for our own use, but for the Army and the Navy. And there was the Ambulance Corps, with forty-five companies of over 5000 men in training and in service.

So through the first summer and fall we drove ahead, whip and spur, gathering in the people, enrolling nurses, erecting buildings, buying supplies and machinery and means of transit, establishing canteens and equipping the Red Cross at every possible point where it could come in contact with the life and needs of the soldier. The War Department issued a call for 25,000 nurses before the end of the year. All over the country we carried on a nurses' drive; and the Department of Nursing in every one of the thirteen divisions tried to surmount many and grave obstacles. We combed the medical profession of the country, too, for doctors to go into service; we organized a Medical Advisory Committee of famous doctors and sanitary experts to give counsel in all matters relating to medicine and sanitation.

I have tried here merely to sketch in outline the various departments of duty which had to be mapped out, peopled, and set in motion, and to produce a sort of composite picture, necessarily inadequate, of the Red Cross in this vast formative period. At times it seemed well-nigh impossible to meet the accumulation of simultaneous demands. While careful and far-reaching were the plans for organization of our domestic work, oftentimes it became necessary to make fundamental changes, experiment having foretold failure to discharge our duties when the supreme test should come; and all this time the heart-breaking cry of suffering Europe was never for a moment still.

The work in France, as I have previously stated, had been started first, but within a very short time we had commissions to Russia, Rumania, Serbia, and Italy. A Commissioner and Deputy Commissioner for England had been chosen and a special department for Belgium appointed under the direction of the Commission to France.

Moreover, in connection with these, we had not neglected to build up a Department of Supplies and Transportation to handle all the millions of dollars' worth of purchases, the collection of the vast supplies from the Chapters, the provision of material, rail freights, the procurement of ocean tonnage, and the delivery of all the Red Cross benefactions to the points where they were needed. Further in the background, but indispensable to every day's labors, were the advisory committees to various departments, legal advisers who canvassed all our transactions, — particularly with regard to international relations, — a general manager whose function was to complete the coördination of all branches, solve problems, and smooth out rough places, a Bureau of Naval Affairs connecting the Red Cross in all lines of its service with the Navy and its requirements, while in the foreground was the Department of Publicity, establishing more firmly, as the work grew, our link with the public which stood behind the work.

CHAPTER III

THE COMRADESHIP

Divisions and Chapters

Orders from Abroad — The Response of Women — Knitting no Longer in the Feminine Gender — New Methods and Machines — Evolution of the System — Total Production of Chapters — Army Mending — Emergency Orders — Red Cross Motor Corps — Canteen Workers — First Aid, Home Dietetics, etc. — Home Service — Total Number of Chapters and Members — Fourteenth Division.

THAT which we call a Red Cross Chapter is a highly perfected piece of social machinery. Its motor-power is supplied by the highest and yet the commonest human impulses and its product, applied humanity, is the bright hope of a war-wrung world; but its high mission is based firmly upon modern business principles. Romance flees from the committee reports, the organization charts, the careful records, the waybills and invoices, and all the matter-of-fact and dreary system that insures the arrival of bandages and nurses in a plague-stricken East and the temperature of the coffee in a local canteen. Only the enthusiast with a pure passion for organization derives a real thrill from the knowledge that "a Chapter is a geographical unit having jurisdiction over a county or large city"; that "it is responsible for all Red Cross activities in its territory"; that it organizes this territory for convenience into Branches which miniature itself, and Auxiliaries which carry on one line of Red Cross service; that its officers and executive committee are elected annually by all the members; that it

23

reports its activities in detail to one of the fourteen Division Headquarters; that it must be a complete miniature Red Cross with a committee in charge of every line of authorized Red Cross activity, so that the line of communication may remain unbroken from Washington to the members of the tiniest branch and none fail to respond to a national call for help.

Dry as dust it seems on paper, with its analysis of administrative committees (Development, Publicity, Finance) and productive committees (Chapter Production, Military Relief, Home Service, Nursing Activities, Junior Membership), with its provision for dividing membership and subscription between local and national activities, yet the perfected machine is the triumph of hard work. It is a skillful compromise between elasticity to local conditions and control from headquarters, and it was evolved under the tremendous pressure of war conditions, while new Chapters were being installed and veterans were running at top speed.

Let it not be thought, however, that a Red Cross Chapter is merely a sublimated sewing circle. It is the applied humanity of its community. It represents the organized forces of friendliness and it applies them in ways as varied and as colorful as human need. Let me select as an example a call for supplies that was flashed underseas from a Red Cross outpost in some No Man's Land of want! Divided and subdivided it sped unerringly along the familiar lines from Headquarters to Division, to Chapter, to Branch, to Auxiliary until in the folds of a hundred hills, along marshaled city blocks, at village cross-roads each item of that order busied the hard-earned leisure of a woman's hands. Or, a depot-master who reported a troop-train headed east and four hours late; though it was in the weary dead of night the Motor Corps brought the Canteeners to the tracks on time to hand out coffee and sandwiches, postal cards, and words of cheer. Under cover of laconic entries in the production reports, "Christmas bags, 500,000," "Repairing 1,000,000 socks," the women in the Chapter workrooms mothered a million boys in camp. Did the Government ask for nurses or fruit-pits or tin-foil or platinum, then forth from Chapter Headquarters went campaigners, speakers, posters, to rake the highways and byways for recruits. The invisible cohorts of the comradeship rode east and west and north and south along the winding ways of all the world, drawing a cordon of safety around the dooryards of home, spreading the wisdom of physical well-being, and guarding the hearth fires of those who had gone to war.

Chapter members had a great deal of hard work during the war and very little glamour. But to those who would see visions and dream dreams Centreville and its thousand counterparts were just behind the trenches. They were the Red Cross bases for money, for supplies, and for inspiration. To such souls all the rest of the organization was merely the line of communication that linked them to a hundred fronts.

Woman's classic part in war is to send her men away with a smile and then wait. Somewhere she must find the strength to bear that waiting; the women of the Great War found it in the countless workrooms of the Red Cross. In the concourses of railroad terminals, in department stores, and in hastily transformed offices, in Sunday Schools, and in libraries the quiet, white-garbed women sat with flying fingers and thoughts that kept pace with the swift whir of machines turning out the endless yards of gauze and cotton for the war-locked lines in France. This is the freemasonry of woman, this white magic that they weave to shield their men from harm, laying innumerable folds of gauze and cotton between them and the bayonet thrusts.

The workrooms in action little suggested the house of dreams. The long, white-covered tables, the lines of busy sewing machines, the shining rows of bandage rollers and knitting machines, the shelves piled with materials, the business-like officials checking out supplies and recording finished work suggested the humming shops of a great factory. They were found wherever people most congregated; but whether they shared tall office buildings with lawyers and business firms or elbowed the general store and the post-office on the village main street, they wore the same aura of up-to-date efficiency. The demand was for expert workmanship and skill in many intricate processes, and this the irregular workers developed to a high degree.

New methods and machines were invented under the high pressure of demand in this new craft. Cotton had a double war use for munitions and surgical dressings, and because in that grim game the guns took precedence over the hospitals, sphagnum moss became in high favor in Red Cross workrooms. Tons of it were gathered in Maine, in eastern Canada, and the Northwest. Its absorbent qualities are so great that when water is poured upon the sphagnum compress it expands to twice its thickness before the under layer of muslin shows a trace of moisture. The preparation of the moss was a tedious process until a woman solved the problem by constructing a six-foot ferris wheel hung with open air trays. In the big workrooms these machines were set up, the current switched on and the wheel left to do its time-saving work in the electric heat of the drying room.

Nor is knitting any longer of the feminine gender! A new hand-machine, turning out socks at a shocking rate, has made hundreds of men and boys successful rivals of the "knit two, purl two," brigade. It turns out a pair of socks in *twenty-five minutes*, and can be adjusted to any size or length. One millionaire groceryman spent his mornings in a New York workroom ribbing and turning heels with the ease and precision of a veteran.

Even chemistry played its part in the Red Cross opera-

tions. When linen and cotton materials for bandages and
dressings were scarce in the market, an immense reserve
was found in the drafting-rooms of manufacturers and
architects. Here were great quantities of discarded cloth
which had to be treated with diastase to remove the drawing
ink and transparent dressing. Great laundry plants volunteered to handle the bulk of this work, but in many places
Red Cross workers set up emergency laboratories in their
own washrooms.

It has been estimated by some genius that to this
work, after America went to war, two million hours
were given, — two hundred and thirty years of labor com-
pressed into eighteen months! Whatever the actual
time the record totals an enormous sacrifice of rest, of
pleasure, of food, and sometimes even of sleep. Some
of those hours represented spare moments between trains
or unexpected lulls in a shopping tour; the bulk of
them were hard wrung from busy lives. They stood
for condensed housekeeping, foresworn frivolities, shortened
lunch hours, night work volunteered by factory girls
when the day's business was done. Miles of material
passed under their busy hands. Every month they put
a five-and-three-quarter-inch girdle of gauze around the
globe; they used two and a half million pounds of wool.
Here was the most marvelous factory the world has ever
known: it kept no hours, and it knew no payroll. Its
shops were erected in every crowded mart and on every
country byway, in the Chicago loop, and in icebound Alaskan
villages. The limit of its production was never reached,
yet every item in its output was known and controlled in
one white marble building — the National Red Cross Headquarters in Washington. The evolution of that system is a
monument to the energy and the self-discipline of the American women.

In the wake of the first staggering news of war in Europe

came tales of awful suffering for want of bandages and dressings. The report that wounds were being covered with sawdust and newspaper sent pitying fingers hurrying to their task; and when with winter came the demand for socks and sweaters to expel the biting cold of the trenches, little groups of workers bravely started out to explore the unknown field of surgical dressings and refugee garments. The Red Cross had issued directions for their making, but almost anything was acceptable. Women made what they could, or what rumor reported to be right. With the result that wherever two or three women were gathered together, a new line of models arose. The Red Cross undertook to forward gifts to any designated country, and a motley stream of packing boxes passed through the New York warehouse. During two and a half years of divided senti-ment, seething under official neutrality, eighteen thousand donors, individuals, ladies' clubs, charitable organizations, and Red Cross Chapters appear regularly on the record of shipments received. Seventy-five thousand big packages went overseas. But by April, 1917, a little order was coming out of the chaos. Classes in making surgical dressings had been established, and trained instructors were now directing the output in Chapter workrooms. In spite of individualistic tendencies a compress from Kansas was, obviously, now of the same family as a compress from New Jersey.

On April 30, the first foreign order was ticked off at Washington: "Ask Chapters for four hundred thousand pairs woolen socks and unlimited supplies hospital garments and clothing." At last a direct line of communication to the front was established. This first haphazard stock of supplies was built up under the pressure of imminent un-gauged demand; during the war, a call from overseas was answered promptly without apparent effort. Often it was only a matter of shipping a certain number of packing cases from the piled reserves in an export warehouse. Segregated by size and kind in uniform boxes, duly inspected, recorded, and labeled, garments, bandages, and socks moved in orderly ways from thirty thousand workrooms, through division inspectors and export stations, by train and ocean liner, to the long line of warehouses that paralleled the Western front.

How the system was slowly perfected and strengthened in every link is told in a slim folder of varicolored forms, filed under "Foreign Requisitions" in the cable office at National Headquarters.

Following the blue sheet bearing the first request for "unlimited quantities" comes the Chapters' answer. Many yellow pages are written close with the serial numbers of packing cases invariably headed by the formal statement, "United States Transport sailing recently New York carried French shipment number 000." Soon the Commission was measuring its needs and weighing the relative merits of bandages and pinafores. In the same files under date of August 17th appears the following: "No more shipments from United States without specific request from France." This, by the way, did not mean a halt in production; it meant that the situation was so serious and the demand so urgent that to avoid confusion and duplication they would determine what was most needed and the order in which it should come.

When the Red Cross Commission — those pioneers facing immense and unknown needs — sailed for France in June, they made preparations for yet unsolved contingencies. In France an endless stream of gray ambulances poured wounded men into army hospitals, and refugees fled empty-handed from the battle-zone. Here, back home, American soldiers were entering the first stage of their journey to the front. These things the Commission knew. But if heretofore they had failed to plumb the capacity of the Chapter supply system they soon began to send enough specific requests to satisfy the most enthusiastic Chapter.

In September the right of way was given to surgical dressings and hospital supplies. In December the ratio of need was stated as seventy-five hospital to twenty-five refugee garments. By July, 1918, the veteran Commission had an accurate finger on the pulse of France. "Requirements for Military and Hospital Purposes for six months following" headed an order of six million items.

Meantime details of transportation were straightened out. After November, 1917, drains and bed socks and boys' corduroy trousers were no longer permitted to consort fraternally in "miscellaneous cases," but were ruthlessly sorted and packed in uninteresting uniformity with their kind. In the spring, the cases themselves were put into uniform. The familiar insignia and a three-inch diagonal red stripe on sides and ends proclaimed their source and destination. The piled boxes on the wharves of France were all of a size, dictated by the door space of the French box-car. The serial number stenciled on each was the key to its recorded march from a far-away workroom to fill its allotted 2×2×3 niche in the need of France.

"Bales or cases" became the subject most discussed in shipping circles. Cargo space was precious and cloth bulked smaller than wood, with the result that a few experimental bales were dispatched on sea voyages to test out various wrappings, fastenings, and markings.

Cabled orders read like ciphers. They referred to all items in Chapter production by their code numbers. This was the last step in a discipline of detail that spoke of the delicate balance of need and supply. Early in 1917 the Red Cross sent representatives to find out by personal investigation what surgeons and nurses in army hospitals wanted in the way of hospital supplies; and what size sheet was best for the regulation bed; also what length nightshirt fitted

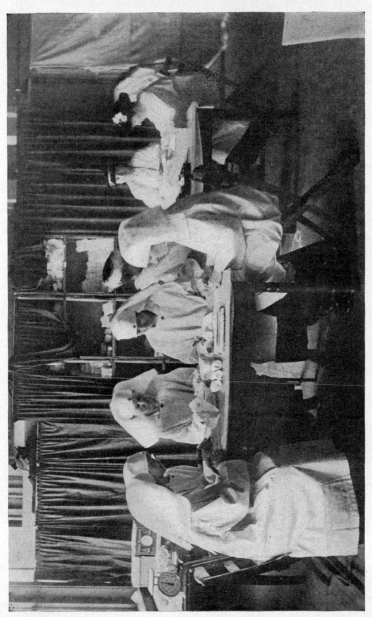

AMERICAN RED CROSS CHAPTER SCENE, BUFFALO, N. Y.

the regulation patient, and what form of surgical dressings came most readily to hand in the operating room. They also went from station to station behind the lines to learn what kind of clothes refugees liked best to wear. Their findings, coded and crystallized in exact directions and patterns, were later in every Red Cross workroom. Number 453 became precisely the same thing in Evian and Palestine and Akron, Ohio. Every American worker knew that the awkward, unbelievable ugly garment she fashioned would be beautiful in the eyes of some refugee, a familiar link with the past, a tiny balance wheel in a life wrenched from its moorings and adrift in the backwash of war.

In the first month of 1918, two thousand packing cases of supplies were coming in daily from the Chapters. The workers had struck their pace. New recruits were gathered daily as reports came in of Americans in the trenches, and production soared. The average monthly production in 1917 was six million; in 1918, it was thirty-one million. Up to September 30, 1918, 275,000,000 articles made by the women and children in the Red Cross had been sent overseas. The bulk of them, 250,000,000 in round numbers, followed the United States transports to France; the balance carried their message of comfort and good cheer to Italy, England, Serbia, Russia, and Palestine.

But, although the shuttle of their thoughts moved through a woof of many lands, the Red Cross women did not forget the cantonments that had sprung up at their gates. Their Christmas bags replaced the familiar Christmas stockings in the great barracks; their socks and sweaters and wristlets warmed the waning enthusiasm of many a novice in winter-camping. What more fitting than that they should do the army mending? In June, 1918, the Red Cross officially took over this duty from the Army quartermasters. In this transaction red tape was conspicuous by its absence. The privilege was restricted to those localities that boasted camps and quartermaster depots. The clothes, which included everything that a soldier wears, were delivered clean, but ragged, to the workrooms. They presented vivid examples of what one man could do to a perfectly good uniform, given perseverance and the facilities of army life. The garments that averaged more square feet of holes than material were cut up for patches. Thread and buttons came with the consignment; the magic of flying fingers did the rest. Trial lots of 5000 were issued to each Division in June; within thirty days 500,000 garments of every size and kind had been returned to respectability. One Division rehabilitated 150,000 on its first order. Sometimes mending was a blanket term for complete transformations. Witness 96,000 collarless white shirts, opening in the back, that strayed into Northern Division workrooms and emerged a short time thereafter dyed, collared, cuffed, opening in the front, regulation O.D.'s. By November 1, 1918, more than one and a half million garments had passed in and out of the Red Cross mending bag.

The volunteer supply system was organized. As nearly as it was humanly possible every garment was made exactly like its model. Moreover, the same number of rolls or compresses was exacted from every yard of gauze, and workrooms turned out no more and no less than their accepted quotas. All materials were bought through the Central Supply Department at Washington and issued from Division warehouses on requisition. The constantly depleted reserves in the export warehouses were as constantly replaced by a steady, unhurried procession of uniform cases, each one containing one size of one article. These were factory methods indeed! One would say that production had become automatic. But let an emergency throw open the throttle and the "machine" responded with an elasticity of effort, a determination to accomplish the impossible that is the greatest birthright of human genius.

One day an army consignment went astray and a transport was sailing minus its equipment of surgical dressings. Could the Red Cross help? The appeal came at 11 : 00 A.M. At two that afternoon the ship was on her way "over there," with the requisite number of Red Cross boxes stored in her hold. When the influenza epidemic reached the United States on its westward journey, the Red Cross Chapters turned out 1,250,000 germ-proof masks in two weeks. One day an S. O. S. call came into central Headquarters. Contagion was rampant in an Iowa camp and the hospital must have ward masks. Chicago had none on hand, but she knew where they were to be had, and in three days, twenty thousand of the precious filters were on their way from a northern neighbor. The thirty thousand and more Red Cross workrooms were cogs in a great machine, but it was a human mechanism, welded from millions of heads and hearts and hands.

The women of America from the day they first took up the burden of war to October 1, 1918, made and packed and shipped 253,000,000 surgical dressings; 22,000,000 articles of hospital supplies; 14,000,000 sweaters, socks, comfort bags, etc., for soldiers and sailors, and 1,000,000 refugee garments — 291,000,000 pledges that America's women were right behind the flag. The value of this gift cannot be measured by its bulk nor by the $60,000,000 or more that it would bring in open market. The manner of its giving put it beyond price. It was a splendid gesture of courage, faith and love, commensurate only to the human misery it has lessened, the human courage it had stiffened to "carry on" against all odds. The little red labels sewed into every chapter-made garment carried the propaganda of good will around the world.

The gray uniforms of the Red Cross Motor Corps were a familiar sight in the streets of many cities. Between six and seven thousand women were enrolled in the Chapters'

D]

transportation system. In trucks and ambulances and in their own cars they went about the Chapters' business; they carried workers and food to and from the canteens; they hauled Chapter supplies and hospital patients and visiting personages. Their obedience to orders and their promptness in reporting for duty were as military as their uniforms. The Motor Corps was no place for faddists; it was a working organization of skilled drivers and mechanics. The prerequisites for the first division of membership included a course in automobile mechanics, sanitary troop drill and first aid, a chauffeur's license, and physical examination. The members gave at least sixteen hours' service a week. Local emergencies proved their spirit. During the influenza epidemic, many drivers stayed on their jobs twelve and fifteen hours a day and slept in the garages beside their cars.

At seven hundred railroad junction points where troop trains stopped to take on coal and ice, Red Cross canteeners were always waiting to greet the cramped and train-weary men with something to add to their comfort. In winter, it was coffee and sandwiches; in summer, watermelon or ice cream. Newspapers, magazines, postal cards, and stamps were popular the year round. The gift, small as it was, embodied enough good fellowship to last till the next stop.

The Red Cross is dedicated to the defeat of suffering. Its work in the face of actual disaster is the last stand of the battle. It begins in the Red Cross classes of instruction. The Chapter is the evangel of physical efficiency. Crystallized in three slim textbooks, "First-Aid," "Home Dietetics," "Elementary Hygiene and Home Care of the Sick," there is enough simple knowledge to shield a whole community from petty emergencies and the insidious encroachments of disease and dirt. First-aid classes were organized in January, 1910. In eight years, 85,257 certificates have been issued. First-aid contests are an annual event in many industrial plants. Sixty thousand women have learned to make their homes strongholds of healthy lives.

Home Service — a strong hand holding hundreds of thousands of families from disintegration under the dead weight of war — may be a matter of economic and social laws among the file cases at Headquarters, but in the Chapter it resolves itself into individual problems in neighborliness, vivid with personality, inspired by loyalty to the absent soldiers of democracy.

In April, 1917, the Red Cross had 555 Chapters. Most of them were in the Eastern States and in large cities. To-day 3874 Chapters stand on the Red Cross rolls, and throughout the land there is no county that does not boast of at least one Auxiliary. The pre-war membership of 486,394 is lost in the mighty army of men and women, boys and girls, who answer with 30,000,000 voices to the Red Cross roll call. Sixteen million joined during one week of the 1917 Christmas drive.

The rallying of the comradeship is, indeed, one of the great romances of democracy. Millionaire and miner, red Indian, white man, and negro marched shoulder to shoulder in the army of mercy. One of the most stirring chapters in the whole series is the tale of the Fourteenth Division. When we entered the war, it was felt that through the Red Cross these exiled Americans scattered around the globe might help do their bit. As a result, the roll calls of the Red Cross echoed from Cairo to Vladivostok and from Buenos Ayres to Tokio. In its workrooms thousands of more or less homesick Americans felt closer to the state than they had for many years. In Porto Rico and Hawaii, in the Philippines and Guam and the Virgin Islands, men, women, and little children found a new meaning to their American citizenship.

Incidentally, it gives me great pleasure to state that when we figured up the result of our second appeal to the country for another $100,000,000, which resulted in a total subscription of more than $182,000,000, we found that the Fourteenth Division had contributed $1,700,000 to this fund, which meant that the Fourteenth Division had gone over six times its quota.

One thing more : in less than a year the scattered Chapters of the Fourteenth Division turned in a million and a half dollars' worth of supplies, knitted goods from China and Chile, surgical dressings from Brazil and Spain, tons of guava jelly from Porto Rico destined for French hospitals, and Havana cigars and cigarettes from Cuba. Red Cross work also was carried on in the little island of Exuma — a scrap of land not to be found on most maps. In Costa Rica twenty knitters called for the second hundred dollar lot of wool in four months, and knitting needles being scarce they made their own from cocobolo wood. The Fourteenth Division planted the outposts of the American Red Cross around the world.

CHAPTER IV

WORK FOR THE SOLDIER AT HOME

Aim of the Government — Relation of the Department of Military Relief to the Army — Service at Railroad Stations — Numbers of Canteens — New Work for Women — Death to a Libel — Canteen Functions Defined by Army Orders — Canteen Records — Washington Union Station Canteen — Many-sided Service — One Month's Statistics — Sanitary Branch of the Service — Camp Service — Red Cross Field Director.

THE United States Government started out with the definite intent that the American soldier should be the best conditioned, the best fed, and the best cared-for soldier in the world; the verdict of a proud and grateful people is that the Government, taking everything into consideration, came very near to realizing its purpose. In truth, the fitness and fighting qualities of these men — men who a year before had been shuffling along in a thousand-and-one different trades — proved to be the happiest as well as the biggest surprise of the war to tired and disheartened Europe.

In lending a hand to the Army, coöperation between the Red Cross and the Government was necessarily close but, oddly enough, no phase of our work is less known than the almost herculean labor undertaken on behalf of the soldier.

To a large number of people the military work of the Red Cross is personified in the figure of a girl in khaki passing out coffee and sandwiches to grinning soldiers who, already, look a hundred per cent nourished. This trite picture does not begin to tell the story. The soldier himself, unless he be a very thoughtful and observant man, does not know how strongly and at how many points and angles the Red Cross has influenced his mental attitude, his moral conduct, and his physical condition.

Reference has been made to the departmental organization of the Red Cross and the distribution of its duties incident to war. Moreover, it may be unnecessary to add that the men and women engaged in all these various departments were, every one, convinced that their own department was the biggest and most vital; but it was this conviction, nevertheless, that inspired their work and actuated the whole machine. It is also true that as we follow the soldier on his long journey to the battleground, and back again, each stage as it is passed seems to yield in importance to the next.

In all the formative stage of the soldier's development and, for that matter, at every step of his service, of all the departments of the Red Cross that of Military Relief was closest to him. In his cosmos that department and no other comprised the Red Cross.

A large part of the work of the department of Military Relief was merged in the Medical Service of the Army. The base hospitals with their personnel, which were organized and equipped by the Red Cross as part of its official business, became automatically a part of the Army organization when they were sent into service overseas. There remained under Red Cross administration, for the purpose of utility and to simplify the Army mechanism, the bureaus whose sphere was broader and more elastic and whose functions were not an actual part of the war-making business. They were, in a way, the left hand of the service. Under this head may be grouped the Bureau of Canteens, the Bureau of Camp Service, the Bureau of Motor Service, and the Bureau of Sanitary Service.

The American boy — up to forty-five — bumped into the Red Cross at the very moment almost of leaving his home door for the training camp. The last thing he saw from the train as the old town faded behind him was the Red Cross girl he had known from babyhood, waving good-by ; and at the first station were a group of Red Cross girls to let him know that the folks back home were not the only ones who cared.

Here is where the illustrative instances begin, showing how this Red Cross factor pervading every stage in the work of soldier-building made for a general cleaning-up. It is related that in the early days of the war the mayor of a western town in the exuberance of his feelings presented each man of the town's draft quota with a bottle of whisky for "deoch an' doris." The next station was a canteen town where Red Cross women waited to welcome the troop train. When the Red Cross report of that visitation reached the War Department the instant reaction was the brassard on the sleeve of every drafted man, and thenceforth it was a penitentiary offense to give or sell him intoxicants.

During the early period of mobilization it was not realized that the services of the Red Cross would be needed at railroad stations. But when the railroads began to feel the strain of moving hundreds of thousands of troops, and trains began to be late, the inevitable emergencies arose : it was not enough to have Army dining-rooms at regular intervals along the route but the Red Cross must be ready to feed and take care of the men at all stations. Secretary Baker's request that the Red Cross take over this work acted like magic on the women of America. The whole nation was mobilized overnight.

And so it was that when the armistice was signed there were in the United States 781 canteens where 70,000 women with military organizations were doing yeoman service. They not only gave the soldier a lift when he needed it, but they themselves discovered a new meaning in service and came to the knowledge that life is real and that there is beauty in its reality. There were women scrubbing floors in Red Cross canteens who had never done a day's work before in their lives. But the thought that they were helping made them happy.

When the canteen women at one of our debarkation ports were first called upon to take care of the wounded men, who had now begun to come back from war, they said they couldn't stand the awfulness of it. But they did. The cheerfulness of these poor fellows shamed them into self-sacrifice. Forgetfulness of self strengthened these women's characters and illumined their souls. In the change that war service has brought to the women of America, many an old fetish has gone by the board.

The incident described in the following letter from a canteen worker in Charlotte, N. C., and of which there were many similar occurrences all through the Southern States after America went to war, shows that the Red Cross is not a thing of race or color and should be the last word of proof of this growth in patriotism : —

"To-day we had a fine example of discipline and its value. Thirty colored sailors stopped at the Canteen hut. When we went to serve them they were drawn up in two lines and stood at attention. As if with one voice, they said, 'To the Red Cross,' and saluted. As we passed down the line, each man as he was served removed his hat and bowed, but did not speak. After all were served, they sang all sorts of songs, gave a rousing cheer for our Country, the Red Cross and Charlotte Canteen. It was one of the most affecting experiences we have had and our Chairman went back to the hut and cried. These men had crossed the ocean eleven times."

The war and the canteen sounded the knell of one ancient fallacy that should long ago have been laid to rest. In order to insure prompt supply of needed food or special service that the canteen could furnish, the troop train commander wired his requisition to the commanding officer of the next canteen ahead. This involved imparting a knowledge of the movement of troops, which had been religiously guarded to forestall the ubiquitous alien enemy and his secret wireless. The service oath of the canteen worker bound her not to disclose this knowledge to "a living soul." For centuries fathers have inculcated in their sons the belief that a woman cannot keep a secret. It is a matter of record that seventy thousand women dispelled this fallacy. In war time loyalty becomes a religion.

The vital importance of the Canteen Service of the Red Cross can be realized from the reliance of the War Department upon it for all sorts of emergency work essential to the rapid transportation of troops. The soldier's need of food and drink was reason enough for the canteen; but the Army orders to troop-train commanders and canteen officers, defining the canteen functions and outlining its use, confirmed its value as a wheel in the great mechanism. This, like every other department of the Red Cross, did the things which the Army could not do without slowing down the business of war. The Red Cross could be depended upon to find a short cut, if there was one, to the furtherance of its ends. Its service was not confined to the maintenance of good spirit by providing soldiers with food, tobacco, newspapers, postal cards to keep in touch with home, shower baths, recreation grounds, medical supplies, and other aids to comfort; on telegraphic order from the troop-train commander the canteen provided supplies of all kinds, whether commissary or medical, and lodging and meals where needed. It is not treason to say that Army stores sometimes go wrong — in fact, it would be strange indeed if such were not the case. There have been instances where detachments of soldiers have rolled into canteen stations without having had a bite to eat or a sup to drink through a long weary, empty day.

But there are other untoward things that happened. The Army called further on the canteens to arrange for surgeon, dentist, or physician to meet trains on wired request; it authorized them to accept sick or even dead men for transfer, and to give receipt for them to the officer in command. There were military books of instruction covering all this service and every train commander had one. They listed all the canteen stations along their route on every railroad, indicating the equipment of each in detail and the service it was able to provide. There were voluminous Army orders covering in minute particular the procedure for the soldier who was left behind or missed his troop train while on furlough or in transit, and for the Red Cross in giving help to him. These orders also provided for the disposition of all sick or injured soldiers who might be turned over to the Red Cross at canteen stations; the contingency of a soldier's death, the care of his remains and the notification of his family were likewise prescribed in detail. Here entered the Red Cross Bureau of Home Service, which is another important story.

These things were not mere possibilities, but actually came to pass. Forty-five canteens in the Southern States during the month of August furnished medical treatment to 1180 men and 22 were removed to hospitals, either military or civil. For record of all removals of men from trains, whether living or dead, there were transfer slips in duplicate with all details regarding the soldier, his service record, his malady, and the hospital to which he was dispatched. By these records the train commander accounted to the War Department for his missing. Simultaneously, cards were sent to the Communications and Home Service officers who, forthwith, established relations with the soldier's family and summoned them, if he happened to be dangerously ill.

There was a wide range of facilities offered by the more important canteens in various parts of the country. In large towns where there were big chapter organizations and war enthusiasm ran high, elaborate equipment was installed

A CAMP STUDY IN BLACK AND WHITE AS IT APPEARED TO AMERICAN RED CROSS WORKERS.

for bathing and, in some places, for swimming, and the menu of refreshments sent back home on the Red Cross postal cards made the home folk think that soldiering was an easy life after all. In many ways, the most noteworthy canteen in the country was that in the Washington Union Station. It was formerly the presidential suite, but was given over by President Wilson at the beginning of the war. Its spacious reception room, conference rooms, and offices, were filled daily with way-bound soldiers. There were refectory-rooms, reading-rooms, lounging-rooms, and all sorts of rooms for the doughboy, who was wont to idle in the station at night waiting for the early train to bear him away. There were baths and sleeping places near at hand where he could go if he wished.

This service of the canteens was many sided : it not only made the soldier comfortable but it kept him from the station-saloon and other temptations of the night, and went further than most people know towards keeping him clean and straight and ready for his big job. In the great inland stations like Chicago, this service had almost no boundaries. Through the confusion, incident to war preparations, it happened, frequently, that the men traveling from the Atlantic coast to far western posts found that their tickets read to Chicago only and money for the remainder of the journey was, likewise, lacking. Here again the Red Cross stepped in to feed and send the men on their way.

In almost every canteen of consequence there was a surgical ward — a neat little hospital equipped for as many as ten or twelve men and a doctor who, without a summons, was patriotic enough to meet the troop trains on the chance that some soldier might need him.

The intimate stories of canteens that are "different," in all parts of the country, would make a huge volume. There were college girls who set up extraordinary canteens in university boathouses that were equipped with everything under the sun; there were canteens that were famous all over France for certain articles of food, and were a pleasant memory through trying days. The Staten Island canteen at Tompkinsville Naval Station was known, probably, in every port for "pie like mother used to make." Little branches and auxiliaries off the main lines of travel which never saw the passing show but were none the less eager to help along, baked, canned, and pickled all manner of things, and the Motor Corps girls came and toted the output to the railroad. The whole business was developed in an astonishingly brief space of time. Who, in pre-war days, would have thought of classes in the art of "handing out lunches on the fly"?

Speed, indeed, was the order of the day. When the detachment of fifty men tumbled into a canteen without notice and empty as drums they were fed nights, days, and Sundays; and when the Sergeant with a dozen sick men asked for invalid food the Motor Corps "hustled it up." And then there was the newly married man from the hill country and his weeping, girl-wife who had just learned that she could not follow her man to war and who lacked the wherewithal to purchase a ticket back home; needless to say the ticket was placed in her hands and everything done to send her more cheerfully on her way. On the Hoboken docks, one rainy night, the Canteen Chief found a hundred or more soldiers who had come from the war to train new troops. They had no food, no money, and nowhere to go — not even the solace of a smoke. When that company got up from a large hot meal and a long cigar, and had slept and breakfasted and had a ticket for their destination, there were a hundred odd more men who knew something of what the Red Cross meant.

In the station at Goldsboro, N. C., was a soldier on crutches who had finished with war and was making his slow way home. When the canteener learned that he had

come through the fighting of Château-Thierry, she gathered
the men, five hundred of them, from the next troop train,
and got him to make them a speech.   That voice, straight
from the front, sent them away cheering madly and vowing
to square him with the Kaiser.

Altogether it is wonderful record of service.   There is no
way of telling half its story.   Statistics, which are more or
less unconvincing, have only recently reached the stage of
compilation, but one month's figures from only about forty
odd per cent of the canteens of the United States, tell this
interesting tale : —

Men served	2,416,000
Sick aided	2,552
Removed to hospital	83
Value of supplies requisitioned	$9,950
Value of supplies furnished free	$81,890
Postals distributed	1,215,000
Cigarettes distributed	2,140,000
Canteen workers	17,168
Canteens reporting	267
Canteens not reporting	399

The Sanitary branch of the service was efficacious in
meeting emergencies, and the things it did, while they do
not appear outwardly as service to the soldier, none the
less reacted upon him in the largest way possible.   An
illustrative one was the work which was done at one of
the Army Camps.   Camps, it may be well to admit, were
not always located in ideal places, not always where the
Army would have put them if it alone had had the choosing.
This particular camp had a swamp beside it — a swamp
where the highly armored mosquito made merry on his
rounds, delivering malaria to any unlucky human whom
fortune might send his way.   To the Army Staff it was plain
enough that the swamp spelled trouble in capital letters,
unless it were promptly drained.   Yet in the statutes there

was a stubborn little law, born no doubt of the iniquitous land juggling of early days in the West, which forbade the improvement of private property at public expense. But there was no law to keep the Red Cross from doing the job, which it proceeded promptly to do, the cost of which was $7000. In the opinion of the Surgeon General's Office, this work forestalled an epidemic which was positively scheduled to appear in the spring and which would have laid on the Army a continual tax in man power and expense.

This Sanitary Service, which was conducted as an adjunct to the Federal Department of Public Health and in co-operation with the state and local health boards, and which shared their powers under state law, was indeed one of the most fundamental and omnipresent of all Red Cross activities for the preservation of Army health. It did not doctor sick soldiers; the Army did that. But Sanitary Service went further back: it doctored the country for five miles around the camps; it diagnosed the fields and streams and ferreted out behind the camouflage of landscape the hidden machine guns of disease, which in one summer can shoot an Army cantonment full of holes; it ditched the sink-holes and swamps that breed and harbor the carriers; it sprayed with fatal oils the streams and ponds and ditches on thousands of ancient and diseaseful well-curbs and sounded the death knell of the "Old Oaken Bucket." It put old vaults where they could no longer spread sickness; it combed the stables of near-by farmers with a rigorous hand and drove them into at least the "B "grade, or else out of business. Dirty or tuberculous milk simply could not be sold to soldiers. Nor were unsanitary conditions allowed to prevail where food was served: A restaurant keeper who had a military policeman before his door for a week warning soldiers away was a poor bookkeeper in not discerning the business wisdom of cleaning house.

To-day, the Sanitary Service maintains medical inspectors

NEW SWEATERS FOR OLD AT FORT OGLETHORPE.

Several million sweaters and mufflers have been distributed by The American Red Cross to soldiers and sailors.

of schools and homes and even churches. It vaccinates everybody who needs it. The Public Health Department's nurses — all graduates — are promptly available for combating epidemics. For bacteriological purposes there are laboratories, sometimes newly established for the emergency. And to safeguard against a crying need the Red Cross has furnished at substantial cost four laboratory cars which, the English sanitarians and car builders agree, are the last word in point of convenience and equipment. These can be hooked on to fast trains and delivered on the front of an epidemic's advance, civil or military, with amazing alacrity.

Thus, on every side the soldier was guarded against all that had in it any potential possibility of injury to his health, and the sanitary forces which were combined for the physical protection of the army camps built up health organizations of the highest order all over the United States. In many lines, standards were established and methods of purification set up which will outlast all wars.

In our supersensitive land we have a fashion of sidestepping reference to what we term social disease. If the Army had been as squeamish there would have been a different story told in the Saint Mihiel salient. The Public Health authorities and the Red Cross Bureau of Sanitation, as well as the War Department itself, recognizing in this thing a peril greater, even, than tuberculosis, laid hold on it barehanded. There are thirty-seven states now that have made venereal ailments reportable; whereas, at the beginning of the war there were but five. The program was to stamp out this thing at its source. The arm of military law is long: It reached into far villages that sent soldiers to the Army, and the Army lever to pry the truth from men is strong. The day is here when the distributors of sex poison, professional or otherwise, will be put where they can no longer foul the nation's life.

In the more wholesome field of Red Cross work for the

soldier in camp, there was an activity that knew almost no rest and no limit. Keeping in close touch with the man from the time he landed within the reservation until he finished his training, it tried to make him bear in mind that it was there to help him get rid of his worries and to smooth his road. An unsung genius who saw how the thing worked out crystallized it in this stanza : —

> 'Don't pack your troubles in your old kit bag,
> Tell 'em to the Red Cross man."

That is the story in a very few words. The Red Cross built houses in all the thirty-nine camps at first established. When the war closed it had nurses' houses in connection with base hospitals in more than forty-two different camps, posts, and Army hospitals; it had convalescent houses in sixty-three military and naval establishments and rooms in others furnished for convalescent purposes. There were nearly six hundred men and women in the Camp Service offices, and fifty-nine directors doing communication service at base, general, naval, and embarkation hospitals. There were no large camps, posts, or stations for the training of soldiers, sailors, or marines not covered by the Bureau of Camp Service, and when peace came the small places were being added to the list as quickly as possible.

It is difficult for the person who has never seen one of the great Army camps, with its miles of barracks and hospital buildings and warehouses, the far-reaching avenues and endless company streets, the brand-new drainage system, the garages and fire houses, commissary stores and officers' quarters, rest houses, mess quarters and remount buildings and all its innumerable housings of soldiery, to form a mental picture of the setting in which the Red Cross Headquarters was located. Through all the hours of daylight the movement never ceased. It was an endless reel of motion filled with the burly, brown figures of a man population, and the air vibrated with their clatter. There was the rhythmic beat of tramping recruits, going through the ever-lasting evolutions of drill, and the murmur of many voices. There were individual figures "hay footing" to and fro on a thousand errands, working detachments whose blue "rompers" were almost a foreign note in the khaki symphony, mule-teams, trucks, and commissary-wagons, loads of hay and loads of drain pipes, tents, and supplies — everybody going somewhere and doing some one thing. Scattered everywhere, singly or in groups, were soldiers, soldiers, soldiers. The thought that every soldier lazing down the road, every disconsolate mule browsing on the scanty herbage, every single thing, animate or inanimate, was a duly recognized and numbered item in either the personnel or the furnishing of an Army summoned up a vision of bookkeeping which staggered the imagination.

Let no one imagine that the day of the Red Cross Field Director at any busy Army camp was a day of rest. He was the officer in command of Red Cross activities at every camp and cantonment. There was no busier man on the premises, and the fact that he worked for nothing never seemed to slow him down. Moreover, the qualification test that he had to pass to get the job was not an easy one : tact, caution, initiative, calmness, firmness, and persistency were a part of his necessary equipment — he need be many types of men all in one.

There were no bankers' hours in the Camp Service. The camp turned out at six when the Red Cross man was on his job mapping out the day's work, examining and preparing to fulfill orders from the camp commandant or the chief surgeon, going through a mail that was full of Home Service problems, a hundred individual cases, official communications, and "axes to grind." There might be requests for help in securing discharges, for the Red Cross — with its facilities for investigation and its standing with the War Department — could present the story of a man who had

E

a just claim for release as well as for the man who had no claim and had yet to learn the hopelessness of asking to be released. There were always a lot of private messes that were coming up for settlement, domestic complications, legitimate and otherwise. The draft brought to light more bigamy than the law could ever punish. It brought one soldier face to face in many a camp with two wives and often with more. There were reunions in Red Cross camp headquarters of several families with only one head. It would take Solomon and Haroun-al-Raschid rolled into one to adjust in these cases the questions of insurance and allotment. The Red Cross Director was not a judge, but he was asked more than once to sentence a foolish soldier to matrimony.

In forty-four of the camps throughout the country the Red Cross built big cruciform convalescent houses to give the sick or wounded soldier, who was on the mend, a lift up the hill — a cheerful place to flee to in his daytime hours to escape the sight of sick men and medicine bottles, of temperature charts, the paraphernalia of surgery, and the smell of ether and iodoform. It was a great thing for a man who, with the help of nurses and doctors, had won a long uphill fight against death, to be transferred into a big cheerful place with couches and steamer chairs and sunshine, with cards and checkers, with curtains and flowering things, where the Library Association furnished him with the latest best-seller, where the magazines and newspapers were handy to restore his touch with American life, where he could smoke and swap yarns, and where his mother or his sister, his wife or his best girl could have a pleasant reception when she came to see him. It cost money to build these houses, but they were worth it.

Then there was the warehousing in connection with Red Cross administration in a big camp. There was all the trucking and handling and requisitioning. Sweaters? A big packing case held a great many. A mathematical genius at Camp Cody, away down in Texas, figured up in his idle moments that if the cases of sweaters that had come in were ranged in a row they would make a fine barricade nearly half a mile long.

Then there were the pitiful things in the base hospital — the things that laid bare the quick of life and drew forever on the reserve fund of nerve and heart. There was the drawing of wills, the adjustment of allotments, and the constant touch that must be kept with all the teeming and changing life of that city which was called a camp. It certainly was a variegated industry, this Camp Service! A man of unsteady nerves or inflammable temper or lacking in resourcefulness would not have kept his sanity in it longer than twenty-four hours. It did not require continual searching to find the "gaps"; other people found them for you; the Red Cross mission was to fill them. To get soap, brooms, medicine-glasses, and hot water bottles for a hospital whose supplies were held up on a railroad siding somewhere; to provide a heater for heating liquids; to get screens to give the ward patients a certain amount of necessary privacy; to rig up a building where junior officers could study nights; to provide entertainment for a delegation of Civil War veterans; to get a Ford car for the Division Surgeon to go his rounds in when an epidemic was overhanging the camp; to hurry in a consignment of horse medicine out of the blue sky in time to save the whole herd of sick and dying remounts from being sent to the horse cemetery; to find laundry tubs on twenty-four hours' notice for a quarantined regiment; to skirmish up quarters for a staff of nurses; and, finally, to get a flag to put on the coffin of a dead soldier on his last journey home, represent a few of the requirements and not even a decimal part of the work accomplished.

CHAPTER V

THE NAVY

Red Cross Coöperation with the Navy — The Naval Reserve Force — Medical and Surgical Service — Hospital Ships Equipped through the Red Cross — Lack of Coast Hospitals — Personnel for Base Hospitals Supplied by Red Cross — Naval Shore Hospitals Abroad — Organization of Naval Auxiliaries — Letter of Secretary Daniels — Rush Order for Surgical Dressings — Camp Service in Naval Stations — Convalescent Houses at Naval Stations — Relief for Survivors of the *San Diego* — Admiral Sims Encomiums.

THE mass of the American people are wholly unaware, I am sure, of the close coöperation that existed all through the war between our organization and the Navy. Nor is it at all surprising when one considers the strictness of the departmental censorship. These strange fighting ships, the lean, trim cruisers, the lithe sea wasps that they call destroyers, the undersea boats, all are members of our family but we are permitted to have little more than a speaking acquaintance with them. They come; they go. They swing in the river at evening and with the last somnolent note of their bugles yet echoing across the waters, they are still with the stillness of sleeping villages. When the sun comes they are gone, and the young ebb tide, which tells no secrets, silently follows on their track. Every now and then, it is true, some fortunate individuals catch a glimpse of these great, gray ghosts of war moving in purposeful majesty down the harbor outward bound, and fading into the murk and mystery of the sea. But the horizon's rim is the end of their knowledge.

Now and again, however, there comes the inevitable leak — the human equation is always to be reckoned with — and word finds its way into the public prints of some brisk bit of business that the Navy has been doing. But that is all. The highest tribute that a loyal people can possibly pay to the Navy is that of unquestioning and abiding faith which, certainly, is the evidence of things not seen.

Public interest and popular enthusiasm turned ever, perforce, to the soldier whom we had always with us. Sturdy, clean, competent, and happy, he was forever tramping up and down the thoroughfares, a welcome visitor at the Red Cross Canteens. Yet, during these anxious years, our ships together with those of our Allies held watch over the German Navy, netted the harbors, mined the runways, keeping up night and day a sleepless vigil while it safely convoyed 2,000,000 soldiers and many more millions of supplies across the Atlantic.

Almost at the start the Red Cross had one of its opportunities to coöperate with, or better, to help the Navy. It was at a time when newly fledged naval recruits were being hurried into the great formation and four hundred of them were rushed east from the Great Lakes station to Washington. They were forced to depart so hurriedly that their account books were left behind. They arrived in the capital with practically no money and there was no prospect that the governmental machine could provide them with funds. A request was made to the Red Cross to finance them over the period of delay, which was cheerfully granted.

But to go back a little: In August, 1916, Congress had created the Naval Reserve, unlimited as to number for the duration of war; the old naval militia became Class Two of the Reserves. By this measure the Navy, later on, was able to reach out and gather in men who had seen service, as well as thousands of recruits. The regular establishment increased in numbers from 55,000 to 88,000 in a few months and, ultimately, reached nearly 600,000 men. The Marines jumped from 10,000 to 75,000.

We come now to what might be called the first move in the naval game which followed our entrance into the conflict : the spectacular arrival of the first flotilla of our destroyers in British waters long before they were expected. For many uneventful years the Navy had been waiting for a chance to make just such a dash as that and the order, needless to say, was carried out in accordance with the best traditions of the service. Within six weeks, also, after war was declared, the personnel of the Navy had more than doubled. Not only was the Atlantic Fleet growing in an amazing rate, but the Navy was called upon to furnish guards for American merchantmen, and it had already been suggested that the training of the new merchant crews, soon to be launched, should be under naval auspices.

Meanwhile, the Medical and Surgical Service of the Navy had been organized with great care and thoroughness. In the naval training schools there was established at the opening of the war, as part of the general preparation for a great emergency, an elaborate system of instruction and training for pharmacists and hospital corps men. The training of these new forces was intensive and involved practice as well as theory. There was instruction in clerical work, microscopy, urinalysis, pharmacy, dentistry, pathology, bacteriology, chemical nursing, X-ray examination and development of plates, the making of splints and surgical dressings, and all the chemical laboratory and field work incident to the care of the sick and wounded. The Army, numerically so great, stripped the field of medical men and hospital attendants. The Navy, especially for sea service, — where women cannot or do not go, — was forced to rely upon itself. To realize the urgency of this need, it is necessary to consider the special character of naval service, its environment, and its difficulties.

The Army can evacuate its wounded from one hospital to another by prompt and, in the case of hospital trains, highly equipped conveyances. Aboard a warship it is different. In an engagement between modern vessels the space available for the wounded is limited, and the intensity of battle permits of little or no work with them until an engagement is over.

The most that can be done for a wounded man is to apply the dressing that every one carries and to remove him, if he cannot remove himself, to the unexposed side of the ship to await attention until the battle is over. Then, if the ship stays above water and there are surgeons enough left, the wounded may be transferred to an ambulance ship, hospital ship, or other transport, if there be one nearer than the nearest land.

This matter of hospital ships was one of vital moment to naval establishments and one in which the United States Navy had long labored under serious embarrassment. The lack of facilities in this service had been obvious for a long time prior to our entrance into the war, and by persistent effort Congress had been prevailed upon to make appropriations for its extension. Two passenger vessels — sister ships of about 10,000 tons — were taken over by the Government and adapted to hospital uses. They were commissioned under the names of *Comfort* and *Mercy*. Through the Red Cross, the Society of Colonial Dames provided money to equip them, which was done in the most thorough manner.

In addition to these there was the *Solace*, a small ship, also converted and which, prior to the war, was the only vessel maintained for this purpose by the Navy. Mention, however, should be made of the yacht *Surf* whose owner offered through the Red Cross to turn her over as an ambulance ship to attend the fleet in Atlantic waters. She was altered to meet the requirements of the service, equipped with all the necessary appliances and placed in commission on May 27, 1917, in New England waters, thus releasing the *Solace* for purely hospital service. Later she was transferred to Chesapeake Bay, and in August to the New York base. When the Red Cross flags and markings were removed, and she was turned back by the Government, she had transported in the neighborhood of a thousand sick men from ships of war. But save for the *Surf* there was no distinctive ambulance ship available for the naval service. In this connection the following will be of interest : —

"A hospital ship," says a writer on naval matters, "does not in any sense replace a base hospital in a coast town. The hospital ship acts as a hospital transport to which ineffectives are transferred to fixed base hospitals. The hospital ship is, in a way, a fleet base hospital moving from place to place as the fleet position changes on the sea."

At the beginning of the war there was a decided lack of coast hospitals, notwithstanding that the Medical Bureau of the Navy had long tried to secure them. However, there was great activity in expansion of hospital facilities based upon the nucleus of the old established naval hospitals, which had undergone material improvement and enlargement. Civilian hospitals in larger cities were specified as collateral naval institutions, and prominent civilian physicians were enrolled in the Navy Aid.

Apropos of this last statement, I have the assurance of an authority that within a year after the United States entered the war nearly five hundred medical officers were added to the present Medical Corps of the Navy, and a thousand medical officers of the Naval Reserve Corps were assigned to active duty. Every sort of specialist was listed in the Navy service.

Nor was the Red Cross at all backward in the way of assistance : it supplied the personnel for five base hospitals. In itself this may not seem, perhaps, to be of much importance, but in the intense work which characterized the

THESE ENGLISH PINES ARE ON THE GROUNDS OF THE AMERICAN RED CROSS BASE
HOSPITAL AT DARTFORD, NEAR LONDON.

naval medical service, it was distinctly an advantage to secure staffs of medical men and nurses who had worked together in civil practice and were familiar with each other's methods. Thus, our Red Cross system of recruiting as many as possible of its hospital units from large cities was the means of providing the peculiar teamwork that is so essential.

On August 22, 1917, the Red Cross had provided eight base hospitals and thirty station units of the Navy with medical officers and nurses. Hospital corps men and expert workmen in various lines coincident to hospital operation were provided by the Navy from its trained personnel. For example, in addition to doctors and nurses, each unit included diagnosticians, X-ray specialists, pay-clerk, commissary steward, yeomen, carpenters, electricians, plumbers, mechanics, cooks, and mess attendants. In perfecting the base hospital system, the Public Health Service collaborated with us in attending to sanitation.

Moreover, at that time the Red Cross stood ready to equip more base hospital units for the Navy, but no further call was made. In addition to permanent equipment it provided articles of invalid diet, which were a boon to the sailor in convalescence.

After activity started in foreign waters, Red Cross efforts bore fruit in increased efficiency of naval shore hospitals abroad. There were two base hospitals in Brest, each of which accommodated 500 patients; one in Queenstown, which held 300; one at Lieth, with an expanding capacity of 800; one at Strathpepper, rated at 500; and a small hospital of 50 beds near London, which was purely a Red Cross establishment.

In the effort to organize its system of service at the beginning of hostilities, in order to supply every possible lack of sailor and soldier and to render instant aid in any direction to all branches of the service, the Red Cross began in September, 1917, the formation of Naval Auxiliaries throughout the country. This was done in compliance with the wishes of the Secretary of the Navy, who addressed a letter to the Chairman of the War Council in which he successfully endeavored to impress upon me the necessity of centralizing all of America's war relief agencies under the Red Cross. It read : —

DEAR MR. DAVISON:

For some months a large number of patriotic women of the country, animated by a desire to add to the comfort of the fine body of youths who have enlisted in the Navy, have been sending useful gifts of their own make. Some of these good women have done this work through the Red Cross and others through different organizations. It has been suggested that it would be wise if the Red Cross, the only National relief organization having official recognition, be asked to extend its large sphere of usefulness by taking over entirely the direction of this laudable work of sending tokens of good will from willing workers to the men in the Navy by creating a Naval Auxiliary of the Red Cross.

I am sure the country fully approves the statement of the President, that "recent experience has made it more clear than ever that a multiplicity of relief agencies tends to bring about confusion, duplication, delay, and waste." In every European country volunteer aid has been rendered "under a well-organized central body." The Red Cross is the body to which the whole country looks. To its appeals the people are ready to respond generously because, as President Wilson recently said : "With its catholicity and its democracy the Red Cross is broad enough to embrace all efforts for the relief of our soldiers and sailors, the care of their families, and for the assistance of any other non-combatants who may require aid." With this broad foundation, with a record of efficiency, I feel sure that the workers of the country who are particularly interested in the men who wear the Naval uniform will be glad if the Red Cross will increase its benefactions by this natural and proper addition to its noble service.

If your organization can do this, the Navy Department and the Navy in all its units and the one hundred million Americans who are proud of their Navy will give cordial aid and hearty coöperation.

Trusting that this suggestion will meet your favorable consideration, I am,

Sincerely yours,

JOSEPHUS DANIELS.

And again at a meeting on November 26, 1917, the Secretary said : —

"The women are in the War because war cannot be conducted without them. Across the water in the early days of the War there were mobilized organizations of patriotic women and patriotic men. They organized in the cities and states to serve and help, but they largely failed of their purpose because of their division of interest. They lacked a uniform and coördinating head.

"I think it time everybody in America should be a member of an organization and helping the Army and Navy.

"In getting the coördination we must not lose the spontaneity and the enthusiasm and the zeal of individuals, but it must be harnessed to organization.

"Since the Geneva Convention the Red Cross has been the chief organization to which people looked for succor, for help, and for wise administration. It has demanded the best thought of the country. They are trying to coördinate all the agencies of America, and we are here this morning to work with them. I shall assure you for myself and for the Navy, we will coöperate with you in every way possible.

"Some time ago, a very patriotic organization announced that unless a certain number of sweaters were sent within a certain time, the Marines would freeze. Now the spirit back of that was to stimulate good feeling and help, but it did more harm than good, because the men in charge of that service had not neglected their duty. The impression got out somehow or another that the Secretary of the Navy, the Secretary of War, and the head of the Marine Service did not appreciate the splendid service women rendered. Of course it was a mistake.

"You know that this Navy is made up of boys. The average age is twenty-one, perhaps nineteen. Sixteen year old boys rushed into the Navy and they said they were eighteen in order to get in, and I have no doubt that if they made a false statement the Recording Angel blotted it out.

"So you are working for boys, and that is the appeal to mothers of this country, you are working for boys, and I come over to thank you and to join with you and with the heads of the Red Cross, who are charged with a great work."

As the ships, large and small, came hurrying to the Atlantic bases and the work of final preparation went forward, many things were found lacking, among which was a supply of surgical dressings. This was essentially a Red Cross emergency. Dressings were called for to supply 133 destroyers and small vessels and 56 battleships and cruisers. The Navy supplied the gauze, but the Red Cross had the willing workers at hand for immediate action. So far as possible, the Red Cross placed the order for these dressings in the home towns of the ships, but as haste was most essential the demand, for the most part, was distributed among the ten nearest large Chapters — Chicago, Cleveland, Pittsburgh, Washington, Baltimore, Philadelphia, New York, Boston, and the Atlantic and New England Divisions. The Chapters turned the order out, packed and marked, in record time. It was all forwarded to the Supply Department at the Brooklyn Navy Yard for distribution to the ships wherever they might be.

The making of this supply of dressings, on Navy specifications, lifted a load from the Navy shoulders and enabled their surgical staff to attend to other pressing business; and, in addition to the dressings, a large number of knitted articles were supplied to these same destroyers and battleships by the Red Cross knitting women, who had now begun to work for the Navy. Sweaters and socks and helmets went out in great bundles to ships and training stations.

In the first outburst of excitement, however, there were a number of people who thought little of knitting needles as instruments of war, but who now sat in the revealing brightness of a great light as the letters began to come from the North Sea in Arctic weather telling of the comfort of Red Cross sweaters and snug woolen helmets. Indeed, many a tar blessed the Red Cross knitter long before his ship poked her nose into the Atlantic for the journey overseas.

One bitter night in the early winter, a battleship came bowling into Norfolk from Guantanamo Station with several hundred very blue noses aboard. Out of the dark they picked up a tug light. The harbor boat swung alongside

BATHING AND DISINFECTING PLANT IN ENGLAND LOANED BY THE AMERICAN RED CROSS.

and Red Cross men from the Norfolk Station swarmed aboard with bundles of Chapter knit goods. That sturdy ship crossed the Atlantic many times afterwards, taking the Army across. To its Commander the Red Cross sweater was the best thing of the war.

Parallel in every respect of organization and work with that carried on in the Army camps and cantonments, the Red Cross maintained a thoroughly organized camp service in camps and training stations and hospitals in fourteen naval districts.

At Pelham Bay, Newport, Portsmouth, Quantico, (Marines) Chelsea, Great Lakes, and Norfolk it established convalescent houses similar to those at Army camps; and other similar work at Philadelphia, Paris Island, (Marines) and Balboa Park, near San Diego, California, was just begun, or partially completed, when hostilities ceased.

In divers ways, some large and important, others small but still important, the Red Cross was able to assist the Navy. The consensus of opinion in the Navy, however, is that the best thing the organization did for the sailor was to provide these recreation places where the convalescent men, away from the unhappy monotony of hospital surroundings and the propinquity of suffering, could for a time forget their own woes and make strides toward health and a return to their homes or to duty.

To facilitate the work of the Navy on shore, it has been the privilege of the Red Cross to assist by provision of motor equipment and service. A very considerable number of ambulances, motor trucks, and touring cars were provided for the use of the naval establishment. Where civilian hospitals are utilized for the accommodation of Navy patients they are often widely scattered and the naval doctor, in order to visit them, is compelled to travel long distances. Congress does not provide quick transportation for these emergencies, but this was provided by the Red Cross.

A very good example of Red Cross service for the naval stations is found in the New York or Third Naval District : the service here was under the Atlantic Division, with headquarters at New York City. There were eighteen stations in this district in which Red Cross work for the sailor was conducted. In and out of New York thousands upon thousands of sailors passed; and we contributed in every way possible to the comfort and content of the multitude.

The same thing is true in other great naval centers, such as Newport News, Boston, Newport, Philadelphia, Norfolk, Charleston, New Orleans, Galveston, at the Great Lakes Naval Training Station, at Chicago, Seattle, San Francisco, and San Diego, as well as in the navy yards where men were at work on the ships which were in process of construction or tied up for repairs.

Among the incidents connected with Red Cross coöperation with the Navy, the strangest, perhaps, was the action of a woman who, by the way, for a year and a half afterwards was the busiest person about the Hoboken Embarkation Station (the old North German Lloyd and Hamburg-American piers). I am positive it will be written in personal if not official Navy records as a remarkable instance of intuition. One day there came a woman all the way from western New Jersey to the Red Cross Station who said that she had an unexplainable feeling that something was wrong. That there was something wrong was demonstrated in less than a half hour from the time of her arrival by a message from the Navy Yard which said that the survivors of the cruiser *San Diego* were coming in. There was fast work in Hoboken getting out warm clothing from the Red Cross stores and commandeering of trucks and tugs for its delivery. The boat to which the woman was assigned took off seventy-eight men from the incoming collier. When she went back for the next load she took the things the men needed for their immediate comfort. And so it happened that half the next day men were running around the docks in Red Cross pajamas, looking for all the world like escaped hospital patients, while they waited for the Government to find them uniforms. That woman surely left the Red Cross engraved on the memories of many sea-faring men!

The same thing happened on the other side of the Atlantic. Out of the busy life which the Navy led over there, there came through various channels thrilling narratives of rescue. It was tolerably well known, in spite of naval modesty and secretiveness, that United States vessels, both small and large, gave a very good account of themselves in the disposition of submarines. On one occasion an American torpedo boat, having rescued crew and passengers from a steamer which had been sunk in the English Channel, brought them into a French port in cold weather almost destitute of clothing. It would have been a very serious matter for the victims of this outrage to have waited the action of the United States Congress for an appropriation for clothing and its delivery to France on contract. Application was made to the Red Cross, which furnished outfits for the entire company.

In summing up the joint work of the Red Cross and the Navy it is not too much to say that our organization wholeheartedly indorses the sense of satisfaction that all our people have for the accomplishments of the Navy. Conversely, the Navy has ever shown itself most appreciative of the efforts of the Red Cross to do their part, and nowhere is this spirit of enthusiastic fairness more happily reflected than in the words of the Commander of the American Naval Forces in British waters: —

"When our men are sick or wounded we need quick action," declared Admiral Sims in an address in London, "and it must be free and unhampered. That is where the Red Cross comes to the front. Disasters like the *Otranto* show how valuable is its work." And, later, in replying to a question that can easily be imagined, he said: "all government activity is governed by rules with a view to what is likely to happen, but all needs cannot be foreseen. When an emergency turns up, we sometimes have not the facilities, sometimes not the legal authority to do all that we ought to do. The Red Cross man can make a law as quick as you can write a check. The Red Cross is ever present to help in time of trouble."

CHAPTER VI

HOME SERVICE

An Inspiration — Number of Families Assisted — Home Service Worker, a Silent Agent — The Picture of the Woman Left Behind — The Range of Home Service — The Peculiar Fitness of the Red Cross for Home Service — Representatives in All Camps and Cantonments — The Machinery for the Work — United States Government Sanctions Home Service in Camps and Naval Stations — How Home Service Is Administered — The Character of the "Cases" — Complications after the Signing of the Armistice — Home Service Institutes and Training Courses — Number of Trained Workers — Lasting Force for the Betterment of Social Conditions.

WHEN a man goes out to fight his country's battles he and all who belong to him are of paramount moment to the Government. The day has gone by wherein his dependents are abandoned to whatever fortune might befall them. Indeed, few things connected with the fighting man are more impressive than the increasing solicitude extended to those whose welfare is imperiled by his absence or death.

Almost at the start of this new conception of duty, — an acknowledgment at last of the importance of every individual, — the Red Cross recognized that here indeed was a long step forward. And since it has ever been its mission to consolidate public effort on behalf of the soldiers and sailors, to concentrate the prevalent good-will towards sufferers in other countries into an organized system of relief, it, therefore, proceeded to formulate a plan for the far more delicate and difficult work of giving to the families of the American fighting men the hand and help that they needed when the need was most pressing.

It is hardly necessary to say that this was an undertaking that required the exercise of tact in no small degree. When the call came for hundreds of thousands of our fighting men, many of them left behind them the tangled affairs of life, some of which it was well-nigh impossible to straighten out.

To enter into these innumerable homes in the capacity of guide, counselor, and friend, to do so many diverse things for so many widely variant people was in the nicety of its requirement no less exacting than the planning of a military campaign, and amounted to far more than the simple duty of giving people a hand to help them over a rough spot.

Home Service was an inspiration. Organized for the purpose just mentioned, there was a human note as well as an assurance of sincerity in it which were keys to confidence. It had no echo of condescension or patronage; on the contrary, it took people back to the time when the scattered and imperiled colonists were all things to one another; in other words, it brought into the foreground of thought the picture of friendliness, of neighborliness, and it won prompt and grateful recognition.

As the work developed the scope of its possibilities became more and more patent. Home Service did not go about its business preceded by a brass band, so to speak; to have done so would have ended its usefulness automatically. It had its very root in the sanctity of confidence, and the people whom it was privileged to serve knew that if it gave assistance it would also keep the faith.

Who of you know of the things that Home Service has done in your community — perhaps even next door? Not many, probably. And yet within a little more than a year it took into its keeping approximately 300,000 families. If one will consider the number of perplexing problems the affairs of one family can present, it is not difficult to understand what it signified in service rendered to straighten out the tangled affairs of a large number of families scattered all over the United States; nor must we forget that it is that very confidence which has made of Home Service the big brother of many a troubled household, the lawyer for counsel in times of stress, the banker in a pinch of circumstances, the doctor in sickness, the nurse, the teacher, the bearer of burdens, and the friend in need that is responsible for its being relatively unknown. The things it did were not on the surface.

Every one knows that the canteens were a picturesque and lively addition to any railway station. That there was glory in hurling a Red Cross motor-ambulance through the lanes of traffic on a crowded city street, and that Red Cross service in France had a glamour and a thrill all its own are, also, well-known truths. But the Home Service worker was a silent agent who, in a way, did good by stealth; so that if by any chance one of his countless deeds did creep into print it was by the very nature of the case utterly depersonalized. As for the glory of the service, it was ever unhonored and unsung.

It follows, therefore, that the narrative of what Home Service did since it entered upon its mission consists in the main of a blind succession of "cases." They are told in skeleton with a studious lack of detail. But it is certain that in these reports, flowing from every corner of the country, from homes and camps, from the embarkation piers, and from the turbulent zones of soldier life behind the lines, that there was more of melodrama, more of the plain, plaintive comedy of human life and of tragedy, even, than would suffice to fill the endless reels of half the world.

No one who has traveled country roads, either by foot or by motor, could have missed the home side of the war. In all the thinly populated places, in the little white cottages of the New England hills, in the farmhouses of the Dakotas, far scattered over their rolling expanses of wheat fields, one saw the war symbolized by strangely muted homes. There was a hush over things, a sense of finality about it all. The smoke rose only from a necessary chimney, the barn was shut up tight, even the "stock" stood around in a solemn sort of expectancy. Rural industry, simple as it was, had lost in such places its emphasis. The fading service flag and Mr. Hoover's mark in the parlor window told the passing stranger what had happened. For the old farm, battling against pests and bad seasons, taxes, and the hungry and long-lived mortgage, was not like a mercantile or manufacturing business in which diversified labor is distributed through many channels; and, besides, war and the munition factories had stripped the farm. More than likely, too, the next-door neighbor was a lone woman whose mainstay was somewhere between the farmstead gates and Vladivostok. And, to make matters harder, even if a woman could manage a farm — and there are some who could — there was not a farmhand to be had for love or money.

In nine cases out of ten the farm woman took over as much of the farm work as she could handle single handed. Such a situation, of course, was a trouble-breeder. All that anybody on earth could do in such cases was to be a good neighbor. It does not require much imagination, therefore, to surmise what the war did to country homes, how still the nights were, or how far the bare fields stretched to the horizon !

The monotony in the cities may not have been so intense, but in cities a family on the floor above might as well be in Manchuria for all they know of you or all the heed they give you. It is an old saying that there is no place so lonely as the city street. And the war brought pathetic changes here. Behind the same old service flag and the food pledge, which in so many cases was a superfluity in the face of soaring prices, the same old misery was doing its work. From the proud habitation uptown to the crowded tenements downtown, where English, Greek, Italian, Yiddish, and even German made the fire escape a babel on hot summer nights, men of the A. E. F. had gone forth, leaving behind them lonely women and still homes.

As will be easily seen, therefore, all the variation of town and country life came within the range of Home Service. In planning the work it was to do it enlisted a wide and a detailed knowledge of life as it is lived everywhere. It was essential to have shrewd consciousness of how people's minds work as well as an almost inspired intuition of things that were apt to happen. It had all been measured in terms of morale to begin with, and the threads of this multitudinous life traced on a chart of inference and theory, which proved phenomenally accurate from first to last in the great drama of war.

It has been said of certain important tasks in this war that there was no agency that could handle them except the Red Cross. This is, of course, an overstatement. It is, nevertheless, doubtful if any other existing instrument could have fulfilled the peculiar purpose of Home Service, for there was no other agency which had ready and equipped an organization so far-reaching, so instantly and so incessantly active and available, and so closely in touch with the homes and the needs they were apt to have. Moreover, in the thousands of Chapters driving away night and day for the soldiers and sailors, there was a perfect line of communication to every home which had sent a man to war.

Ever since the war began the outstanding thing in all Red Cross work was the alacrity with which its wide-branching plan of organization enabled it to meet demands on the minute. The actual accomplishment was noteworthy, but the sentimental unity of the machine enabled it to perform many more delicate functions — functions which in their nature required a high pressure of personal tact and sane judgment, not to speak of the necessity of a business-like faculty of execution. Foremost among these was Home Service. The framers of Red Cross plans knew the American man. They knew — what a great many narrow-gauge people had never suspected — that he was domestic to a degree never imagined, and that while he was perfectly willing to throw up his job and put his life to the hazard, if his country asked it, the only virtually important thing was that his family should be free from trouble.

"My time in the service," wrote a Texan, early in the war, "is the happiest time of my life. It is great! But you pack up your home affairs when you go in, and you can't help wondering all the time about the folks at home."

Home Service proved the most effective possible agent for establishing in numberless homes a new view of life and a new schedule of values, which was seed for future growth and betterment; it created new ideals where they would do the most good; it was, without doubt, the most effectual kind of shock absorber for the Government, and by its good offices a silencer of the note of resentment and discontent which echoed far in war time.

There are women, as we all know, who are natural-born dependents and whose training has added to their native tendency; on the other hand, there are those who have inherent resources of courage and self-help and will fight their way through any obstacle. So, naturally, it was the former class who needed the ministrations, for the most part, of Home Service. A man who left a strictly dependent wife at home with a few little dependents looking to her as acting manager could do very well for about three days. Then he began to realize, as he never did before, how helpless she was. One wailing letter has made all the wondrous new life of the training camp a gray and dismal thing. The mental picture of an empty pocket-book, with a weasel-faced land-lord in the background insisting that "leases are leases,"

THE HOME SERVICE OFFICE OF THE AMERICAN RED CROSS AT THE UNION STATION, WASHINGTON, D.C.
Here men in service could secure information about their families, and the families of enlisted men, information about the boys.

summoned in its train visions of misery that made a man deaf to the brisk accents of a drill sergeant and replaced martial ardor with a longing to be back home for just half an hour. It is a corollary of modern war that you can't manufacture a first-class soldier out of a man who is thinking all the time that his personal responsibilities are going to the dogs, and whose barrack pillow is hardened by nightmares of trouble in the home.

I have been told that there were practically only two kinds of desertion from the American Army : one of men who deserted in France from their regiments in the rear in order to join regiments at the front ; the other of men who deserted because of unhappy letters from home. When we went into war it was established beyond any shadow of doubt that there must be intimate and direct connection between the family and the trenches, that the home fires as well as the flames of patriotism were essential to proper military temperature.

There had to be a way to send soldiers and sailors 3000 miles or more across the sea and yet assure them that their families alike deserved and would enjoy the good faith and watchful kindness of the nation. The roots of the thing struck deep. The easiest way to keep the service man from being worried by unhappy letters was to make the letters happy. The only way to accomplish this in so many homes was to establish a neighborhood feeling that would embrace all. And the chapter organization, — a growth whose roots ran into millions of homes in every section of the country, — was there for the spreading of the Home Service gospel and the doing of the Home Service work.

Three months after the declaration of war, Home Service had already begun to send representatives to all the camps and cantonments in order that Home Service workers in the Chapters might always be sure of a good attorney, whose duty it was to locate the soldier in camp when his family wanted news of him, and vice versa. There were camps, notably in the vicinity of New York, with its strangely diversified population, where for three weeks the major part of the Red Cross field director's time was taken up with the home problems of men in the new levies. All the Red Cross machinery, all its resources were called into use in the prosecution of Home Service business: it enlisted trained men and women of every sort, some skilled in the care of the sick, others whose trade was to unravel legal and business tangles and who knew the resources of a community. These could minister to people caught in war's complications far better than an untrained individual, no matter how well meaning, could ever hope to do. To solve properly any problem, even the failure of an allotment check to arrive, required a system, with agents both in the Chapters at home and in Washington; it required some means of access to the War Department where the mystery of soldiers' money could be elucidated. True, the troubles of some lonely woman could be settled, but it required machinery, brains, telephone, telegraph, cable, letters, railway journeys, and professional assistance, all working together. Home Service could set a thousand forces at work, thousands of miles apart, to find the right answer to any question.

At first it was hard to make this purpose clear. The Red Cross pursued no one. It did not intrude into people's business. This would have been the first step to failure. But wherever its lantern shone on the darkness of a camp street, wherever the chapter centered its war activities, the latchstring was always out for the man and his kinsfolk to enter.

Now, like every one else, the American soldier, or sailor, has his traits, and it required thorough knowledge of his mental processes to introduce the business to him and tell him that he was entitled and welcome to all that the Red Cross could do for him. So in the training camps, in the railway terminals, and in every place where sailors and soldiers congregated big signs were displayed at points where no eye could miss them. Some of these signs asked pointed questions — they were never impertinent, however direct, for a question is pertinent or impertinent according to what is behind it. Here are some examples: —

"Have your allowance and allotment failed to come through satisfactorily?"

"Are you worried about the home folks? If so tell your troubles to the Red Cross man."

"We keep your home safe while you fight to keep the world safe."

All this was reassuring news to the fighting man who had just learned from a letter that everything was going wrong.

It is eloquent of the sagacity with which the Army was constructed and managed that these placards, in curious contrast with the purely military atmosphere of the camp, where every conceivable thing has been bent to martial purpose, were placed at the request of the United States Government in the interest of military efficiencies, a governmental recognition of the fact that a worried fighter is a poor fighter. At most of the stations the men in trouble — and there were a multitude of them — had the same everlasting problem of the bread-winner. But where a civilian, if he had any gumption, could get out and administer "Civilian Relief" to himself, the service man was tied hand and foot. He knew that if his checks did not come through there would be no groceries in the house, and he was plainly between the devil and the deep sea.

It was just because Home Service was equipped to step in and save this situation that it found its greatest field of endeavor in the camps. But all the promotion work was not done by the signboards; there were other ways by which the Home Service representative found out who needed his assistance. He got it from the chaplains, from patriotic and relief organizations, from camp paymasters, and in other ways known only to these earnest practitioners. What Home Service did when the much needed moneys lagged was to file the claims again for preferred consideration at the Bureau of War Risk Insurance or the War and Navy Department, as the case might be. It got into immediate touch with the Red Cross Chapter in the man's home town, which sent some one around to see the family, advance the necessary money, adjust their legal tangles, get the doctor, get the nurse, and reconstruct the housekeeping schedules so as to lessen the anxiety incidental to the high cost of living. When the mother was able and of a mind to work and help out the family income, the Home Service — through its wide connection — got her a job. If she was about to do foolish things to banish loneliness, well, there were cures for loneliness, too. These are things that do not go by formula and never can be standardized.

It may be said, therefore, that Home Service was pretty nearly all things to all men and women. But it is an interesting human fact that much of the work that it did for service men's families has been in response to demand from the service man himself. Many of the applications were made by men in camp who, in desperation, had been driven into seeking a way out of the dreary letters and who leaned on the Red Cross as it was meant to be leaned on. As for the women, some of them — perhaps because of their pride — did not go to the Red Cross to tell their trouble but wrote instead to their husband or son about it; and he, not knowing how simple a matter this was for the machine to handle, immediately hated the sight of a rifle and began to think in the back of his head that the Kaiser might just as well have the earth since it was no longer fit to live in, — which was a perilous state of mind for a man who was headed for France with the country's fate in his hands.

THE AMERICAN RED CROSS SERVING OUR COLORED TROOPS.

Confronted with a situation like this, Home Service stepped in and checked it; and when it had once taken a family under its protective and advisory wing, it "carried on" with them, kept tab on them, and mothered them properly. After that the letters that went to camp or overseas had a new color and Uncle Sam had a new soldier.

If Home Service in Italy was reflected in the victory at the Piave, Home Service in America gave an account of itself at Château-Thierry and along the stubbornly contested reaches of the Meuse.

The "cases" which constitute the Home Service record were multi-colored. In the main they pivoted on money, and the tough old question of subsistence, but their details varied as people do. There was every conceivable sort of plot. It was to the credit of the system that most of these had a happy ending. Where it was merely money or business complication that caused the trouble, it was easy of adjustment.

Still further complications arose after the signing of the armistice, because then began the real test of the fighting man's morale. The fighting was over and the fighters wanted to return home. Their families were insistent that their boys should be returned to them. Home Service workers now had the additional task of explaining why their boys could not be returned immediately and of dissuading them from sending their boys morale-destroying letters, of investigating family conditions of men who applied for discharge and, at the same time, not allow their sympathies to warp their judgment. Instead of decreasing, the work of Home Service kept increasing for many months after November, 1918. Who can estimate, therefore, the effect of Home Service, before and after the signing of the armistice, on the mental attitude of the millions of people who either fought or gave fighters in the Great War?

There was hardly a department in the work of the Red

Cross in which Home Service aid was not invoked or in which the home principle was not involved. The prompt acceptance of this service and this principle by the people whom it was meant to aid, and the realization of its meaning in the new life of America, demanded an extension of its scope, which meant a greatly increased number of workers. In order that there might be at hand a force to meet the growing need, the Red Cross established Home Service institutes, — a six weeks' training course planned to fit students not only for war work among soldiers' and sailors' families, but to serve in equally specific ways returned fighters themselves, who have been crippled in action and for whom definite programs of reëducation and industrial adjustment will be necessary.

The syllabus of instruction prepared for these institutes, which were started in the fall of 1917, was wide and comprehensive. It included not only the fundamental principles and procedure of Home Service, — health, employment of women and children in reëducation, — but went into all these departments with thoroughness in order that certificates of the institute should imply a knowledge of the ethics of family and community living. Manuals of instruction were carefully prepared, covering the whole ground of Home Service activity. In this way the emergency was soon met.

In the end it took 30,000 mature and tactful people to carry it on and at a cost approximately of three million dollars. But it did more than help win the war; it raised the standards of health, efficiency, and happiness in the homes that had sent men to France, so that the man returning should find small reason to reproach his country for the way his family had been treated in his absence.

At the time that this is written we are about to enter upon wider fields of international activity and these, obviously, necessitate new development in industry and thrift. But it has been part of the work of Home Service to teach these lessons with everyday application. It has shown in a practical fashion the effect of intensified effort, intelligent management, the worthlessness of outworn formulas. And precisely as the Red Cross labor in France was directed to the conservation of child life as insurance for the imperiled future of the republic, so in America we have made an effort to improve living conditions for soldiers' and sailors' families, always aiming at a steadily progressive and wider betterment for the time that is ahead.

The work that Home Service has done is merely a sowing of good seed; future generations will reap the harvest. In spite of what was ostensibly an emergency origin, the whole undertaking was constructive in its inward purpose for the long future of our national life. Throughout the war Home Service taught English to women of foreign birth who had husbands in the war. Every instance of this kind meant one more family on the road to Americanization. Again, a multitude of soldiers' and sailors' wives found it hard to resist the temptation to set their children at wage earning in order to increase the family income. But Home Service, mindful of the future and recognizing in this recourse a net loss in which the whole country shares, set itself persistently against it. Not only did it labor by every possible means to keep the children in the schools, but in many cases it contributed money outright to tide the family over. In others, expert assistance in the adjustment of household expenditure averted the necessity of turning soldiers' children into the factory.

Lastly, it was in such things as solving imperative problems and performing, at the same time, an educational office which looks to future widening of horizons, improvement of living conditions, maintenance of higher ambitions in the young, that Home Service assumed its highest position and that through it the Red Cross attained to a greater plane of usefulness.

CHAPTER VII

SOLDIERS OF THE CROSS

The Nurse, a Crusader — The Red Cross Stands Sponsor for Her — Enrollment of Nurses — Called for Disaster — Relief Ship *Red Cross* — In Many Lands and Climes — Typhus in Serbia — Mobilized for Immediate Action in April, 1917 — Base Hospital Units — Reserve for the Army and Navy Nurse Corps — Unit System Later Abandoned — Changes in Character of Base Hospitals — Emergency Detachments for Cantonments and Camps — Conditions in Camps and Stations — Coöperation with Public Health Service in Sanitary Zones — Duties of Nurses in France — American Nurses for American Men — Nursing Service of Red Cross in France — Call of the Italian Government — Honor Roll of the Red Cross — Expenditure for Equipment and Uniforms — Provisions for Comfort of Nurses — Work for Health of the World a Post-War Duty.

THE Soldier of the Cross is a very human crusader. Where civilizations have crashed in disaster she makes living clean and possible; with the modern magic of medicine, food, and cleanliness she banishes hunger and dirt; with infinite patience she builds up the lives of broken men and, seemingly, at times, is the only stronghold of sanity in their reeling world.

To render such service worthily demands more than pity and a white cap! It requires years of hard mental and physical training and the self-control that makes good discipline possible; for she must stand ready to tax herself to the utmost at need and, at the same time, not indulge herself in the hysteria of overwork. Moreover, it requires the physical strength to endure long journeys and hardship; more than all it requires high endurance of the soul —

courage to bear vicarious suffering. The Red Cross nurse looks on mortal agony day and night, yet she holds fast to sanity and cheerfulness that she may rekindle spirits snuffed out by too much horror. She denies herself the luxury of emotion because lives depend on the steadiness of her hand. The stuff of her days is woven of the two great realities — life and death; yet those she tends must not suspect that she is a woman of many sorrows and acquainted with grief.

Such is the nurse. For her the Red Cross stands sponsor. She has carried its symbol into the plague spots of every continent where disaster has left its mark — whether in San Francisco or in the far islands of the sea; she has carried it to within a few short miles of the European trenches. Everywhere, the Red Cross has backed her up with money, with equipment, with supplies, with uniforms and recreation rooms and words of cheer. It has increased her value by giving her her tools and sending her where she is most needed. Around the work it has opened up the path of mercy for her to tread. That is the great mission of the Red Cross — to take the funded money, strength, and skill of the world and send it to fight against disease and ignorance wherever they may be found. That is the democracy of humanity.

Five years before the European war brought a supreme duty and a supreme opportunity to nurses, the Red Cross began preparation to meet the unheralded need. In the fall of 1909 it affiliated itself with the American Nurses' Association and began to enroll nurses as a reserve for the Army and Navy. These young women were required to have had at least two years' training in a hospital that averaged fifty patients a day of both sexes, to be registered in their states, and to submit satisfactory evidences of fitness, and to be between the ages of 25 and 40. Enrollments increased year by year. Although no war clouds gathered, the Red

Cross called again and again on its nurses to save the victims of fire and flood, conspicuous among which are Dayton, Salem, Luzon, the *Titanic*, and the *Eastland*. Each name recalls havoc wrought by fire or flood, by earthquake or shipwreck, and it recalls, too, the heroic work of Red Cross nurses.

. . . .

In August, 1914, when the World War broke over Europe, the American Red Cross, true to its watchword, offered its trained personnel and hospital supplies to every belligerent country; acceptance was unanimous. On September 13, 1914, the relief ship *Red Cross* carried surgeons, supplies, and 120 nurses for England, Russia, France, Germany, Austria, Belgium, Serbia, and Bulgaria. Four days before, the Serbian unit had gone on a slow steamer, crowded with several thousand Serbian reservists, to meet what proved to be the most heroic task of all.

It was, indeed, in many strange and unique shelters that the tiny American units set up the outposts of their country's generosity: for instance, there was an estate at Paignton, the Palais d'Hiver at Pau, a Lyceum at Kief, hastily erected pavilions on the sands of La Panne, a modern schoolhouse in Vienna, the Victoria Kabaret theater at Gleichwitz, a tobacco factory at Ghevgheli, a tent on the desert sands of Wadi-el-Arish; other detachments were at Yvetot, France; Nish, Serbia; Kosel, Germany; Budapest and Belgrade; and Constantinople and Hafi, Turkey. Part of the German unit went in September, 1915, to work among the German and Austrian prisoners in Russia.

When, however, in the spring of 1915, typhus broke out in Serbia and men, women, and children died like flies, two Red Cross surgeons fell victims to the fever, and the ranks of the fit grew daily thinner. The Rockefeller Foundation and the Red Cross coöperated to rush volunteers and huge quantities of supplies into the infected country. Serbia was, literally, drenched in disinfectants and smoked in sulphur, and only after a bitter battle was the scourge conquered.

The tale of suffering that the pioneers sent back to America in 1914–1915 is familiar now to our ears, but in those early days its horror was unbelievably strange. In this, their first contact with modern warfare, American nurses won a place of honor on the medical rolls of all Europe. Their experience was to prove valuable in later days. The units were recalled in October, 1915, after the promised year of service, but many members remained as volunteers. When America went into the war, Red Cross nurses were still serving in all of the Allied countries.

Thus, the stirring and troubled days of April, 1917, found the ·Red Cross nurses mobilized for immediate action. Eight thousand and fifteen names stood on the Red Cross rolls. Of these the Red Cross could mobilize 2970 immediately, enough to care for an army of a million, according to the calculations of that early day. (The first military assignment was with the United States Marines at Vera Cruz in 1914. During the year ending in July, 1917, there had been assigned to the Army Nurse Corps 817 Red Cross nurses. Of these, several hundred were sent to take care of the 113,135 troops guarding the Mexican border.)

For a year before the storm broke along our shores preparedness had been trumpeted down every wind. Active official preparation in a neutral country, however, is apt to verge on mobilization and let slip the dogs of war too soon. The Surgeon General, therefore, requested the Red Cross to organize Base Hospital Units, and allowed it the privilege of building up a hospital system that was to be the backbone of the Medical Corps during the first trying months of war.

In the Base Hospital Units the doctors and nurses of

G

each group were accustomed to work together. When they moved they carried with them the personnel (from pharmacist to scullion) and the equipment (from scalpel to laundry plant) to set up a complete five hundred bed hospital wherever needed. The value of this close formation had been tragically proved by the countries already in the war and by the experience of the Red Cross relief units abroad. The great civil hospitals of America were called on to organize teams from their staffs, and soon a score of units were established. Twenty-two doctors, two dentists, sixty-five Red Cross nurses, one hundred and fifty-three corpsmen, six civilian employees, a chaplain — the complete personnel signed the muster roll of each and pledged to report for duty whenever called within two years. The personnel of each list called for careful study : the staff of the parent hospital must not be unduly weakened, yet every man and woman must be of the best, and they must "pull together." Personal knowledge was the basis of choice. Together with the Medical Director of the unit and the Director of the Bureau of Red Cross Nursing Service a Chief Nurse was selected whose duty it was, subject to the approval of the Director, to select the nurses, the dietitian, and the nurses' aids. Naturally, she chose those whose value she had proved, preferably graduates of the parent school, while the nurses' aids were prepared under her direction. It was the only possible method where compatibility was an essential, and it resulted in a team that "played up" with mutual knowledge and confidence.

Beds, bedding, ward furniture, drugs, surgical instruments, laboratory supplies and equipment, mess-gear, sterilizers, ambulances, touring-cars, motor-trucks, a motor-cycle, complete X-ray plant, kitchen, disinfectors, surgical dressings, and hospital garments, some refrigerating and laundry equipment, telephone system, and machine shop — all the supplies that would not deteriorate in storage were collected at a convenient point. It was at first estimated that the total cost of equipping a Base Hospital Unit would be $25,000. In the end each unit averaged $75,000. The Red Cross has spent $1,500,000 first and last on its fifty Base Hospitals, and all but $54,000 was contributed locally by patriotic citizens.

The names of the nurses were submitted to the Bureau of Nursing Service at Red Cross Headquarters, checked up with the enrollment files, duly carded, and held for final assignment to the Army Nurse Corps; the personnel was inoculated for typhoid, paratyphoid, and smallpox; corpsmen were enlisted in the United States Army Medical Corps Reserve; doctors and dentists were commissioned as Army officers; a commanding officer from the Army Medical Corps and a member of the Quartermaster Reserve Corps were assigned to the unit; the two carloads or more of equipment were stored; the completed unit was turned over to the United States Army Medical Corps — and life went on much as before. The personnel scattered to their daily jobs, the Director put the key to the warehouse in his pocket, and the storage bill and the muster roll were the only outward signs of the powerful machine that could be assembled on such short notice.

A Base Hospital Unit was mobilized for the first time in October, 1916, at Philadelphia. Base Hospital No. 4 (from Lakeside, Cleveland) came together on record time and with the precision of clockwork. The tentage covered a space 1000 feet long and 500 feet wide. The trial mobilization cost $5035.75, and proved beyond doubt the practicability of the "canned" hospital.

When America recognized the existence of a state of war with Germany, twenty-five Base Hospital Units were well under way. The first call for specific aid came to America through the British Commission for doctors and nurses. Six of the waiting Base Hospital Units were assigned to duty with the British Expeditionary Force. The Surgeon General decided, however, not to use the nurses' aids mobilized with the Base Hospital Units. Number 4 (Lakeside Hospital) was the first to leave New York in May, 1917; No. 5 followed two days later; and then Nos. 2, 12, 21, and 10. It was over the hospital unit in Rouen that the Stars and Stripes first floated as the flag of an ally on the soil of France.

In this first summons, war sent a clarion call to all Red Cross nurses. The members of the six units were scattered over the face of the land in the pursuit of their personal destinies. Hard on the heels of our entrance into the war came their summons to report in New York for overseas duty. The Base Hospital Unit was suddenly a living thing instead of a paper chart. Thousands of others in clinic, hospital, and home watched their going, knowing that their time would come; while others quietly entered their names on the Red Cross rolls, that they too might have a share in the great work.

In the first seven months after America went in, seventeen Base Hospital Units were rushed to France, and the others were held in readiness for immediate departure. Meantime, a serious outbreak of contagious disease in the mushroom-grown cantonments and camps in the United States demanded new quotas to battle within our very gates. Our first winter in the war was a severe one and thousands of boys, just drafted and unhardened to the rough life, succumbed to pneumonia and meningitis. It was hard to make it understood why the waiting units could not be used for this duty but must be kept free to go abroad. The Red Cross worked desperately to recruit enough emergency detachments to fill the terrible needs of the camps. No attempt was made at unit organization; the nurses were assigned as fast as they could be recruited, singly or in little groups. Later the nursing personnel of the Base Hospital

Units was sent to the cantonments. This was an advantageous move, as it gave the nurses preliminary training in a military hospital and also gave the hospitals an adequate nursing staff. Throughout that winter and spring they worked gallantly in the face of appalling, though unavoidable physical hardships, while not a few gave their lives on one of the first American battlefields of the war.

The Red Cross turned with a will to meet its responsibilities as "the chief reserve for the Army and Navy Nurse Corps." During the summer months enrollment was speeded up to the limit. On October 1, 1918, over 30,000 names stood on the card index at Headquarters. Of these, 14,368 had been assigned to the Army and 903 to the Navy, while 2454 were awaiting orders. The greater number of the nurses were assigned as part of complete organizations. Fifty-one complete Base Hospital Units were turned over to the Army with a personnel of 3734 nurses. The Navy mustered in five Base Hospital Units of 250 beds apiece. Nineteen Hospital Units, each manned by 21 Red Cross nurses, were organized at a cost of from $3000 to $7000 apiece. Various groups of specialists in mental and nervous diseases, in fracture cases, and orthopedics, were gathered together at the request of the Surgeon General.

The unit system of organization was under the circumstances a splendid plan. It gave the Army Medical Corps a running start in the war, which its official limitations prevented its making for itself. In the stress of later events this system was abandoned. The great civil institutions from which Base Hospital Units could be organized had for the time being given all the personnel they could spare without dangerously weakening home defense. Moreover, the War Department was now in a position to organize units for foreign service from nurses already serving in camp hospitals, who had learned to pull together under the peculiar circumstances of military life. So the Red Cross bent all its efforts to the task of recruiting nurses, equipping them for active service, and turning them over to the Surgeon General, singly or in little groups.

These nurses, sent fully equipped by the Red Cross into the military establishment, have passed through the Red Cross clearing-house in a continual quiet stream. After the war began, 65 or more were assigned to duty with the Army or Navy every day. In August and September, 1918, this reached its highest daily average of 100 assignments. Most of them reported in New York, where there were several Army mobilization centers. They received their uniforms, their blankets, and the "extras" that oiled the machinery of living in strange places, from the Red Cross Equipment Station. They met co-workers and leaders of their profession while waiting at the center for weeks, oftentimes, for a ship to take them "across"; but sooner or later they left for their posts — perhaps to Europe, to Siberia, or even to Porto Rico. The "military" took them; even the beloved Red Cross insignia they resigned in the interest of discipline, and thereafter their story became one with the Army or Navy Corps of which they became a part.

But, although they laid away her symbol until the war was over, the Red Cross did not forget its nurses. By September 30, 1918, in forty-five camps and cantonments she had expended $1,586,563.75 for uniforms and equipment for nurses, for recreation houses and their furnishings of bright hangings, easy chairs, long reading tables, and electric irons, all spelling home and a release from narrow barrack quarters. In France the Red Cross meant something beside the label on a package of surgical dressings or the protective insignia of the long lines of incoming ambulances; it meant friendly club-houses, convalescent and rest homes, and a special hospital if they fell ill. Always and everywhere it meant a strong friend to whom the welfare and honor of the nurse was near at heart.

THE GREATEST RED CROSS PARADE EVER HELD IN AMERICA.

15,000 women, many of whom at that time either had served on the battlefields of Europe or were waiting orders for overseas service, marched down Fifth Avenue through lines of cheering spectators.

The military map of the United States indicates the location of the camps, cantonments, aero and naval training stations, and marines' barracks. Here the nurses did no less valiant work than overseas. They took up arms against the epidemics of our first war winter. During the autumn months of 1918, while the Allied forces swept victoriously across Belgium, they fought stubbornly against the ravages of Spanish influenza — the dread disease that swept from the Atlantic to the Pacific.

Conditions in America were sometimes as rough as those in France, as the following letter from an Army nurse in one of the camps will show: —

"To begin with, when we seven arrived here we found ourselves the first group of nurses that ever crossed these grounds. It seems we were not expected so soon and nothing was ready for us. The place which was to be our home was an empty barrack with nothing but a coal stove in every room. But let me tell you that no department store in dear old New York ever delivered things more rapidly than they were brought in here. It seemed to us that our arrival set the camp a-stirring and everybody seemed to be busy in our behalf. Within a few hours we had our beds complete, the most welcome thing to us just then, we were all so tired. Meanwhile we were shown through the hospital, and then through the camp proper, and we were just amazed at the enormity of it all. The camp grounds occupy some 17,000 acres and the Base Hospital takes up about 62 acres and so far has 32 wards and more in process of construction. A few months ago this region was a stretch of wilderness and the first division of men worked this place through to what it is at present."

Another, a Navy nurse this time, wrote: —

"After the preliminary business of arrival I was taken over to a barrack-like building and found a bed allotted to me in a dormitory with about 50 other nurses. I must admit that this for the first impression was rather daunting. The place was littered from end to end with clothes, trunks, and grips, to say nothing of the beds themselves; some occupied by night-nurses trying to sleep, some by day-nurses reading, writing, sewing, or resting. I could see no possibility of the faintest trace of privacy, neither was there any, and later I learned that there was no water for any purpose nearer than the main building. We had rough wooden shelves to put our things on and a few nails to hang our clothes. To get a bath we had to walk outside of the main building two blocks away. When it stormed the rain came in upon us from the roof, and when it blew the sand came in and almost buried us, and the flies were a veritable plague — but all this, I am glad to say, was only a temporary discomfort, for now we have a very nice quarters, brand new and clean. I often look back and laugh and think of my chagrin, and realize that it wasn't so bad as it seemed after all, and that it was a good experience for me, for now I appreciate the good things as they come along."

The work of safeguarding our men in training could not all be done within camp bounds. It might begin in every city within range of a soldier's leave. To this end, the Red Cross joined hands with the Federal Public Health Service, which held watch and ward over sanitary zones and marine hospitals. Red Cross nurses helped in the everyday work of keeping the extra cantonment zones cleaned up and healthy; their prompt aid stamped out incipient epidemics of many contagious diseases. In Muscle Shoals, Louisiana, they were called in to inoculate interminable lines of munition workers for typhoid fever. At Newport News, Fort Riley, Hattiesburg, and Camp Beauregard they isolated threatening cases of meningitis. At Nitro, West Virginia — a munition town stretching twelve miles along the Ohio River — the 96 nurses at the Base Hospital insured an open line of communication between the powder plants and the big guns on the Western Front.

"We have had great changes at the hospital," wrote a nurse from France; "all the regular Army nurses were transferred, also our commanding officer, and instead of having 500 beds we have 2000. Doctors, nurses, and corpsmen were all put out of their quarters and these were made into wards at the beginning of the big rush. We received the wounded from the battlefields about twelve hours after they were hurt, all in need of operation. This kept up for days; it just made my heart ache to see them coming in in such terrible condition, — officers as well as privates, — lay on the floor or on stretchers in the corridors for hours awaiting their turn to be operated on. They were so tired, hungry, sleepy, or suffering, that they didn't care what happened to them. The first week of the big rush we worked eighteen or twenty hours a day. I would be in bed about three hours before I would be called again. I never felt tired, nor did I want to go to bed, for when I did go I could not sleep, the excitement was much too great.

"It was wonderful how the nurses kept up. Each one was on duty from eight in the morning until ten o'clock at night, taking only five or ten minutes for her meals. We had at that time only about eighty nurses, twenty were in the operating rooms, we were running ten tables both day and night, and stopped only on the top floor during an air raid. We had an air raid every night while we were so busy and two nights they were right over our heads; the shrapnel fell all around us, and hit on the tin roofs like big hail. The boys rushed out and picked up big pieces of it."

"American nurses for American men," was a famous recruiting slogan for the Red Cross, but only those can appreciate its poignancy who have seen the eager welcome that leapt to meet the nurse who "talked American."

Especially was this true of the nurses sent by the Red Cross Commission to take care of American wounded in French Army hospitals. Despite the close bonds of friendship between France and America, these little groups could not help feeling lost — strangers in a strange land. They were suffering and immeasurably weary, and they "didn't get the lingo." No wonder they were pathetically grateful for the American nurse; no wonder the nurse's aid who went along to speak French for her was kept on the jump by day and by night. It is said of one American boy, and there were many such cases, who had undergone an operation as soon as he reached the French hospital, that, on hearing an American nurse speaking to him when coming out of ether, he became almost hysterical with the relief and excitement that followed his surprise at not finding himself among Germans.

These nurses were among the 604 that served directly under the Red Cross. Of these some 250 formed the nursing service of the Red Cross in France. They manned the great hospitals run by the Red Cross for the French and American soldiers and Red Cross personnel; they stood ready to go on call to the French or American Army Hospitals near the front or to the convalescent hospitals in the interior; they were the sword arm of the Red Cross in its fight against tuberculosis and of its work for children and refugees.

Work with the Red Cross was essentially emergency work. A Chief Nurse writing casually of the Children's Bureau states that "The hospitals have a way of doubling overnight." A shift in the offensive, a sudden flood of *repatriés* into Evian, evacuation of a strip of bombarded territory, and the hospitals were swamped and personnel commandeered wherever they could be found. Red tape tripped no one on field service for the Red Cross.

Later in May when the stream of wounded ebbed slowly back into France, the Red Cross Department of Civil Affairs turned sixty of its nurses over to the nursing service. They were all experts in baby welfare, tubercular, or other social welfare work. One afternoon found them peacefully at their work in the interior, washing babies, dieting old men, lending a kindly ear to neighborhood gossip; the next night they were miles away, gone by motor truck to the rescue of six American nurses, a few doctors, and twenty wounded at Beauvais, and were assisting major operations with the aid of flashlights in pitch-black wards during an air raid.

France was the battleground of nations. In France beat the heart of the Red Cross work in Europe, but to each of the principal Allied countries there went Red Cross Commissions, the flying squadrons of mercy. Milan was the clearing-house for the nursing service in Italy. Here, new recruits from America learned Italian ways before they scattered to centers of relief or instruction; in England, Russia, Greece, Palestine, Rumania, Serbia, and Siberia, the soldiers of the cross to-day are laying foundations of knowledge and affection for greater work to come.

Many French surgeons who have witnessed the work of American nurses say that they stand preëminently high in the practice of their profession. Their work during the war will be supplemented by equally valuable reconstruction service. Already foreign countries are beginning to look toward the American training schools for nurses for guidance in developing schools of nursing. The Italian Government has recently asked the advice of the Red Cross Commission in the organization of a national association of nurses. The little groups of American nurses in French military hospitals consider the eagerness of the French women to learn their methods a high and touching tribute, while the elementary courses given in baby saving at Paris, Marseilles, Lyons, and Bordeaux, where French women received theoretical instruction from American public health nurses and had practical work in the civilian hospitals, have served to interest French women in developing better public health standards of their own.

The immediate desperate needs of war have appalled the world. The nurse must still hold her battle line long after the guns are stilled. To-day she must help defend the health of the world. The fight has already been begun by the growing ranks of public health nurses now keeping watch and ward over congested city districts, industrial communities, and scattered mountain farms. A great field of health education also awaits her, so that every wife and mother may know the elementary principles of keeping her family well by the knowledge of proper food and sanitation, and of nursing them through minor illnesses by her familiarity with simple nursing procedures. The Red Cross looks even beyond this long reconstruction. War has taught the world the tremendous possibilities of applied humanity, and the spirit of the crusaders is still abroad.

On the honor rolls of the Red Cross stand the names of 197 nurses who, since 1917, have given up their lives. From overseas come reports of American nurses decorated for valor : several received special military mention, while others received Royal orders or the *croix de guerre;* here, in this country, a number were awarded the Distinguished Service Cross. Those nurses, however, who now rest quietly in France and England, have received the highest honors which war can give to the soldier.

Among the ranks of these heroic dead looms the figure of one nurse to whose vision and tireless work the Red Cross Nursing Service owes its development. Born in a little town in New York, educated at the Bellevue Hospital Training School for Nurses, — from which so many famous pioneer American nurses have been graduated, — and serving a long apprenticeship in the practice of her profession in its various branches, she came to Washington in 1909, as the Second Superintendent of the Army Nurse Corps. In 1912, she resigned this appointment to devote all her time to the development of the Red Cross Nursing Service. Slowly she built up this reserve corps until it was recognized as the foremost medium through which the nurses of America might respond to patriotic and humanitarian service in time of national crises. She saw this organization, to which she had given the best years of her life, meet the gigantic burdens of war ; she saw the nurses holding up the hands of the Medical Department of the Army ; she saw them turning with equal success to the tremendous problems of peace ; and then, when at the height of her power and achievement, death calmly, almost unexpectedly, claimed her for its own. Among the American dead in the little Army cemetery on the hill above the great American Base lies Jane A. Delano, First Chairman of the National Committee and Director of the Department of Nursing of the American Red Cross.

"After Life's fitful fever, she sleeps well."

CHAPTER VIII

MOBILIZING THE CHILDREN

Creation of Junior Red Cross — Reasons for Organizing the Children — The Plan Evolved — Means of Replenishing the School Fund — Financial Activities Had an Educational Value — Raising Money Only the Beginning — Coöperation with the Chapter — Correlation of the Red Cross and American Schools — Reaction on the Home — Reaching Foreigners — Thirty-five Minutes a Day — Notes from Reports — Awakening for the Country Child — Definite and Permanent Beneficial Results.

PRIOR to September, 1917, the Red Cross had only grown-up people in its membership. It started out with every intention of doing good work, but was seriously handicapped by the loss of men taken for service and for the ten thousand or more other things that a nation at war had for them to do. This, of course, meant that not only the grown-up women but the young women who expected to be grown-up very soon would have to knit and sew; and, by and by, when more men went away and the demand for supplies and shipments increased, they would have to step in and do men's work.

Up to this time, at any rate, nobody had given much thought to the children. As the months followed each other, however, there were more and more little girls knitting wristlets, helmets, and sweaters, and doing it about as well as their wonderful mothers did. There were little girls marching to the Chapter rooms and working there like troopers as long as anybody. And then some one saw them and what they were doing, and just for a kind of curious mental exercise multiplied it by a million. The result was past dispute.

Now all the time that the Red Cross was trying to do for the soldiers the things the Army could not do ; while it was trying to do for the stricken civilians of other lands what their own overburdened governments could not do, — what in fact nobody else could do, — the Red Cross needed somebody to do what its own organization and all its army of adult Chapter members had not time or fingers for. So the War Council created a Junior Red Cross, by which process "the Greatest Mother" adopted all the school children in the United States, and many more besides in Tokio, Shanghai, London, and the Cape of Good Hope. In other words, the children of America became active partners of the Red Cross. It was to be a family affair, and it meant an immense amount of organizing in the field and at Headquarters, as well as an added bureau to the Department of Development and a new committee in every Chapter.

As can well be imagined we did not attempt to select work that could be done in the schoolroom and at the same time be eligible for "service in France" until after we had made a careful study of Red Cross supplies. Obviously, this involved a delicate adjustment of the established educational system ; it necessitated a great many more things besides ; in short, the Red Cross had cut out for itself another big section of hard work.

And, although this was brought to pass sometime ago, people even now, and not infrequently, have asked us "why did you do it? Why did you bring into the organization millions of new untrained members, children at that?"

At this distance, and in view of what has been carried into effect, it seems almost unnecessary to give the reason : but we did it because we believed that no greater opportunity could be presented to the children of our country.

"Let us give the children of to-day a share in the nation's business," reasoned the War Council. "We will let them see democracy at work so that they may know what to do to-morrow. What better way to train a generation for service than to give it a share in the active application of Red Cross principles? Would it not catch the child in a moment of enthusiasm and organize all this uncentered force in such a manner as to insure perpetuity of effort in the right direction?"

As for the children themselves, there was never a doubt of their eagerness to serve. From the day that that brother got into khaki and mother started her daily pilgrimages to the Red Cross workroom their question had been, "What can I do to help win the war?"

That the school was the existing nucleus, the machine through which all this force flowing everywhere could be most promptly and systematically concentrated, was made clear to us from the very beginning. Our primary appeal was to the idealism which fills the child's mind and colors its view of all things; to its bubbling patriotism, which knew no bounds. But to make it a factor in promoting the world's well-being it was necessary that it should be reduced to practical terms and placed upon a working basis. Through the school the child might be brought at the earliest age into an understanding of national life and participation in the world's big things. He might learn intelligent care and preservation of health through teaching of first aid, dietetics, and nursing, all objectively useful; the understanding and care of animals as a source of human supply, and a knowledge of growing things. Over all was necessary the inculcation of thrift. It required a new course in school — a teaching of the first truth that service, the essence of patriotism, is the keynote of all real accomplishment.

The idea of course was not wholly a new one. Some of the greatest minds in the world had been trying for years to formulate such an idea in practical shape, and had been endeavoring with a discouragingly small measure of success to translate it into action. The task before us was to develop some workable plan which should give the new purpose its proportionate place in the school life and procedure, so that the spirit it represented might permeate all school work and radiate through that work and its attendant industries into the daily life of every community. In this way there could be impressed upon the children the understanding that they were an active and responsible part of the whole world's life; that they were brothers and sisters of the race; and that the human family would be happier and better when unselfishness and cleanliness were the rule the world around. The plan we evolved was as follows:—

The Junior membership was a group membership. The children joined the Junior Red Cross as a school. They raised a sum of money, equal to twenty-five cents per member for the school fund and which went to finance their own Red Cross work, though under unusual circumstances a school could earn its membership by proving its value to the Chapter as a working unit. The School Auxiliary was a part of the local Red Cross Chapter. In all Red Cross matters it was guided by a special group, the Chapter School Committee, which represented the school interests of the locality. In the quantity, variety, and management of its productive work, the School Auxiliary, officered by its own teachers and principal, was practically autonomous, which usually resulted in the Chapter being endlessly besieged for larger quotas and more work.

This was the simple plan by which the School Auxiliary — a powerful motor of Red Cross energy and enthusiasm — was organized. It was the same story from Battle Creek to San Francisco and back to New York. One morning when "Red Cross" had been in the air for several days, a poster appeared on the wall of the schoolroom. The teacher explained that every time a quarter was added to the school fund another little cross could be added to the poster. What a scramble there was for odd jobs after school! Everyone wanted to paste at least one cross. Father, mother, and the neighbors never had so many offers of assistance — for pay; and for a while the quarters rolled in steadily.

After membership was assured, the school fund needed constant replenishment to meet the demands of the "supply service." But since the school fund could not be kept up by odd jobs alone, there being a limit to the woodboxes to be filled, the heads to be shampooed, the leaves to be raked, and the babies to be taken care of, it was then that the day of real business arrived, and every pupil joined forces to swing a project of real magnitude — an entertainment, a sale, a school garden, or one of the innumerable "business opportunities" that the mind of youth could devise. Perhaps it was a bazaar run by all the schools of the city, like that of the city of Minneapolis, in the year of 1917, where the stock was all made by the children in school time. For six weeks before the sale the sewing classes and school carpenter shops were scenes of keen rivalry and commercial ambition. The children worked as never before in the knowledge that the fruit of their labor — running the gamut of transformations from knitting bag to silver coin, from coin to hanks of wool, from unknit yarn to socks — at last would reach the soldiers overseas.

In other instances it was some arrangement producing a steady income. The children of Los Angeles and the Red Cross children in many other places derived unfailing support from the collection of unsalable waste. Periodical calls were made upon householders, who gladly surrendered the week's accumulation of waste paper, old rubbers, tooth-paste tubes, and broken pans. The booty was carried off triumphantly in "two-boy" power-cars, to be turned into real

H

money by a senior Red Cross Committee. The Los Angeles school fund averaged about a thousand dollars a month from this source.

In Southern California the Juniors harvested castor oil beans from vacant lots. In Lenhi County, Idaho, they collected five hundred pounds of wool from the trees and the wire fences of the sheep ranges. Some New Jersey children marketed arbutus in Atlantic City. During the season of sudden rains a Minnesota youngster capitalized the weather by standing on the street corner with an umbrella, ready to take people home from the car for five cents.

Frequently, the children's financial activities were of double value — they seemed to have a faculty for hitting both birds with one stone. The war gardens added to the national food supply. Toy making in school workshops aided markets that were depleted by the boycott on "Made in Germany." The collection of junk saved time and raw materials for overcrowded war industries. Though their efforts were occasionally amusing and their successes frequently amazing, it was not to be forgotten that the first value of all this work was not the resulting dollars and cents; young America was learning from the school fund the value of money, and acquiring some little skill in the business of handling it. One youngster remarked thoughtfully, "You are really giving when you give to the Red Cross, because all you get out of it is the good feeling that you have 'done your bit.'" No, young man, that is not all. When you put your "movie" nickel in the Red Cross box, you found out something about budgets and the relative value of money for you and for the starving refugee, something that you did not know before the war came to America and the Junior Red Cross came to your school.

But raising money was the beginning, not the end, of the Junior's work. As fast as the coins came in they were turned into supplies for the Red Cross. Everybody had a share! The girls sewed and knitted in sewing-class; the boys in their manual-training shops turned out hundreds of pieces for the Red Cross convalescent houses, and thousands of peg legs, potato mashers, equipment chests, bedside tables, splints, etc., for the use of the United States Army. Even the youngest kindergartner could string together the right number of buttons for a garment.

In four months last year the Junior Red Cross delivered 255,000 refugee garments — garments that saved lives in Europe. In an even shorter time the boys contributed over 4000 articles, which included writing tables, chairs, benches, rugs, etc., for the furnishing of the Red Cross convalescent houses in our American camps. Most of this valuable supply work for the Red Cross was done by the children as a part of their school work. Instead of making model aprons, taborets, and pencil-racks, in order to learn the processes of laying hems and joining corners, they made pinafores for children who really needed them and splints for wounded Yanks. The stimulus to proper hemming and joining was immediate and wonderful. The following incident relating to a little girl of ten years is vouched for: "Well, Mary, are you learning to sew?" asked an interested visitor to the Red Cross sewing class in Arizona. "I don't know," replied Mary, who was taking out a seam for the third time that hour, "but I'm certainly learning to rip." It may not be out of place to assert here that work for the Red Cross opened the stage door to the great world drama.

What little girl laying careful stitches did not visualize the French four-year-old who was to be wrapped in that very cloak, or see a gallant "doughboy" charging across No Man's Land wearing her socks? What boy did not drive his plane straighter for thinking of the wounded Yank whose life might be saved by this very splint?

The Junior cog fitted happily into the Chapter machinery. Numberless were the ways in which the children could help.

They were tireless enthusiasts for parades and pageants. They oiled the wheels of administration, not in a haphazard way, but in orderly relays of stenographers, clerks, messengers, and odd-jobbers. Bare workrooms acquired tables and cabinets from the school carpentry shops, while standard packing cases appeared in the storerooms with yarn winders and knitting needles without end. The print shops turned out creditable stationery and office blanks. "Call up the Junior Red Cross," became a familiar phrase on the lips of the Chapter chairman.

The success of the Junior Red Cross was founded on the correlation of two great systems, the Red Cross and the American schools. It was made possible only by enthusiasm and hard work on both sides. Fitting the Red Cross program into 60,000 schools, and doing it in the first year of the new membership, was not a small task. But the school is the children's natural workshop — it must teach him to deal with life, or its mission has failed. He can learn to control human situations only through meeting them. Together these two great forces, the school and the Red Cross, gave the boys and girls of America their rightful place in the nation's work.

By opening the road of mercy beyond the town orphanage to the pain-racked thousands of France, the Red Cross offered the children of America an active part in the great issues of to-day. It put the schoolhouse in perspective with the world situation. For children, as well as for men and women, work strengthened the emotional thrill aroused by the Stars and Stripes into something more durable and active — the will to serve.

In many cases the thing went farther than the children. For instance, in a Chicago school a whirlwind campaign had won 100 per cent membership and the children were very proud of their new Red Cross buttons. At the end of the day one boy brought his badge to the teacher with a request

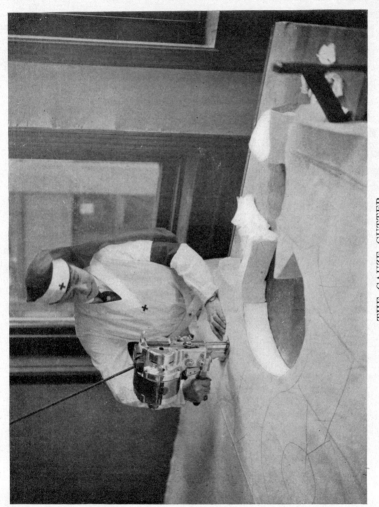

THE GAUZE CUTTER.

American Red Cross workrooms use these electrical machines.

that she keep it overnight, his father having promised to give him a beating if he came home with any such nonsense. The teacher explained that the button was his own responsibility; that he had wanted to join the Red Cross and he could not be a member in school and a non-member outside; and that he could not check his membership with her to be called for the next day. The boy saw the issue at once and wore his button home with a good deal of trepidation. The next day he was looking cheerful. He had not been punished, though family disapproval was deep. Work progressed, and with it the Junior's enthusiasm. A month later the boy's father appeared at the school. The teacher prepared for a struggle. "Say," he asked, "can I get one of those buttons like my boy wears?"

All through the Southwest the Junior Red Cross broke through the barriers that confronted foreigners too shy to go to Chapter workrooms or talk with strangers. These aliens had no contact with the patriotic life of their communities, until women came to school with their children, asking to be allowed to sew for the war sufferers.

American children of many nationalities are in the ranks of the Red Cross workers. Tim Ford, the prize draftsman of the Tonopah, Nevada, Auxiliary, made furniture for Red Cross houses. In spite of his name, Tim was a fullblooded Chinese. The Blue Bird Club was a group of Chinese girls, somewhere in the Pacific Division, each of whom made at least one garment for a soldier. Little Italians, busy in their American schoolrooms making clothes for other Italians who fled across the Piave before the oncoming Austrians, felt a great pride in the big-hearted, long-armed country of their adoption. Race prejudices gave way before sympathy of ideals.

There were twenty-six small Japanese in the Rick Spring School in New Castle, California. A year ago they organized their School Auxiliary to sew for French refugees. East and West met in the great American schoolrooms. Out of the war must come a brotherhood that will reach the national frontiers; and the children, still free from prejudice and bitterness, the inevitable concomitants of war, learned this wide sympathy from the Red Cross.

The plan for fitting Red Cross work into the school system allowed a maximum of thirty-five minutes in the school program of every day as a service period. The service period gave opportunity for discussion of the interests and activities of the Red Cross, the aims of the war, thrift, conservation, and all the other things in which the child could coöperate. This fixed the Red Cross idea in school life and in the school mind, — dignified it by making it a fundamental part of education, a preparation for life. It was a practical reply to the call of human society on every person for his contribution toward the world's welfare.

The school work did not end with the school hours. The activities discussed in the classroom were followed up by the teachers who, in this service, became the officers of the child army; from principal down, they had the handling of their Red Cross forces to think of and plan for. There was actually work to do, and the system injected a new purpose and a new interest in the school life.

The rural schools, where an overtaxed teacher coped with a multitude of subjects, offered a somewhat difficult situation. The meeting of that situation happily involved assistance on Red Cross afternoons from the parents of pupils, who helped in conducting the many lines of Red Cross work. This worked two ways; the lessons of coöperation and service went straight to the home in double measure.

It was obvious from the beginning that Red Cross teaching, to enlist popular favor, must interfere to a minimum degree with the process of scholastic instruction, and also show convincing results in increased practical ability and development of character. The returns were most gratifying. The range of benefits, material, moral, and social, surprised even the people who had devised the plan and who had the faith in its efficacy that enthusiasm gives. Reports from schools all over the United States make an interesting contribution to the literature of education. They are a volume on juvenile psychology, a revelation of a keen intelligence in children which had never before been suspected.

A number of things came to light. The school child of America proved himself possessor of resourcefulness, invention, ingenuity in finding ways and means, faculty of organization, capability in execution, competitive energy, and understanding of the objectives and the inner meaning of the war in such a degree as to put him fairly on a plane with his elders; the demand on his generosity disclosed unselfishness and intelligent sympathy for the sufferings of children in other countries.

From an extensive file of reports on Junior Red Cross work in schools in all parts of the Union, these sentences, taken at random, tell a story:

"War has laid its hands upon American children as well as those in Europe — they are taking the responsibility seriously, as is shown by the readiness to sacrifice leisure time and candy money to the success of school war work."

"The need of raising money for the school fund has brought business ability to light in unexpected quarters. Children who hitherto have had no sense of money values have worked, saved, and sacrificed to get money for the Red Cross."

"War work leaves no time for loitering. Labor is dignified, and they manifest a desire to earn money rather than have it given to them. They hoard pennies with the enthusiasm of the miser, but only to give the money to the Red Cross. Thrift is no longer a dull personal virtue, but a patriotic service."

"Time and money, of which youth is by nature prodigal, are taking on new values to the children."

"Coöperation is essential to the success of such undertakings as sales and entertainments, and this ability to work together is carried into more personal relations."

"The hard work which the children have done has impressed them with the necessity for neatness, accuracy, and teamwork."

"From the tragedy of war, children are learning the lessons of co-operation and service."

"Active generosity and the power of working with other people are by-products of these financial enterprises."

"The Red Cross is not an outside organization. The children have made it their own. Their enthusiasm for its interests has drawn out their best virtues and proved that children can do much bigger and more important work than is generally expected of them."

"Hitherto we have dwelt chiefly upon the benefits, privileges, and immunities of a democracy, without sufficiently stressing the responsibilities implied in its citizenship. Now every child is realizing that he, as well as the greatest and wisest of his seniors, has a share in winning the war. The habits and the ideas that he is establishing are a national gain."

"For years there has been a conscientious effort to teach patriotism to the children of our American schools, but because the teaching was only verbal it often remained as a school association rather than as a reality of after life. The Red Cross has vitalized idealistic patriotism."

"There is no evidence of lowered standards of school work — rather boys and girls feel the necessity of studying hard to lay a foundation for future work. The children accept personal responsibility and the binding values of a pledge of service."

"Common interest and labor shared make a real basis of democracy. Home and school are drawn closer together. Through the work of their hands the children have won fellowship with their schoolmates, with the millions of men and women who are working for the Red Cross, with soldiers in the trenches, and the refugees behind the lines. There has come a wonderful awakening for the country child. He realizes for the first time his own importance as a part of the country — he is surprised and stimulated with his new outlook upon life. He develops an altruism hitherto unsuspected among these somewhat self-centered out of the way boys and girls. He is not to be outdone in his sacrificial service by his city cousin, but gives himself, his interests, his time, his money, and his energies."

"Without seeming pessimistic, one may truly say that the average modern child had become self-centered. The next generation is learning lessons of responsibility and honest service."

These are not editorial observations. They are the first-hand reactions of men and women who saw this Junior Red Cross work start and watched its progress, who knew the old conditions and noted the changes, who saw un-imagined blossoms of character and ability grow swiftly out of the soil of selfishness, carelessness, and sloth. There has come a new vitality into all school life, even into the slow old routine of its exercises. The imitative impulse of childhood has a new goal: The lad no longer imitates the bad man of his village but has a new dream and a new model. He wants to keep fit like the soldiers, who have so nobly thrashed the Huns.

Arithmetic loses its terrors when its problems are practical and urgent ones. The dismal maps of the school geography become a stage on which is passing the most thrilling "movie" of all history. Continents and peoples that once had for the American boy no more vital meaning than Noah's Ark animals are alive with interest that is intensely personal to him and to the boy next door. The threads of all the world run straight to his own house, and in the great picture of mankind's activity he feels himself a recognizable figure. The responsibilities and the vivid interests of world citizen-ship, the thrill of a proud nationalism, have gripped him with a hold that can never be loosened. He reads history now, as no parental pleadings have ever been able to prevail upon him heretofore to do ; it is the new history that every tempestuous day of war has written. He is gathering from every possible source the answers to questions that are ever-lastingly asking themselves in his busy brain.

This is education in its best form. This is the leading of the home-bound mind out into the light of the wide world's life and learning. But there is the reverse action of all the enthusiasm of interest. The school child, with the intuitive deduction which is a child property, gets at once the truth that if the strong and the clean are to win, if right and decency are factors in leadership, then these virtues must begin at home. It is "many a mickle that makes the muckle" and his town must not be the only decadent spot in Denmark. The Red Cross says "community service," and it translates itself instantly into terms of a clean town, a healthful town, a progressive town, a busy town, a town full of thrift and empty of rubbish, and lending every possible hand to the world's big work.

It is hard to overestimate the value and weight of the endeavor which was evoked in all these millions of children — at the time that I write their number is given, 10,728,715 — by this call for personal service. All the vitality, all the invention, all the sacrifice, which in the old lazy days used to go to finding some way of dodging work, were transformed and galvanized into righteous industry.

By the wisdom and ingenuity of the teacher and those who worked with him, this new understanding was converted into national habits. It was systematized and dramatized, it was provided with workable methods, and it was surrounded with a living interest which was to continue after the stimulus of war had passed away.

The Red Cross, with all its wide labors for the good of others, has done nothing more vital to the making of a better and more livable world than this stimulation and organization of child energy, this establishment of new aims, new standards, and a new field of ambition for the young.

CHAPTER IX

SUPPLIES AND TRANSPORTATION

Trying Problems of Organization — Personnel Department — Demand
and Supply — Some Illuminating Figures — Address of the Italian
Premier — "Emergency" Provision — The Earthquake at Guatemala — The Halifax Disaster — "Hurry" Calls — Red Cross Purchases Combined with Those for the War Department — Bureau of
Stores — Shipping Space for Red Cross Supplies — Bureau of Transportation — Report of Baltimore Export Warehouse — Some Figures
from Report of New York Warehouse — Free Space Accorded Red
Cross — Insurance Problem a Difficult One.

ALTHOUGH founded on sentiment and built on purely
idealistic elements, the Red Cross was, nevertheless,
called upon to perform the most mechanical of all functions
and upon the biggest imaginable scale.

With free hand and unstinting faith the American people
gave to the Red Cross large sums to be converted into
everything that our fighting men might lack, everything
that a wide and woeful world might stand in need of. The
money was given with the intention that it would be made
to go as far as energy and business intelligence could make
it go. It was a big trust; a stupendous contract.

As might be expected, the Red Cross had many trying
problems of organization, but none that were greater than
this. Obviously, the men to solve it were those who had
been identified with industrial and commercial institutions;
men who could apply to Red Cross operations the lessons
of long and successful experience in business life.

It was to such men as these, therefore, that the War

Council turned to constitute the Red Cross Department of Supplies and Transportation. In the handling of this huge business of buying and shipping supplies they utilized the wisdom of which commercial competition is the shrewdest teacher. They were the men who converted the sentimental dollar worth into anywhere from one to three dollars' worth of clothing, food, medicine, and a thousand other things, and saw to it that they reached the people who needed them in the shortest possible time.

The operations of the Department of Supplies and Transportation must not be translated by the familiar and prosaic lexicon of trade, but in the language of the need and suffering that war brings. Its interminable invoices and correspondence ever reflect a picture like that, for instance, which France presented in 1917. Back of its continuous transfer of commodities, of shifting debits and credits, was the spurring consciousness of the sick and starving thousands of Macedonia and Serbia where brutality had left a graveyard and waste; through the hours of its buying and the rapid fire of its typewriters echoed the cries of the hundred and fifty thousand unfed babies in the city of Petrograd.

There was a stimulus in this world's cry that chained these men to the job, that humanized and fairly put the breath of life into the bills-of-lading, ships' manifests, and monthly statements, and not the reward that was in it, for there was none.

With noiseless and methodical routine they went on filling the orders and getting the ships away. Everything marched with speed and with lost motion reduced to a minimum. In business this would spell dividends; in the Red Cross its profits were counted in lives saved. For these purposes $9,000,000 a month in supplies passed overseas to our fighting men, to our allies, and to the needy of many lands, in addition to the great quantities purchased abroad and the things purchased for our soldiers at home.

A few men kept this extraordinary work moving. Each had faith in the force of the saying "the fellow who gets to the top is the one who can see what is going on outside without looking through the window." Thanks to that faculty the trains and trucks were always trailing to the seaboard; the warehouses always had cargoes waiting; and the ships with Red Cross money changed into victuals, clothes, and hospital supplies followed each other to the lands where the lack was. Organization wise, the Department of Supplies and Transportation was self-descriptive: it meant and did just what it said; it exchanged the money for the thousands of things needed and transferred them from one part of the earth to another. On the chart, like any other business mechanism, it looked like A B C. The details were multifarious but invisible. The fingers of this Department nevertheless reached out into every field and phase of industrial, agricultural, and commercial production and into every market place. There was scarcely a product which could be used for human comfort that it did not gather to its warehouses. The diversity of commodities was surprising. The manifests of these shipments for Russia, France, and the Mediterranean, were as catholic as a mail-order catalogue. They seem fantastical until one stops to visualize the countries for which they were bound; then every item explains itself; every column of figures supplies a vision.

Take, for example, the figures that represent the January, 1918, shipment to Italy: —

Surgical Dressings	1,495,270
Hospital Supplies	454,536
Hospital Garments	384,517
Articles for Soldiers and Sailors	52,369
Total	2,334,323

And again in February: —

Surgical Dressings	1,349,026
Hospital Supplies	258,075
Hospital Garments	226,214
Refugee Garments	4,059
Articles for Soldiers and Sailors	1,601
Total	1,838,975

What do these figures conjure up, I ask, if not the after-math of the Italian disaster at Caporetto! What do they instantly summon to mind if not a picture of wounded and homeless men safe, at last, and cared for behind the barrier of the Piave! But if visualization is lacking and words needed to understand the appreciation of the Italian people of the prompt action taken by the American Red Cross in forwarding supplies, I take the liberty to quote from an address at the opening of the Italian Parliament: —

"Our soul is stirred again," said the Premier, "with appreciation and with admiration for the magnificent dash with which the American Red Cross has brought us powerful aid in our recent misfortune. We attribute great value to the coöperation which will be given us against the common enemy by the prodigious activity and by the exuberant and consistent force which are peculiar to the American people. . . ."

But to return to the items: Take them straight down from the A's; there is purpose and use for them all. In the distance that you travel between adding-machines and yolk-powder you can see the whole panorama of war and of the people whom it has made forlorn; and, inciden-tally, when you get to the Y's, you have passed an astonish-ing amount of money. An entry of "ambulances and automobiles" brings into view with photographic clearness the ancient French and Italian highways, cluttered with the impedimenta of war and scarred with the ruin which the Germans left behind them. The long list of "agricultural supplies," formerly itemized under "farm-machinery, tractors, farm-tools, seeds, and fertilizers," reveals the French peasant — sturdy women, men broken on war's pitiless wheel — trying with new American methods to restore the lost food production of France, or the unbending Serbian working out his own victualing problem again on the rich acres that the Austrians could not hold.

There was an unbelievable quantity of hospital supplies and equipment and tents and portable buildings to shelter them and which moved promptly in case of need. There were drugs and surgical apparatus without end for the intricate operations which have come into common practice with the frightful wounds of this war. They tell their own stories of the scientific care which the Allied soldier received.

There are household goods in variety that is disheartening in these days of high prices : Games, clothing of every known fashion and size, camp things, auto parts, oils, gasoline, blocks, rope bottles, blacking, catgut, Bristol board, bailing machines, cement, arm and leg supports, rubberized caps, carborundum, earthenware, glass sides, fire extinguishers, enameled goods, crutches, cork, comfort kits, thermometers and photographic films, baseballs, dental goods, cutlery, nails, mouth organs, hooks and eyes, incubators, hammocks, ovens, mattresses, grindstones, razors, rakes, pillow-cases, tree-sprayers, stretchers, scales, stoves, pens, pill-rollers, syringes, shop tools, wax, threshing-machines, sweaters, tubing, washing-machines, puzzles and sewing-machines, oil-heaters and moving-picture apparatus, operating-tables and spool cotton, trench candles, etc., etc. This list taken from the files is sufficient to reflect the strange and almost absurdly variegated life that was lived in the zone of war.

The Bureau of Purchases, whose business it was to buy all these innumerable things, divided its supplies into two sections : one was made up of what it had to buy and, furthermore, to buy far in advance of the need in order not to be caught short when the hurry call might come. These were the raw materials for Chapter production which the women of America had turned out in a ceaseless stream with an astonishing total. The other section included supplies requisitioned by Foreign Commissions and supplies used for our boys at home. It is just as impossible to set forth in detail the infinite processes and steps by which these tons of diverse commodities were assembled together from everywhere and set afloat as it is to depict with particularity the great scenes in which they later appeared.

It will give one but little idea to know that 1,229,016 "pounds" of men's shoes were shipped — practically all to France, Rumania, and Serbia — up to July 31, 1918, and that 150,000 pairs went to Vladivostok in August for the Czecho-Slovaks. All of the women's shoes were bought in Europe. Surgical instruments do not weigh much singly, but they cost prodigiously, and in July the Red Cross delivered over 170 tons of them across the seas to mend shattered and twisted bodies. In sheer weight, it is interesting to observe, cigarettes and tobacco ran a close second to automobiles and ambulances, which show a total of over 1300 tons. In three months alone 280,000,000 cigarettes were sent overseas. There were 237 tons of bandages and 209 tons of absorbent cotton; 400 tons of drugs; 320 tons of soap; 274 tons of sheeting; 48 tons of slippers; 32 tons of pillow-cases; 170 tons of surveyors' instruments, and 30 tons of towels. There are some of these totals that are mystifying, for example, 40 pounds of yardsticks; but 63 tons of chewing-gum confirms the oft-reiterated declaration that the Red Cross tried to make the American soldier feel at home.

In war time "foodstuffs" was the most comprehensive word in the English tongue; it meant everything from pepper and jam to priceless ham and white wheat flour;

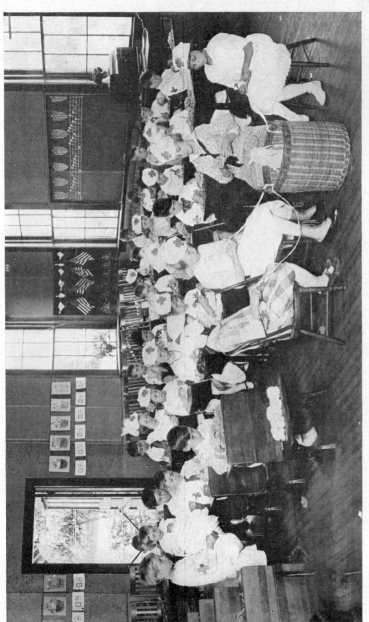

MEMBERS OF THE JUNIOR RED CROSS AT WORK IN A SCHOOLROOM.

even big business economizes on the clerical items when it comes to foodstuffs.

There were times also when emergency was a most descriptive word. In contemplation of its task the Supply Department classed all the provisions it made for civilian relief, military relief, and foreign relief as "emergency." In the crisis of necessity all the red tape was cut. For instance, when the earthquake shattered Guatemala, there came on Saturday afternoon a cry for help. It was in the middle of winter and, naturally, the next day was Sunday, but Monday was New Year's Day; a telegram brought the information that a ship was clearing from New Orleans for Guatemala on Tuesday noon; at once a list of food and drugs and clothing was telegraphed together with instructions to a Red Cross man, a New Orleans banker, that these things must be on board when the vessel cleared, which they were.

When the explosion of December, 1917, shook Halifax, it was the same story: the Red Cross got together carloads of everything that could possibly be needed and had them in Halifax within twenty-four hours. It would seem, therefore, that provocation is all that is needed to effectuate results for, again, when the Bureau of Foreign Relief handed over a cable to the effect that the people in the Madeira Islands were starving to death, there was a response from the Supply Department that surprised even themselves. What the Madeirans wanted to maintain life in their little island was corn. On the Atlantic Coast there was no corn. In Illinois they were making fat steers and 60-cent bacon out of it. A ship loading in Norfolk for Madeira was scheduled to sail in four days and Chicago, in those times of congested traffic, was far away. The Supply and Transportation Department cracked this nut in three taps: first, it got the Navy Department to delay the sailing; second, it bought, by wire, a thousand tons of corn in Chicago; third, it got a priority order from the Railroad Administration; with

I

the result that the corn was hurried into 38 cars and rushed out of Chicago on a special train. It was followed through, and ten days from the date of receipt of the cable the corn was on its way to Madeira. Again: When, shortly after our entrance into the war, the Red Cross hurried off a Commission to relieve the crying distress in Russia, the list of commodities included a large quantity of drugs and medicines. There was another case where the ship was due to sail. Orders were telephoned to the chemists in Philadelphia; the supplies loaded on motor-trucks for New York; and $300,000 worth of supplies were put on board in forty-eight hours.

There are many such instances. I remember that at the time the Palestine Commission was getting under way, it happened that sudden demand was made on us for essential supplies which were not at hand. It was on Friday that the requisition came, the boat was due to sail on Sunday, and the shortage was not definitely discovered until late Saturday afternoon. But all this mattered little to the people at the Atlantic Division Headquarters when put in charge of this order. In a jiffy they had enlisted the service of a fleet of automobiles, located a number of dealers, induced them to open up their establishments on Sunday morning, and when the ship passed Scotland Light every last item was in the hold.

Nominally, a dollar is worth a hundred cents. There were many obvious reasons for making the Red Cross dollar worth more if it could be done, and not the least sound reason was that it was a Red Cross dollar and was being gladly and graciously given in the interest of mankind. So when the markets became excited in the latter part of May, as everyone knows, and prices rose entirely beyond reason, the purchasing department sought to protect itself in its purchases; with the result that an arrangement was effected with the War Industries Board whereby Red Cross

purchases were combined with those made for the War
Department.

With the talent at hand and the spirit of helpful co-
operation everywhere it would be strange, indeed, if there
had not been many savings made. But why attempt to
recite them. It must not be overlooked, either, that the
various departments of the Government extended every
facility, which resulted in the saving of precious time and
hundreds of thousands of dollars.

In the days of submarine and overtaxed shipping, it had
become the rule to forward nothing from America that could
be bought on the other side. When this plan was first
considered we first explored the French market. But,
appalled at the volume of red tape necessary to conform to
French regulations, we turned to England. That Government solved the situation by putting the American Red
Cross on a parity with the British Red Cross. The Red
Cross dollar went up in value. England got the business at
a reduced margin of profit, and a vast amount of trans-
Atlantic cargo space was saved for munitions and guns and
Army supplies. As a matter of fact, during the year ending
June 30, 1918, the purchases abroad for France, Italy,
Great Britain, and Belgium exceeded in value the purchases
made in America during the same period for shipment to
Europe.

We come now to the Chapter Supplies. These were
small troubles to the Department of Supplies. There was
a Bureau of Stores which did nothing else but look after
the supply of material furnished to Chapters and the avail-
ability of the resultant product for shipment. Every
woman who knitted or sewed for the Red Cross knew that
the whole business of Chapter production, which had a
bureau all its own, had undergone a change since the early
days of 1917, when every patriotic soul in the Chapter was
buying yarn for herself and nowhere two sweaters looked

alike. Those were parlous days! If there were three business houses in a Chapter town that handled wool and none had a sufficient quantity to fill a Chapter order, all three would rush a call into the New York market; the demand thus ran wild and the market was fluctuating and uncertain. Then the War Industries Board put its adjusting hand on the wool supply. By and by, through a studious process of coördination, Chapter production was put on a business basis. The Bureau of Chapter Production provided specifications for all Chapter production, so automatically definite that sick soldiers looked like twins in hospital garments and socks were always mates. There may have been a better way to run this business, but no one ever found it. A million or more of silvery-haired grandmothers who had made stockings for four generations had to change their method, showing that it is never too late to learn. To further aid in adjusting supply to demand, the Bureau of Stores was formed. The value of Chapter effort, always great, was multiplied many fold. It was estimated most conservatively at anywhere from sixty to a hundred million dollars.

The principal business of the Bureau of Stores was intermediary. It was more a Bureau of Records, limited records, but of large importance. It had a set of books, — one for each Division, — which was turned in from the Division monthly and in which were set down the demands for material for articles which the Bureau of Production had allotted for manufacture; against the totals of these requirements the Bureau of Stores inscribed its stock on hand, and thus was enabled to know from month to month the state of its supplies by Chapters, which, when made up into finished articles, were shipped to the Division Warehouses, where they awaited demand. It was a very simple cog, but it kept the whole system of Chapter production protected against lack of materials; and, in conjunction with

AMERICAN RED CROSS MOTOR AMBULANCES, HOSPITAL TENTS, AND OTHER SUPPLIES IN THE COURTYARD OF THE PALAIS ROYAL IN PARIS.

These supplies were destined for Russia.

the Production Bureau, was of use in assuring a supply of finished goods on hand. I said in the beginning that it required purely mechanical processes to transmute sentiment into relief. This is an intensified illustration.

When the market goods were bought and the Chapter goods were made the thing was to get them to the people who needed them. The nationalization of the Red Cross has been a great aid in securing for it every possible advantage in ocean tonnage. The Allied Governments had been called upon to give space for Red Cross supplies to France, Italy, England, Russia (Kola, Archangel, and Vladivostok), Serbia, Greece, Switzerland (for American prisoners, Serbian prisoners, and the Swiss Commission), Palestine, Denmark (for American prisoners), Virgin Islands, Madeira, Guatemala, Haiti, and Madagascar. In negotiating for space the Bureau of Transportation perfected arrangements for shipment in steamers controlled by the French High Commission, the United States War Department, the British Ministry of Shipping, the Italian Ministry of Shipping, the Greek Legation, the Russian Embassy, the United States Shipping Board, and the Commercial Steamship Lines. The Red Cross Ports of Export were New York, Newport News, Norfolk, Baltimore, Philadelphia, Boston, New Orleans, Montreal, Seattle, and San Francisco.

Beginning with a simple organization in 1917, it required many changes, in the face of increasing difficulties, to perfect the present system of transportation. No smallest item that could contribute to increased efficiency was omitted, nor anything that would reduce by the smallest amount the cost of the operation. War tax, for example, was exempted on all Government freights. The Red Cross appealed to the Treasury Department for similar recognition on the ground that it was a governmental agency, and thereby secured exemption on all domestic transportation. It did not apply to foreign shipments. Revenue tax amounting to hundreds of thousands of dollars was also omitted on soldiers' tobacco. Under private ownership it was the custom of the railroads to extend to shippers two weeks' credit on freight charges. The Railroad Administration, upon taking control, cancelled this custom but exempted Government freight. The Red Cross claimed like exemption and the administration circulars were reissued to that effect. This concession contributed substantially to the smooth working of the Red Cross system. It enabled the Division to check their goods on shortage and simplified the processes of claim and recovery. To further profit in this direction, the Bureau of Transportation placed a traffic man in each Division and Port Warehouse for the purpose of checking freight and express bills, claims for overcharge, loss, and damage on raw materials delivered to, and finished supplies received from the Chapters, as well as supplies handled through the warehouse. Each Division and Port Warehouse was responsible for materials received and shipped, and made its own recoveries. Expense bills remained in the records of the Division and Port Warehouse so that they might be available for use in prompt presentation of claims to common carriers. Many of these fundamental changes in transportation regulations solved embarrassing problems in the actual handling of material.

At first, it was the custom of the division warehouses, and even of the Chapters, to ship to New York export warehouses small quantities of articles as finished. It was afterwards decided that no Chapter goods should be shipped unless in carload lots and without first obtaining necessary authority from the Bureau of Transportation — a step which established control of the movement to ports of embarkation, and did away with congestion, demurrage, and many difficulties in the adjustment of steamer accommodation. Under the old system Chapter goods were piled into New York in large aggregate, entailing heavy operating expenses, particularly for truck delivery. The cartage charge alone at New York City, railroad station to warehouse, was 35 cents per case. This was eliminated. The congestion in New York was troublesome until arrangement was made with the Italian Ministry of Shipping to transport all cases for Italy from Baltimore.

A substantial saving was effected in securing short hauls, as will be shown in the following order for 400 tons of rice for Italy: under the old conditions this shipment normally would have moved from the port of New York. The Food Administration quoted on rice delivered in New York, but the rice was in New Orleans. Through the Italian Ministry of Shipping, the Bureau of Transportation secured space in a vessel clearing from New Orleans, and thereby saved freight revenue amounting in all to $4559, based on all-rail rate to New York at 56½ cents per hundred pounds.

A great amount of material which, ordinarily, might have required rail transportation to the eastern seaboard for export, was shipped from the Pacific coast in direct vessels. Much of this consisted of the products of the Chapters in the Northwestern and Pacific Divisions. The Bureau secured from the United States Shipping Board an allotment of seventy-five weight tons per vessel in the new merchant ships which were being constructed on the Pacific coast. The vessels from Seattle, Washington, and San Francisco, California, carried to France flour ground out of Australian wheat; Pacific salmon and dried fruits from California went directly overseas in the same way, which resulted in a saving in overland freight transportation of one dollar and fifty cents to three dollars per hundred pounds.

There was scarcely an angle from which one could approach the purchase and transportation of Red Cross supplies to-day without finding a saving in money, resultant from business efficiency and from the uniform consideration shown by the Allied governments, the departments of our own Government and commercial interests everywhere. An interesting showing is made in the operation of the Red Cross export warehouse, even at the busiest ports. The operation report of the Baltimore export warehouse from April 1 to September 30 revealed a satisfactory economy in the handling of seaboard traffic. The total expense in the warehouse for this period — including warehouse and office rental, demurrage, cartage, lighterage, salaries, labor, and every other miscellaneous expense — showed a total of seventeen thousand and some odd dollars. There were shipped at this time 135,072 cases, with a total value of $6,727,928; the total weight was 7996 tons. The cost of handling was 12¾ cents per case, and by the ton $2.17. This ton cost — every ocean shipper will confirm this — was actually lower than a stevedore company would contract for the warehousing and loading or unloading of any vessel. The low cost per case is almost extraordinary when it is borne in mind that many of these cases were five-ton trucks, kitchen trailers, and other heavy equipment requiring steam derricks for handling.

The New York export warehouse in its report covering the year ending June 30, 1918, disclosed an increase in shipments handled monthly from 26 to 55; and an increase in packages handled from 43,000 to 48,000 per month, but the cost per shipment decreased from $1.655 to $.508 over 242 shipments; the cost per package from $1 to 53 cents; the cost per ton from $15.31 to $9.06; and the cost per $1 value declined from $.0373 to $.0157.

But the greatest saving in all the business of transportation is shown in the record of free space accorded to the Red Cross. Before the Government took over the shipping lines the rates for ocean transportation appeared to have no limit. The average quotation was $110 a cubic ton, and it ran from that rate up to all the traffic would stand; on the assumption of governmental control the Red Cross fixed a commercial average rate value of $100 per ton.   As the total shipments from April, 1917, to February 28, 1919, amounted to 196,000 odd tons, it will be seen that the value of this space ran well over $19,000,000.

The problem of insurance upon these tremendous shipments of Red Cross materials was, necessarily, a difficult one.   It conformed to the usual business practice of insuring shipments at sea against risks of war and marine peril. The greater portion of the war risk was covered by the Government War Risk Insurance, and the balance was offered to leading insurance companies at net rates and without commission to any one.   As the volume of Red Cross shipments increased, it became possible to establish a plan of partial self-insurance whereby the Red Cross, guided by its technical insurance advisers, assumed a part of the war risk on each vessel.   Altogether there was carried on Red Cross shipments $32,000,000 of insurance, of which by far the greatest part of the premium was war risk.   Out of $1,400,000 of premium, $1,200,000 was on insurance of this nature, and only $200,000 on marine risk.   Chapter goods were insured on cost of material only, since the value of the labor is given by the Chapter workers.

CHAPTER X

THE DISABLED SOLDIER

New View of the Disabled — The Vocational Rehabilitation Law — Coöperates with the Department of Labor — Experience of European Countries — Five Recognized Forms of Disability — Places Where Treatment Is Given — Cure for the Mind and the Will — Illustrated in the Reëducation of the Blind — The Keynote in Cure — Fields Open to the Blind — Training in France and England — Red Cross Institute for Crippled and Disabled Men — Home Service in Reëducation — Treatment of the Tuberculous — Institute for the Blind — Hospital for Shell-Shock Patients — General Résumé.

INJURED men have been an inevitable residuum of wars since wars began. To militant rulers of old they were merely an item in the wastage and were left to fate and their own powers of recuperation.

The aim of modern science and of sociology is not only to leave nothing undone for our crippled soldiers that will make them productive members of society, but to go a long step further, while mending their bodies, and lift them forthwith out of the ruck of dependency and give them standing as co-equal workers in the working world.

It would be at once foolish and insincere to pretend that this is a small undertaking. With its obstacles and its inevitable corollaries it presents a heroic problem. It is the unhappy testimony of history that after the first outburst of emotional gratitude the consideration shown to crippled veterans loses grace and spontaneity. The madness of popular appreciation — vocal at first in free-handed proffers to the home-coming soldier — dwindles as the war recedes and the concentration of business intensifies.

So far as the disabled soldier is concerned there are two principal elements involved in making a new man of him: one is the extent to which surgical science and reëducation can restore his efficiency. But the first and primary essential is the will of the man to profit by his assistance, his ambition, his desire to be a doer rather than a dependent. We must season our gratitude to the wounded soldier with common sense, that it may not evaporate in the violence of its initial warmth. If we treat this wounded soldier like a man and a brother he will be one — for he has proved his quality.

People "by-and-large" will scarcely credit the advance that has been made physically in the restoration of the disabled and their refitment for work. In order that every use may be made of the world's learning and invention in this field, and that the work may be pursued to its conclusion without interference, Congress enacted, and the President approved, the Vocational Rehabilitation Law, embodying a national plan which provided not only for the reduction of a man's disability to its owest terms by surgical and medical treatment, but, also, when this shall have been accomplished, to furnish him with the most perfect artificial limbs and appliances obtainable to render his injury in some degree inconspicuous, but primarily to restore locomotion and manual ability.

Upon this follows reëducation to whatever extent may be necessary to assure substantial earning power and, finally, the procurement of employment for him in the trade or business for which he has been equipped. Wise provision has been made in the law that this acquirement of profitable occupation shall not reduce his pension, but shall supplement it to an extent which will enable him to live on a parity of comfort with other men pursuing similar lines of industry.

In charging the Federal Board for Vocational Education with the mobilization of resources for all necessary courses of training, the Government places at its disposal all the employment facilities of the Department of Labor. It is intended and provided that there shall be complete coöperation between the Army and Navy Medical Boards and all other departments that in any way contribute to the plan; that the work, curative and educational, be so coördinated and combined that rehabilitation shall constitute one uninterrupted process, beginning in the base hospital and ending only when the disabled men, restored, equipped, and trained to the point of industrial efficiency, shall be definitely and permanently placed in lucrative employment. The upcoming generation will not see so much of the paupered veteran soldier, forced by his disability to depend on a precarious and ever diminishing charity, all too thinly veiled by the purchase of lead pencils on a street corner.

In making large provision for this work, the Government took lesson from the experience of European countries. Plans are already under way for the creation of large centers, specially located, designed, and equipped to meet the problem.

The schedules contemplate, with some latitude for complications and minor variations, five general forms of disability: (1) Surgical, involving primarily the loss of one or more limbs; (2) Blind; (3) Shell-shock, including the various phases of psychoneurosis; (4) Tubercular; (5) Deaf. In the reception hospitals at ports of debarkation, the men were classified and distributed to various general hospitals where provision had been made for specific treatment, surgical, medical, and occupational. The following institutions have been designated and equipped: General Hospital No. 2, Fort McHenry, Maryland; General Hospital No. 3, Colonia, New Jersey; General Hospital No. 4, Fort Porter, New York; General Hospital No. 6, Fort

AMERICAN RED CROSS MOVING PICTURES IN WARD AT WALTER REED HOS-
PITAL IN WASHINGTON.

McPherson, Georgia; General Hospital No. 7, Roland Park, Baltimore, Maryland; General Hospital No. 8, Otisville, New York; General Hospital No. 9, Lakewood, New Jersey; General Hospital No. 11, Cape May, New Jersey; General Hospital No. 16, New Haven, Connecticut; General Hospital No. 17, Markleton, Pennsylvania; General Hospital No. 19, Azalea, North Carolina; United States Hospital, Waynesville, North Carolina; Army and Navy General Hospital, Hot Springs, Arkansas; Walter Reed General Hospital, Takoma Park, Washington, D.C.; Letterman General Hospital, San Francisco, California; Fort Bayard, New Mexico; Plattsburg Barracks, Plattsburg, New York; St. Elizabeth's Hospital, Washington, D.C.; Whipple Barracks, Arizona.

The establishments at Fort McHenry, Colonia, Lakewood, Walter Reed, Letterman, Fort McPherson, and Hot Springs are for general reconstruction. Blind cases in which surgery is required are treated at Cape May, but all reëducational work with the blind is carried on at Roland Park, Baltimore. Otisville, New York; New Haven, Connecticut; Markleton, Pennsylvania; Waynesville, North Carolina; Fort Bayard, New Mexico; and Whipple Barracks, Arizona, are reserved for the tuberculous. Deafness is treated at Cape May, and insane cases are taken to Fort Porter, Plattsburg Barracks, and St. Elizabeth's, Washington. The Indian School at Carlisle, Pennsylvania, has also been made available for reconstruction work.

It was the custom in former times to discharge immediately from the Army all men who developed chronic disease or physical disability. At present, under the War Department's ruling, no member of the service disabled in the line of duty will be discharged until he has attained the fullest measure of recovery possible.

In the treatment of these forms of disability there is involved a wide range of medical and surgical skill. The infinite complexities of physical derangement tax to their last resource the ingenuity of physicians and surgeons; they bring into service the latest fruits of scientific development and research. But in one sense all are alike. Their successful management, the attainment of right results in the end, had a common basis and background — the mind and will of the patient. The victim of war, from the moment his life is assured, becomes the object of care and attention with a view to making him useful to the world he lives in.

A perfect illustration is the man blinded, from whatever cause. If in the first stage of hospital treatment it is thought possible that his vision will be permanently lost, the work of reëducation begins without his knowledge. From that time on, — even while he is yet ignorant of the truth, — the doctors are "teaching him to be blind." While his eyes are still covered with an unnecessary bandage, perhaps, he is taught to do for himself things that the blind do, such as shaving and finding his own way about. It is one of the everlasting marvels of life that dormant nerves and muscles and brain cells, waked by necessity, learn in so short a space to do their work. By the time the blinded man discovers the truth the crushing force of the blow has been broken. From that point onward, — on the journey home and at every stage he must pass before the last hope of saving his sight is abandoned, — he, unconsciously, is being trained in the rudimentary lessons of blindness.

With other forms of injury the same general theory is pursued, though perforce more slowly and in less degree. But back of all the physical problems still stands the mental one. In the first days, weeks, or months after realization, there comes the hard, incessant fight against depression, discouragement, relaxation of hope. The winning of this battle is the most vital factor in the work of reconstruction, in the remaking of the man's life. This mental infection of despair is the malady that requires most skillful medicine,

REBUILDING THE HUMAN FACE.

The American Red Cross Artist, who is shown in this picture, has achieved some wonderful results.

and that if uncured may make all the drugs and surgery of no avail.

It is a labor requiring infinite patience and tact and most delicate intuitions. But it can be done. The keynote of the majority of cases has without doubt been struck in a letter written by a teacher, himself a cripple, to the Surgeon General : —

"You must," he says, "not only fit a man to become a wage-earner, but fully as important, you must fit him to enjoy the wages he has earned with his fellows. . . . Unless you prove to the cripple that there is joy ahead, you cannot help him. . . . When a man is wounded and crippled the realization of the crippling comes upon him at a time when the nervous system is least able to bear the additional shock which the realization brings. . . . The mental suffering is very acute, though the doctors and nurses may not know of it. . . . Couple with a shattered nervous system weeks of inactivity, with the idea of helplessness, with the idea of life abnormal, outside the pleasures of the world ; it is wonderful that all cripples are not helpless. You must kill the idea of helplessness almost as soon as it is born, for in a few weeks it becomes very strong. You must show moving pictures of men who are crippled enjoying themselves in normal ways, dancing, skating, paddling a canoe, swimming, playing billiards, and hundreds of things they cannot or do not know about. I could multiply these things a thousandfold, things which you would refuse to believe. But they must be 'put across' to the men early, and it must be done by men who have had experience first hand."

An industrial engineer in the Government employ, whose business it is to make surveys for the purpose of finding fields open to the blind, states as a result of tests and investigations that approximately three per cent of the manufacturing industries involve work which blind men can do satisfactorily. It has, in fact, been found that in some branches of work blind men are more efficient by reason of their closer concentration and that the sense of touch, when developed to requisite nicety, is often more alert and more discriminating than sight.

Fortunately for the work of reëducation in this country, France and England faced the problem before us. In their experience the perfection of mechanical arms with a "chuck" for holding work or tools has opened to armless men occupations in which they would at first sight have been counted helpless. One-armed men, and even blind men, develop incredible skill in the operation of a typewriter from dictaphones, the shift key being worked by pedal. The running of lathes, agricultural tractors, drills, and other machinery, carpentry, tool making, the manufacture of surgical instruments and tools of precision, watch-making, telegraphy, photography, typesetting — all these have been found possible. At the *École Joffre*, near Lyons, which the French established early in the war, accounting and commercial work are taught, also toy making, bookbinding, shoemaking, mechanical drafting, woodwork, tailoring, wood carving, gardening, and machine tool work. It has been found here that industrial drafting and design attract the greatest number of pupils. The National Institute in Paris teaches tailoring, shoe and harness making, tinsmithing, cabinet work, accounting, and the operation and repair of farm machinery.

Both in England and France there is a decided trend among the disabled men toward agricultural pursuits, particularly the raising of poultry. It is the aim of the reëducators in America to fit many men for agricultural life in some form. English schools teach carpentry and cabinet making, carving and gilding, frame, toy, and basket making, metal work, building and construction, decorating and electrical fitting. At Roehampton and Brighton are the greatest centers of training for the amputation cases. It is found that both in England and France the disabled men have proved expert in the making of artificial limbs. This is a specialty in this country, which produces the best appliances of this sort.

In anticipation of the task which lay ahead, the Red Cross established in 1917, with funds made available by gift, the Red Cross Institute for Crippled and Disabled Men, in

A SENEGALESE SOLDIER WHO HAS LOST BOTH ARMS, WRITING TO THANK THE AMERICAN RED CROSS FOR HIS NEW PAIR OF ARTIFICIAL ARMS.

New York City. The purposes of the Institute are chiefly
experimental and in the line of surveys. It has compiled
and republished papers setting forth the results of the best
reëducational work in Europe; it has made a census of the
cripples resident in New York City, with records of their
accomplishment in various occupations; and it has begun
experiments in vocational training in a large number of
trades to determine what the cripple may derive from them.
Teams of disabled persons, thoroughly trained, are put at
work side by side with the sound to determine their relative
capabilities. In some lines of work, the cripple has proved
the better of the two. It is essential that after the classroom work is advanced the beginner in a new trade should
have experience in shop practice, and in securing such facilities from employers these surveys will be of service.

In selecting a trade for the disabled man the most thorough
search is made into his past history, his business or industrial
record, his home life, into every detail, in fact, which may
have weight in the planning of his future. It is desired,
wherever possible, to return the man to his own town and
to his own home and to select for him some branch of industry
in which the place affords employment and a promise of
permanence. The conditions of the home, its atmosphere,
the mental attitude of members of the family and neighbors,
the opportunity extended for further study and for helpful
social relations are of the utmost importance as bearing on
the encouragement which is so necessary to him. In all
these lines of investigation, in preparing a man's family to
be a help rather than a hindrance to him, the Red Cross
Home Service is organized and equipped, by the very nature
of its mission, to carry on a wide and helpful work. In
looking after the welfare of the soldier's family it has
established a relation with them as it has with the soldier
himself during his training and transportation, at the front
and on the way home, which makes for confidence and trust.

K

In what reëducators call "follow-up work," — seeing the man well along on his new adventure in life and giving him a lift when he needs it, — the Red Cross, represented everywhere as it is by the Chapters, is "on the ground" the whole country over. It saw the soldier off and it welcomed him home. It is merely sticking by him now.

The records thus far available indicate that the wounded, and especially those who have lost limbs, are in relatively small proportion of the total number engaged, and the blind, even a smaller number. Medical cases outnumber the surgical, while tuberculosis is chargeable with a particularly large share of the discharges. Fortunately, the United States had developed before the war thorough practice in the treatment of tuberculosis; and in planning its work for returning soldiers the Government has made preparation for them. There were nearly six thousand beds available in the hospitals already set aside for tuberculous patients. The function of the Red Cross in this work was to prevent, through its connection with the families of soldiers, the withdrawal of the man from treatment before his restoration should be complete and he cease to be a menace to the well-being of others.

As an aid to the work of the blind, the Red Cross has established in Baltimore an Institute for the Blind, of which the medical officer responsible for the Army program for the blind is the director. The institution is situated conveniently near to the General Hospital. It provided quarters for the relatives of soldiers who come to visit the hospital. In this, and in furnishing transportation for such relatives where necessary, it is helping to overcome the first and, perhaps, the most serious obstacle to reëducation, — the listlessness or discouragement of the men themselves.

Of all the American soldiers returned from France, it is recorded that twenty-five per cent are suffering from some phase of "shell-shock" or nervous disorder. The treatment

A SCENE IN A CONVALESCENT HOUSE OF THE AMERICAN RED CROSS IN THE UNITED STATES.

of these, in many cases, is extremely difficult and requires time, patience, and extensive equipment of appliances for electric treatment, baths, etc. The special center for these cases is the hospital at Plattsburg Barracks, which includes in its personnel only those who have had to do with treatment and care of similar cases in civilian life.

Medical authorities estimate from the British Army records that the great majority of all men discharged will return to civil life with but little more need for medical care than might be expected in the case of a man of somewhat more advanced age in ordinary surroundings; but for the "disabled," the provision that is being made is broad and liberal, in the highest degree human and kindly, and governed by intelligent counsels. If understood and wisely availed of by the men for whose benefit it is devised, a great part of the poverty, demoralization, and unhappiness which, in other times, have followed long in the wake of war, will have been done away with and comfort and contentment exist in lives which, at first, may seem to have been utterly blighted.

PART II

CHAPTER XI

ON THE BATTLEFRONT

Workers at Every Point in the Red Cross Service to the American Soldier
— A Gap in the Continuity of This Service — Coöperation with the
Army Medical Corps — Research Bureau Maintained — Work of
Communication Bureau — Picture of a Canteen — Rest Stations —
Girl Heroes — Mobility of Red Cross Formations — The Narrative
of Compiègne — The Hospital at Annel — The Rolling Canteen —
Extract from *The Washington Post* — The Ambulance Drivers —
Ambulance Sections Absorbed in the Army Medical Corps — Hos-
pital Service in the Army — Appropriation for *Ravi Taillement* Serv-
ice — Hospital Supply Service — Fifty Base Hospitals Furnished
to the Army — Examples of Special Efficiency — Scientific Triumphs
— The Cause of Trench Fever Discovered — Diversions in Hospitals
— Comforts Furnished — Letter Writing for the Boys — American
Wounded in French Hospitals — Searchers for the Bureau of Com-
munication — Searchers and Help for Prisoners — Care for the
Dying and Dead.

THE hugeness of the war and the detailed awfulness of
it will never be told. For those, like myself, who
touched the edges of it, there can, of course, be no telling
of it save that each recite his vision of the little fragment
that was his lot to see. It is written in the Book of Ages,
and military science will analyze its strategy, but before the
tragedy in its entirety can ever be fixed in human record
the waters of God-forgiven-forgetfulness will have washed
away a great part of it.

It is better that it is so. The hope of mankind lies in the

revelation of inborn human kindness; the task of mankind is to heal the scars that the war has left. Fortunately, as the-horror has grown so has grown the unremitting cry of sympathy and pity. And certain it is that men of vision have never ceased to believe that the world will be saved and that hope's patient litany will save it.

For the soldier, the Red Cross had workers in the field at every point where they could by any chance serve him: at the port where he landed, in the stations through which he passed on his way to camp, at the camp itself, at the stations between the camp and the trenches, and, finally, at the very front. The canteen convoyers brought up supplies of hot food for him despite the weather, shells, or gas. They were ready through the cold, rainy night to comfort him; while a little back from the lines was the canteen where he could wash off the mud in which he might have been standing for nights, where his clothes could be disinfected, and where he could sleep if he had a few hours to wait. In short, it was our intention that the soldier should never be without anything that could express the appreciation of his country and lessen his sacrifice. Unfortunately, however, in a war that has to be told in fragments, it was all too easy, as will be seen presently, for gaps to appear in the continuity of this service.

"It is absurd," said a French soldier who had just come out of the trenches, "to talk about Red Cross work. It has not existed. . . . How could it? A few litter carriers went with us on some of our expeditions but they were soon shot down. . . ."

For the wounded the Army Medical Corps provided the best and quickest care. Alacrity in this department was the essence of effectiveness. An hour might have meant the difference between life and death. That hour was saved by mounting on wheels everything conceivable so that the wounded might be met at the nearest possible point. The

Red Cross contributed ambulances with operating equipments, dental operating rooms, ophthalmological ambulances, plants to make ice to pack head wounds, heating plants, and disinfecting plants. In the American Medical service there was surgical skill that is not surpassed in the world; and to supplement the medical work the Red Cross, with Army coöperation, maintained a research bureau, the value of which has been recognized by all medical authorities. For operations there was a plant manufacturing nitrous oxide gas which, otherwise, could only be obtained in France after long delay. There were shops to manufacture artificial limbs; there was a department — the Communication Bureau — which searched for the missing man and gave his family news concerning him and which, like the Home Service in the home camps, straightened out a thousand tangles and did a multitude of things that were seldom twice alike.

All the permanent or semi-permanent Red Cross plants in France, — following the practice of the Army, — were built and equipped for future requirements. The French onlookers had a thought in reserve when they saw the preparations that were being made for debarkation of the American armies — the unconscionably huge buildings, the ponderous railroad equipment and hundreds of miles of rails; they looked dubiously, too, at the preparations of the Red Cross and wondered if the finished fabrics of accomplishment would ever fit their vast foundations. But within eighteen months they saw two million soldiers walk off these same docks and move forward promptly to business over the iron pathways; they saw incalculable stores of everything under the sun following in uninterrupted procession, food and raiment, engineering supplies and building material, and all the paraphernalia of war.

A well-known Liberty Loan speaker upon returning from France, referring to the big line of stations, said: —

"I didn't know what a canteen was like. I didn't know whether you rolled it or kept it back in the kitchen somewhere; but here is what it's like: if you took one of those piers in the North River that you tie a big steamship up to and converted it into a business enterprise to rest and feed and sleep and wash people, that is about the size of the proposition. The kitchen came first — a huge room full of caldrons and chopping blocks and meats and things — and next was a lunch-counter affair with some tables where they could probably feed five hundred at a clip. Next was the living room where the soldiers could throw off the accouterments of war and rest themselves and write letters. Outside they had some very pretty gardens which had been decorated by the camouflage artists of France. Next came a large theater, — mostly moving pictures, — I was told, but occasionally the men got up entertainments of their own. Next came a place where I suppose 2500 men could sleep, and they had baths and ways to make their clothes sanitary and things of that kind, all very essential.

"The women workers in this same outfit are entitled to some kind of a memorial, if it is nothing more than in our hearts and minds. They are doing a wonderful work. There is a group of women over here taking care of about seven or eight thousand soldiers every day. It is at a railroad center where they transfer off the trains and are redistributed. That thing is done twenty-four hours a day in three shifts of eight hours."

The American soldier interpreted "Rest Station" — with its subtle and more or less elusive course dietary of the French — as something more or less like home and the good old dishes of childhood. Home, therefore, became the keynote in all the buildings and furnishings of the Red Cross way-stations on the road to war. There was the home flavor in the seasoning of the food, and a home atmosphere in the chintzes and various commodities at hand, such as soap, towels, reading matter, and phonograph records. The facilities which the Rest Stations afforded for writing letters back home made the censor of one section, who had to handle them, old before his time, and brought forth a plaintive, if humerous, protest against the stimulation of correspondence.

It was not easy work that these women did. As a matter of truth it involved the hardest kind of physical labor.

Moreover, they were accomplishing unconsciously, perhaps, what even they did not realize at the time — the keeping uppermost in his mind the home idea of women.

Thus, until the day came when the trains of wounded began rolling back to the coast, the soldier's journey was not such a bad journey, after all. And when he got within sound of the trouble he was clean and fit. That was what the Red Cross aimed to make him.

The war has brought to light many heroic deeds. However, not all heroes were men : there are girls who went out in all humility to lend what help they could in the service of the Red Cross canteens and who came home with the *Croix de Guerre;* there are girls who stayed at their posts of duty in the canteens while the soldiers were at the front and when the windows of their huts cracked from shellfire, and the roof fell in pieces — stayed through nights of tumult and danger where their lives were worth scarce a penny whistle; and, again, when on the jammed roadways in the great advance, where the crowding thousands of troops were choked and stayed by ambulances and trucks with their hundreds of wounded, these Red Cross girls were there to help dislodge the tangle so that the great currents could flow normally on their way. This, surely, was getting into the road and makeshift of war.

"We feed 4000 or 5000 soldiers a day, and our canteen is never closed," wrote a Red Cross canteen girl. "All of our boys on this line of communication stop and rest and have meals and refreshments. After every battle and at intervals we see them coming back. Over 1500 came in lately and practically none had ever had first-aid service. Blood-soaked, weary, but oh, how brave! With shell-wounds and bayonet-wounds, they will tell you quickly, 'I can wait, look after Jim, here.'"

It was a long hard grind with existence always in the balance and with no rest or change other than the precipitate retreat or advance as ground was lost or gained. The pictures did not vary except in minor details and in intensity.

The canteens were located in all sorts of places, — any shelter, almost, that would keep out the rain, served the purpose, — but the vital creature comforts were there. The worn, mud-marked, often bloody faces of war-weary men swarmed in out of the night. There was no light save candles or a guttering lamp. They did not eat, — they fed, gulping the hot coffee, munching ravenously. They were spent, but the urge and rush of battle was still on them. The great guns punctuated the talk and the clatter; there was the sibilant half-moaning whistle of the German shells and the muffled roar of their breaking; one had the sense of being depersonalized, or the dual feeling that comes of hasheesh. And yet, for all its awful reality and nearness, it seemed like a dream. The last exchanging columns having passed away into the night the canteeners slept — these men of varying age and calling who, with gray in their hair but with youth's dreams still weaving in their hearts, were keeping Mercy's outposts on the borderland of doom. And the evening and the morning were another day with a flight to the cellar when an air-raid began or when the rangefinder picked up the little area where the canteen was situated.

In times of violent action, when the lines changed under the weight of new forces, the mobility of these Red Cross formations was invaluable. In the broken chronicles of the great German drive in 1918, there were thrilling stories of the quick shifts made by hospital and canteen workers: a sudden gathering of food and equipment, of medicines and instruments, and that heaviest of all known impedimenta, the wounded men under treatment; a swiftly executed move rearward, trucks loaded with gear and personnel and wounded, but never farther than was absolutely necessary; the establishment of new quarters and the quick resumption of work, for men's lives spelled victory and delay was death.

The narrative of Compiègne, where 100,000 men a day

poured forward and back as through a narrow gateway, is a
moving picture. It started on the morrow of the great
German attacks of March, 1918, when French Grand Headquarters had been moved away to Tevlis and the civilian
population had fled; away back in the days when Lloyd
George was cabling President Wilson to send men — and
send them quick; away back before the main American
Armies came. In a big hotel, long abandoned, the Red
Cross took lodgment, threw open the doors and never closed
them for two weeks, intent on its work of general relief. It
was indeed a world cast from its moorings! Soldiers were
lost, — separated from their commands, — foodless, shelter-
less, cold, and wet; and the streets held crowds of refugees.
There were doctors and nurses, executives and handy men of
every nationality and every faith, who gathered in this
center and joined in its work. The kitchen held steaming
stew-pots which were never empty. On the floors of the
great reception-room and ball-room, soldiers of all armies
slept side by side. The city's stores were opened and dry
food given away to the crowding refugees. The truck
drivers, with aerial bombs falling all around them, gathered
terror-stricken people from their houses and making their
way over bridges that were under vicious fire hauled them
away to safety. In the railroad stations an improvised
infirmary was established where doctors dressed the wounds
of fifty to a hundred soldiers a day — wounds that had been
inflicted two days before.

In the hospital at Annel, six miles from Compiègne, in an
old *château*, were two American doctors who had stayed on
the night of March 25, 1917, after seeing the wounded carried
away by canal boats. The artillery near at hand thundered
on with scarcely a pause. It was a night when the Germans
were hammering at Noyon and threatening to break through
any hour and start down the main road to Paris. But the
American ambulance drivers, from force of habit, kept

AN AMERICAN RED CROSS ROLLING CANTEEN.

American boys at a kitchen wagon near the front.

coming with loads of wounded. The American doctors stayed on and worked over the tables for two days or more. Five Red Cross trucks arrived with supplies and their drivers administered anæsthetics while these two American doctors operated on *poilus*, Tommies, or whoever came along.

Some canteen women came in from Compiègne, and with the big German planes soaring overhead and the grumble of the battle drowning speech, these two lion-hearted Americans remained at their posts. This was the sort of courage and the sort of faith that carried the American wherever his job lay in the hurly-burly of war.

After the fighting became open — after the second battle of the Marne and after the Germans started moving toward the Rhine — the rolling canteen proved the prime solution of the quick-lunch question.

In the zone of war the Red Cross workers did not think of safety beyond the sane precautions of the soldier. The Red Cross man offered his life as a gift to his country and to the cause of humanity.

The picture of the ambulance drivers and their venturous task has become more or less familiar. Their peril was incessant. On the other hand, considering their numbers, the forbearance with which death passed by their charmed ranks since the day the first American units went over in 1914, has been a wonderment of the war. Trying as these young *ambulanciers* did to get the wounded from the most forward point possible, they carried their cars through raining shells and bombs, through gas, through every menace that the fire zone knew. In and out, journey after journey, waiting the summons always by night as well as by day, there is a long record of their courage and their ungrudging devotion to one of the most trying duties of the war.

This letter from a Red Cross ambulance driver at Verdun, in the awful summer of 1916, merits preservation as a picture grimly faithful of the scenes in which these non-combatant heroes played their part, and a pathetic record as the agony by which France made good the promise, *"Ils ne passeront pas."* (They shall not pass.)

MY DEAR ——:

To-night I am sitting in a small underground cellar of one of the public buildings of the town, acting as a sort of time-keeper or starter for the cars going up to our most dangerous post and handling the reserve cars for wounded in the town itself. I wish I could describe the scene as it is before my eyes, — for the whole world is passing here — French, American, living, wounded, and dying.

A long heavily arched corridor, with stone steps leading down to us; two compartments off to one side lined with wine-bins, where our reserve men and a few French *brancardiers* (stretcher-bearers) are lying on their stained stretchers, some snoring; beyond a door that leads into a small operating room, and to the left another door that leads to a little sick ward, the most pathetic little room I have ever seen — with four beds of different sizes and kinds on one side and six on the other, taken evidently from the ruined houses near by — and one tired *infirmier* (hospital attendant) to tend and soothe the wounded and dying.

In the bed nearest the door, a French priest, shot through the lungs — with pneumonia setting in — his black beard pointed straight up, and whispering for water. Next to him, a little German lad, hardly nineteen and small, with about six hours to live, calling, sometimes screaming, for his mother, and then for water. Next to him a French captain of infantry with his arm off at the shoulder and his head wounded, weak, dying, but smiling; and next to him a *tirailleur* in delirium calling on his Colonel to charge the Germans. The *infirmier* is going from one to the other, soothing and waiting on each in turn. He asks what the German is saying, and I tell him he is calling for his mother. "Ah, this is a sad war," he says, as he goes over to hold the poor lad's hand.

A *brancardier* comes in with a telephone message, — "A *blessé*" (wounded man) at Belleville — "very serious." This is a reserve car call, so one slides out and is gone like a gray ghost down the ruined street, making all the speed its driver can — no easy matter — with no lights. In twenty minutes he is back. The *brancardiers* go out — they come in again bearing the wounded man on a stretcher and place it on the floor beside the little stove. One of them, who is a priest, leans over him and asks his name and town; then in answer to what his wife's name is, he murmurs: "Alice"; while on the other side another *brancardier* is slitting the clothes from his body and I shiver at the pity of it, the sight I saw.

The surgeon comes out of his little operating room. Weary with the night's tragic work — after so many, many other tragic nights, he douses his head in a bucket of water. Then he turned to the wounded man. He looked long at him, gently felt his nose and lifted his closed eyelids. Then, at his nod, the stretcher is again lifted and the wounded man carried into the operating room, and soon after into the little room of sorrows.

In answer to my eager question the surgeon shook his head. Not a chance.

A *brancardier* and I gathered the soldier's belongings from his clothes to be sent to his wife, but even we had to stop a few minutes after we saw the photograph of his wife and their two little children.

An hour later, as our night's work was slacking down and several cars had driven up and been unloaded, the *infirmier* came in from the little room and said something to the *brancardiers*. Two of them got a stretcher and in a moment "the *blessé* from Belleville" came past with a sheet over him. They laid him down at the other end of the room and another *brancardier* commenced rolling and tying him in a burlap for burial. As you looked he changed to shapeless log. Then out to the dead wagon with it.

Soon after I went into the little ward again to see how the others were coming through the night, and was glad to see them all quieted down; even the little German seemed less in pain, though his breathing still shook the little bed he lay on.

Through a chink I saw that day was beginning to break, and as I noticed it I heard the Chief's car coming in from the "Sap" and I knew the night's work was over.

In France after the American Army began going over in volume, the ambulance service, in common with that of the hospitals and early work with the wounded generally, was militarized almost as completely as the fighting forces themselves. Many of the ambulance sections which, previously, had been allied with the Red Cross, were absorbed into the Army in the same manner as the nurses and base hospitals: In all, the Red Cross organized forty-seven ambulance units which operated under Army management and as parts of the Medical Corps of the Expeditionary Force; it maintained its ambulance units in the nature of reserves, engaged in transporting wounded men, who were on the way

to recovery, from base hospitals to the convalescent establishments maintained by the Red Cross in all parts of France;
it also maintained service for the Marine Hospital at the
port of debarkation.

The line of demarcation established in General Pershing's
forces between the Red Cross ambulance service and the
units definitely identified with the Army itself had a measur-
able degree of elasticity, which made all Red Cross force
and equipment available for the service in advanced territory
in case of need. At the Château-Thierry fight when the
flood of wounded was overtaxing the space and the Army
machinery for their removal after treatment, Red Cross
ambulances were called into service, carrying their unhappy
burden of injured straight from the front to Paris.

This official relation of the Red Cross to the Army — a
supplementary and coadjutant one — was through the
whole field of military activity, whether in the supply of
materials or of service. In a sense, it is for this purpose
that the people of the United States maintain the Red
Cross as a quasi-government institution and for this ultimate
purpose that it was nationalized.

In the average mind, confused in contemplation of the
war's swiftly moving picture, it is doubtful if there exists
any clearly defined idea of the perfectly regulated system
by which the Army effected immediate removal of its
casualties, and the continuous and progressive treatment of
their injuries while, at the same time, relieving any congestion that hampered the steady back-flow of wounded
from the fighting lines.

Under the Army system there were in hospital service
three parallel zones — somewhat roughly defined, and varying with conditions — in which it was intended that all the
elements involved shall be of the Army service and not
voluntary. In a mobile Army each division had four companies, each company twelve ambulances, with dressing

station equipment. These stations were set up in some sheltered place, if such could be found, and to them the wounded were brought. They were provided with a certain amount of equipment, food, and supplies, such as could be easily carried and would suffice for initial treatment of injuries. Back of these — marking the second zone — were four field hospitals under canvas, each capable of caring for 216 patients. There were beds but no cots. These stations carried operating equipment and adequate kitchen outfits. At the next stage — the head of the line of communication — was the first evacuation hospital. The capacity here was double that of the field hospitals, since the transportation facilities farther up might in time of intense action be over-taxed. This was a more or less permanent station, usually located in some suitable existing building. It was not mobile in the sense that it had no transportation equipment. The wounded were dispatched by ambulance or by hospital trains. It was equivalent to what in the British Army was known as the Casualty Clearing Station and was, usually, located in the nearest town. Its function was to clear the field hospital for future emergencies and was permanent save in cases of retreat. If an advance was made, a new evacuation station would be set up in the acquired ground, thus shortening the distance from the mobile area.

From this point the patient, when in fit condition, was removed to the base hospital. Back of this lay the so-called "home zone." From the base, progress was to the convalescent hospitals in Paris or other parts of France, some of which were maintained by the Red Cross.

This, in short, was the process by which the soldier caught up in the instant of his injury, or as soon after as possible, was passed along on the way to his recovery with progressive medical and surgical treatment. Outwardly, and in its operation and control, it was exclusively an Army organization, but the function of the Red Cross, other than in crises where the system was overloaded and the Army service needed reënforcement, was still an important one. The largest single appropriation of the Red Cross for the United States Army in 1917–1918 was $4,330,760, for what is known as *ravitaillement* service. Under this title the Red Cross furnished all sorts of things contributory to the proper and convenient care of the wounded, to the end not only of humanity but of military effectiveness. It included portable kitchens, heating and lighting plants, laundries, baths and disinfecting outfits, dental ambulances, and material for what are called mobile complementary hospitals; also it furnished huts, barracks, and miscellaneous supplies for the purpose of facilitating restorative work among the wounded and maintaining such work in the advanced territory at the points of greater availability. Under the advice of Army Medical authorities the Red Cross established two plants, one in France and one in America, for the manufacture of nitrous oxide gas for the purpose of anæsthesia in cases where the patient was in too critical a state for ether. The total normal capacity was over 25,000 gallons a day.

The hospital supply service, to both American and French hospitals — and the latter are nearly 4000 in number — was very wide. It was operated by having agents call at the various hospitals and obtain from them lists of needed articles not regularly supplied by the Army, such as special surgical instruments and apparatus, convalescent garments, bandages and slings for special operations. These were delivered from the Hospital Supply Service. There was a diet-kitchen service maintained to supply invalid foods for wounded men. Large stores of these foodstuffs were held in Red Cross warehouses, subject to requisition by the Army. These, in a way, were emergency contributions to the wounded man's welfare. The organization of base hospitals, of which the Red Cross furnished fifty to the Army Medical

THE AMERICAN RED CROSS AT THE FRONT IN FRANCE.

Service, at a cost of over $2,000,000, was most fundamental in its character and value.

The Marne fighting of July afforded striking illustration of the importance of the Red Cross supply system in supplementing the work of the Army hospitals. In one shipment seven tons of surgical dressings and five tons of diet foods were dispatched to the front for use in evacuation hospitals for American wounded. The Red Cross medical officer's storehouses and pharmacies were open and busy day and night throughout the counter offensive. On July 18 the chief of the medical section arrived from the front and started back at three o'clock the following morning with a load of emergency supplies, including fifty gallons of alcohol; 2000 doses of tetanus antitoxin; surgical instruments; several gross of surgical needles; and dressings and operating material of all kinds. There are no speed laws in war, and the means that are quickest and nearest at hand were taken for every service. Drugs or hospital equipment needed in a hurry have been rushed to the front by motorcycle. There is a record in Paris of the establishment and preparation of evacuation hospitals behind the front, which makes all previous performances look painfully slow. A hospital officer left Paris with ten nurses and ten tons of equipment. They found a desirable building, rented it, equipped it with everything needed, including operating room and X-ray outfit, and were receiving patients within three days.

Thus through every phase and department of hospital work the Red Cross sought in greater or lesser degree, as opportunity served, to upbuild and maintain the most effective and most modern service for the healing and restoration of the wounded man. The millions of dollars of popular subscriptions that were placed at its disposal have not only worked in every possible direction to insure his comfort, but the Army's shoulders were lightened of a time-consuming

L

load and the paramount business of saving lives has been sped.

The war signalized more than one triumph which was not of arms. One of the most conspicuous of these was the conquest that medical and surgical science achieved over scourges which devoured man power in the armies of the past. In July, 1918, the Red Cross mobilized in this country a six months' supply of the bacillus Welchi serum for the cure and prevention of gas gangrene, amounting in all to 120,000 doses. Tetanus had been mastered, but the decimation of forces by the cruel agency of poison-gas was not overcome until by exhaustive research the immune serum was discovered. The Red Cross assumed responsibility for dispensation of it to the Allied armies. The providing of splints, of the six types now developed for confinement of injured members in cases of fracture, became another large-scale activity of the Red Cross. The boys of the Junior organization acquired high proficiency in their manufacture and produced them in volume. The Red Cross also maintained five factories for the purpose in Paris, with a total output of 16,000 splints each month.

At the American base hospitals the Red Cross installed various forms of diversion, which shortened the weary journey of the soldier back to health. A little garden enterprise was started at one of the bases which proved of such benefit that the Red Cross sent to America for men and equipment to extend the work to all the base hospitals. These little farms proved a perfect medicine for the "shell-shocked" men, and furnished tons of vegetables toward the food supply of the institutions.

In 1917, the Red Cross had provided funds for a Yule party and entertainment in every base hospital, and a Christmas tree in every ward where a soldier or sailor lay. There were 1,750,000 Christmas cheer packages distributed at home and abroad, which cost approximately one dollar each, and which contained socks, handkerchiefs, tobacco, chewing gum, cigarettes, and other useful things. In 1918, the Red Cross, complying with the Army rule that permitted each soldier to receive only one package of specified dimensions, supplied the cartons and distributed them. Just to make sure that each soldier received one it prepared and filled several thousands of these packages for those who might be overlooked.

During the war the Red Cross furnished each wounded man — who in the stress of the battle lost all his belongings — with a comfort bag that contained toilet articles, razors, handkerchiefs, and many other necessities. These were especially appreciated by the soldiers. A toothbrush was often the first thing a wounded doughboy would ask for on arrival at the hospital.

"These things," said General Pershing, "bring the soldier to remember that the people at home are behind him. You do not know how much they mean to the soldier who is over here carrying the flag for his country."

With a view to centralizing the activities of relief organizations overseas, and to facilitate the work with the Army, General Pershing designated the Red Cross as the only relief society to work in locating and administering to American wounded who had been removed to hospitals in France. There were 4500 hospitals. To simplify the task it was conducted on a zone system and wounded Americans convalescing in France were enlisted to carry it on.

The work of giving information regarding soldiers to their relatives was organized under the Bureau of Home Communication. Primarily, this work consisted in gathering full and detailed information as to casualties and for this purpose "searchers," both men and women, were sent to France, their numbers increasing with the numbers of overseas troops. It was the duty of the War Department to give notices of casualties to families, but these notices

were necessarily laconic and businesslike. No War Office
in the world could be asked, in the multiplicity of its duties,
to write families detailed reports, but there was need of
just this thing. Families sending their boys overseas could
not understand why, when their son was wounded, he should
not come home immediately or why the mother should not
go out to nurse him. Here was a new opportunity for the
Red Cross to be of service. It placed women in the hospitals
abroad to write letters or reports about the young men who
were ill or wounded or dying, and these were transmitted
by the Bureau of Communication in Washington to the
families. Sometimes these women were overwhelmed with
work, as, for example, in some of the evacuation hospitals
where the wounded passed through in a steady stream.
They could not report on all the cases, but they tried to report on the more serious cases and to write to the families
a personal letter about those who had died. With the divisions near the front there were men searchers. Their business was, in the first place, to answer the inquiries forwarded
from America concerning men who had not been heard from
or who had troubles which might be assisted by word from
home. Sometimes they, too, reported on casualties without
any request. Such a case as the following occurred very
often : in the Château-Thierry drive the wounded men were
poured into a hospital, the most seriously wounded to be
treated, the others to be sent on. The searcher had to give
most of his time to assist the stretcher-bearers and the surgeons. He still had time, however, to lie on the ground
beside some seriously wounded man and to jot down the last
message he wanted sent to his family. It was impossible
that a searcher, under circumstances of this kind, could talk
with all of the wounded or even a large proportion of them,
but the few who were seen made the whole work worth while
in that it brought one ray of comfort to a few bereaved
families.

All the information collected abroad was sent to the Paris office where it was classified and forwarded to the Washington office. The little group of letter writers was rapidly augmented and it was always the plan to send the families letters which gave the facts as completely and as kindly as possible. There was also kept a card file of all casualties, which file finally grew to contain some 400,000 cards giving, so far as possible, on each card the history of the case. The Army was thoroughly coöperative in that it realized the need and understood that the Red Cross could be of service not only to the families but to the military authorities. The files at the Central Records Office were always open to the Red Cross workers stationed there and much of the information received outside was checked by the official reports. The only work under the general supervision of the Bureau of Communication which did not actually go through the Washington office was that of keeping families informed concerning men sick in the camps and cantonments in this country. Here, also, men were placed to send out the so much needed information and probably many thousands of letters went daily to families from these camps and cantonments in addition to the thousands concerning the troops overseas which went out from the Washington office.

But to return to the work abroad: particular attention was given to all cases of missing men or prisoners. In addition to its search work the Bureau received through the International Committee at Berne, Switzerland, a list of American prisoners in Germany, officially provided by the German government. After announcement to the relatives, the prisoner's case was transferred to the Bureau of Prisoners' Relief. The Red Cross supplied to each prisoner, for account of the given unit, twenty pounds of food. As a matter of record, there was return receipt card for proof that this food was delivered.

And so to the last possible notch the Red Cross followed the way of the soldier. If he was wounded and came round fit and went back, as he was always restless and eager to do, well and good. His family knew it and he didn't go back hungry or in need. If his injuries unfitted him for further service and he was sent home, then Red Cross men or women met him at the home port and stayed at his side until he reached the hospital to which he had been assigned. And, finally, there remains the one last service — the saddest of all : it was to watch over the brave souls who had given all for their country and for humanity ; to stand by them to the brink ; and to soften, in whatever way possible, the sorrow of those who mourned.[1] If there be any service in the world that is nobler, more faithful, or more inspired by love than this, I do not know of it.

[1] Through the Department of Communication the Red Cross has a corps of photographers, working under the Graves Registration Service in France, whose task it is to take photographs of all identified graves and these, as soon as received, will be sent by the Red Cross to the families of the dead.

CHAPTER XII

"BACKING UP THE FRENCH"

The American Red Cross in France — First Request — Pioneer Work to
Find Families and Keep Them Together — Belgians in France —
Coöperation with the French Government — Coöperative Union
with English and American Society of Friends — Coöperation with
Other Relief Organizations — Dispensaries — Purchasing in France —
Warehouses Secured — Assistance to the French Army — Ac-
knowledgment to the French Government and French Officials.

ONE of the first things I was told when I arrived at our
headquarters in Paris was that the French people had
said that the American Red Cross came to France so silently
that they did not know it had come. It was a particularly
graceful way, wholly French in its subtlety, of paying a
compliment to the newly arrived Commission and, needless
to say, was much to the liking of men almost overwhelmed
with the magnitude and strangeness of their mission. For,
although men may have gone on greater missions, — and
even that is doubtful, — surely none could have been
stranger than that which left the United States in June, 1917,
— two months after the declaration of war, — with only
the vaguest idea of what they would be able to do in the way
of all kinds of relief. Nor was the full meaning of their
undertaking revealed to them until they touched French
soil and had become eye-witnesses of the great havoc caused
by three years of valiant wrestling with the huge and, at
times, all but overwhelming labor of maintaining an unbroken front against the invader.

That the ranks of soldiery had been terribly depleted,

there were signs on every hand; nor were there evidences lacking of the acute suffering among the civilian population, where whole families found themselves separated: fathers were in the trenches, mothers worked in the munition factories, while the children were adrift in a world of disorder; in short, there was not a man, woman, or child that was not a vital factor in the situation!

The crying need, therefore, was not only to keep up the morale of the soldier but also to build up and maintain the spirit of the people behind the line, — something which could not alone be accomplished by the first handful of American soldiers that went over to take the assurance to the military authorities that America was in the war. Early, it had been demonstrated that weeks and months must, necessarily, elapse before the American Army could find her place on the battlefield. So it was not mere soldiery that would serve to hearten the French people, but something that would tell them that the soul of America was, and would be, with them in all their multifarious needs, to the depth of her universal strength and the length of her great resources.

From a purely practical viewpoint it was argued that every particle of strength and confidence which America could give to the French people, would be a real contribution not only towards relief but towards shortening the war. Furthermore, that all care for her sick and wounded and all relief for her destitute people would tend to reduce the number of killed and wounded among Americans in France. So, from the utilitarian as well as from the humanitarian side, the work of the Red Cross in France, in those early days, was altogether worth while.

With the American passion for reducing every project to a business formula, the Commission built in advance on the old Red Cross basis of military and civilian relief, thinking that the work would readily divide and subdivide itself under these heads for purposes of organization and develop-

A ROOM IN THE OFFICE OF THE AMERICAN RED CROSS IN PARIS.

ment; but its calculation went for naught. What it did was to begin relief first and work out the organization afterward.

It took counsel with the men who were controlling the soldiery of France. General Petain went down the lines and put it up to his *poilus*: "What is wanted more — care for yourselves or your families?" To a man, they answered: "Forget us — look after our families."

Before the Commission had been in France a fortnight it cabled a request for food, clothing, hospital supplies, and lumber to help the refugees and begin relief in the devastated regions in the north of France — that long strip of country from which the Germans had been driven out and which they had left shattered, polluted, and stripped of everything that might be of beauty or of use.

On July 12, the War Council set aside $1,000,000 for the relief of sick and wounded French soldiers. And when, on July 16, word came by cable of the immediate need of doctors and nurses, especially those expert in the treatment of children's diseases, the War Council engaged at once the foremost pediatrist of the country who, with a staff of child specialists and a corps of nurses, took ship for the other side where he and others established a most extraordinary series of homes.

So they began with the children, — the most pitiful as well as the most numerous refugees, — and at Toul established a refuge for them, one of many that has been set up between that day and this. Toward the end of 1917, there were at Nesle a thousand little broken down Belgian children under treatment, while preparations were being made for taking in other thousands to be cleaned and braced up and placed somewhere in comfortable homes. From this, the natural advance was to the refugees of larger growth. Work was started in Paris, where the congestion was most acute, and carried out into other cities and towns of the devastated departments.

For the refugees, as for everybody else, the work was done in coöperation with the French Government, which had a system of its own with which it had been trying vainly to stem the tide. It consisted of a Department Committee in Paris, theoretically with a member from each of the eighty odd departments, but actually with only two or three represented, who passed on the applications for relief and the identification papers of the applicants. The Government turned over the task to the American Red Cross, which enlarged the organization so that each of the invaded districts, whose outcasts thronged the rest of the country, had a committee at work. But at best it was hopeless to endeavor to meet such a problem with the bureau. There were only phantom meals to give away, the supply of clothing was not a fraction of what was needed — for these people had been practically blasted out of their homes and had hurried to the highway with German shells bursting behind them. With distress and tragedy written in their faces and their souls, they headed for the centers with the love that misery has for company, and Paris was the Mecca of the great pilgrimage. The result was inevitable. There were families of six, seven, and eight herded in one room, and thousands that had no roof over them at all save as the chance of a night might offer. By converting great public buildings and unused structures of every sort into "apartment houses," by supplying stoves and furniture and other requisites, the American Red Cross set out to move twenty-five thousand families into comfortable quarters before the advent of cold weather.

In handling this multitude of the homeless the Red Cross did not have normal people to deal with. The adults, like the children, were worn to the bone by their vicissitudes, broken in strength, in nerves, and almost in hope. A great part of them were ill, some shattered in mind, while the tubercular were an army in themselves. It was not alone the misery of these last that called for abatement : it was the menace they presented to the future of France. The Red Cross took over, by courtesy of the French Government, and also in some instances from private organizations, already established hospitals which, for lack of funds or of forces, were unable to maintain maximum operation ; it completed half-finished buildings, refurnished abandoned barracks, papered, painted, and put in glass solaria and partitions to make private rooms for those victims who were near the end of the struggle ; it singled out from the battalions of the homeless and exhausted many upon whom the "white death" had set its mark, and even those whose physical depletion might render them easy victims ; it established for such, both old and young, preventoria, where by careful treatment and nourishment the doom might be turned aside.

Health, — health and strength were the things needed, not only for the fighting which was to come but for the peace which was to follow the fighting. France, with her decline in birth rate, representing a huge net annual loss, with her sacrifice in war, with the future all black before her, could not neglect any means of saving life if she was to remain a nation and enjoy the freedom she had worked for so valiantly. And, with the back-breaking burden of the war's expense still piling up, to permit this increasing multitude to settle down as absolute dependents, inactive and unproductive and consuming the food of idleness, spelled ruin so plain that the blind might read. Gradually the solution of these composite puzzles began to outline itself. Taking the cue from the French Government, whose efforts had all been directed toward the return of the refugees to their provinces, so far as the conditions might permit, and availing itself of the consuming love of home which is ingrown in the nature of the French race, the Red Cross combined its efforts for the care of the refugees with a broad and carefully evolved plan to start them on the way to self-maintenance. To this coherent

purpose it added provision for the maintenance of health
and sanitation, and the instruction of its new wards in the
ways of hygienic living.

Little by little the situation began to unfold and the way
of progress to reveal itself. The work gathered speed
and volume. The machine, now increasing its scope and
strength, began to register. Every ship that passed the
German sharks brought new additions to the Red Cross
forces, both men and women; and every day saw fresh
details of them moving out to some new field, pioneers of
pity, soldiers of the new creed.

The refugees from the farming country were keenest
of all to go back to the home acres. And the French committees, by way of stimulating this tendency, withdrew a
moiety of their assistance and promised to refund, after the
War, whatever the land tillers would expend for their own
rehabilitation. So the stream began to move northward into
the territory the Germans had left. On ahead of them, at
their side and behind them, moved the columns of the Red
Cross, ready with food, with lumber, and other materials
for reconstruction, with seeds and tools for the restoration
of the land, with labor provided by a coöperative union with
the English and American societies of Friends, who had done
heroic work from the beginning of the War. There are long
records in the Red Cross archives in France showing in detail what roof was replaced upon this farmer's barn, what
glass put in the windows of another's farmstead, and endless other repairs to fit the places for human habitation and
rural industry. There was an amazing shipment of pumps,
for it is well to remember that what the German apostle of
Kultur could not carry away he smashed and what he could
not smash he fouled.

Like homing birds, these French farmers settled down
among the ruins to resume the tenor of their placid lives.
The like of it could not happen elsewhere in the world!

The Red Cross was with them, ready to lend a hand at anything they needed; it showed them short cuts in agriculture and rebuilding; it taught the lessons of modern sanitation. It established dispensaries, with doctors and nurses and facilities for transit, and the sections mapped off with medical routes after the fashion of Rural Free Delivery.

All up and down the districts established behind the lines, away to the valleys and sloping mountains of the Vosges, the Red Cross set up dispensaries to do the work of the village doctors who had gone away to war. There was scarcely a community in France that had not suffered in health, and for the good of all concerned, particularly of the American Army that was to come, it was imperative they should have the ounce of prevention. In fair and foul weather these American doctors and their assistants traveled the roads of France, visiting the villages and holding office hours in some public building or going from house to house where more serious sickness existed. There were maladies of all sorts, and in some cases incipient epidemics. There were children with mumps, measles, and other things; there were the aged, weary with years, upon whom the War had laid the final straw of pain, and others who never lived to see springtime renew the green of their home hillsides. All through the winter, staying neither for wind nor weather, these Red Cross doctors went toiling over the snow-drifted and wind-swept highways of France, "practicing medicine" with an assiduity which was not inspired by hope of gain, and helping far more than they knew to win the War.

Like the agents of empire in far places of the world, these "struggling" doctors in the "listening posts" of health never knew of the great drama of relief which was being enacted elsewhere. By this time in France the people had begun to dismiss all doubt and incredulity, and had come to the realization as to what the American Red Cross really meant. They saw the cloud of miserable refugees dissolving from the city streets. By day and by night the trucks and trailers of the Red Cross motor corps roared along the roads of France or through the streets of the cities, burdened with the material of relief. It was providential that there already existed in France so many relief organizations whose members were familiar with the field and its difficulties. With each of these, when possible, the Red Cross promptly struck partnership in the common cause ; and lacking at first personnel sufficient to handle the mass of detail, that so vast a problem presented, it shared in the burden of their work. By November, 1917, it was financing and assisting seventy-five of them. To the French Red Cross, struggling with the awful labor of service to the Armies, the American organization gave liberal sums of money for supplies and, indeed, furnished upon demand any and all drugs and equipment of which there was lack. The Civil Affairs Department took over the varied activities of the *Tuberculeux de la Guerre*, established by Mrs. Edith Wharton, of the *Secours Américain* at Amiens, and the American Society for the Relief of French Orphans. In other cases, such as that of the American Hostels for Refugees and the *Vestaire l'Accueil Franco-Américain*, the Red Cross assumed financial responsibility, leaving the administration in the hands of the former governing boards. In all, 397 grants of money were made in the first six months to 322 institutions, whose work had been an immense contribution to the aid of suffering France.

The French, when they came to know us better, coined a complimentary name for the American Red Cross which, even now, is current : "The Godmother of Good Works."

But the Godmother of Good Works was an overtaxed fairy when it came to the delivery of her benefactions. Time was of the very essence of the situation. The lack of everything was so intense, the Atlantic so wide, the ships so few compared with the huge load there was to carry of munitions and inter-Allied supplies, of advance materials for the housing of our Armies and the building of the transportation system, that the Red Cross Commission accordingly found it wiser to buy in France, Spain, and England the many thousand-and-one commodities that were instantly required, than to wait for the long process of purchase and shipment from the United States. It was supplying the French Army with hospital appliances and drugs; to the refugees it was furnishing caps and pinafores and other articles of children's wear; to the societies in the devastated region went clothing, implements, and even animals; and to the organizations in Paris the multitude of indispensable things for making homes. Buying in advance of requirements the Red Cross enumerated on its sheets 470 standardized classes of articles, many of them with numberless sub-classifications. The greater part was stored in Paris, where a dozen warehouses were established. As the calls came, these things were requisitioned and started on their way in the motor transport, the formation of which had been begun early in the campaign. It will shed some interesting light on the scope of these operations to reproduce here the requisition slips of one day, — thirty-six in all, — which was less than the daily average. They represent grants of 4009 articles sent far and near to nineteen organizations. An "article" may mean anything from a poster to four hundred yards of flannel.

Woolen caps, mittens, coats and capes, scarfs, condensed milk, jam, sugared cocoa, meat juice, cheese.

Tapioca, lemons, checkers, backgammon, croquet, playing cards, face towels, kitchen towels, bedside tables, bedcovers, armchairs, chaise longues, bowls, candles, candlesticks, undervests, woolen socks, house slippers, woolen pajamas, phonograph records.

Books (Dumas, Verne, Hugo, Daudet, Mérimée, Loti, Anatole France).

Galoshes, blouses, underskirts, stockings, sabots, finger bandages, beans, hams, sugar, canned meats, wool, posters, roller toweling, serum, drugs, folding beds.

Blankets, pillows, sheets, wardrobes, stock pots, saucepans, enamel saucepans, small dishes, basins, roasting pans, children's blankets, eider-downs, straw mattresses, dust cloths, tea cloths.

Earthenware, hot water bottles, wash-basins, sterilizers for milk, sheeting, bath toweling, flannelette, calico, white flannelette, apron print, gray wool for stockings, flannel.

Soup ladles, tablespoons, butcher knives, peeling knives, kitchen knives, chopping knives, large coffee pot, roasting pans, graters, flat pans, serving pans, black sateen.

Girls' drawers, stockings, handkerchiefs, shoes, stove to cook for sixty persons. Assorted boxes clothing, nightgowns, shirts, part wool, long drawers, girls' bloomers, boys' pants, shirts, girls' dresses, woolen sweaters.

A diversified business, such as this fragmentary list indicates, called for sheltering places. Facilities for handling and shipment were imperative, and there was always the bogie of future growth in volume, which it was now clear would be swift and enormous. The warehouse of the American Relief Clearing House was soon outgrown, even for existing business. Three more of much larger capacity were at once secured with railroad connection, and the Red Cross cleaned up and installed modern equipment. One establishment was leased, cleaned, altered, and ready for business in forty-eight hours despite the fact that labor was the scarcest thing in Paris. The Red Cross employed soldiers on leave. French, red-fezzed Moroccans, and Indo-Chinese; with them as laborers a system of transportation was built up of light and heavy trucks which balked at no burden of traffic to any part of France.

In one room of a Paris warehouse there were thirty tons of tobacco; in another wing foodstuffs were stored in quantities to tax belief. Three hundred tons of coffee for example, a greater tonnage of beans, and everything else in proportion. It was not a storage; it was a gate, through which this volume of supplies flowed in a ceaseless stream. Attached to the warehouses were garages where repairs and reconstruction were done upon the hundreds of machines which were

HAPPY TO SEE THEIR OWN COUNTRY AT LAST.

Repatriates arriving from the station at Evian where they were welcomed by French and Americans.

employed. Even in September of 1917, the motor transport was up to handling in and out of the Paris warehouses
150 tons of freight a day. Even American threshing machines were set in motion. In all the districts back of
the lines were divisional warehouses to which the goods
were carried for distribution. One of these was an old
seminary which, when the Red Cross took possession,
had fifty-two shell-holes in its walls. Most of these warehouses were overrun in the German drive of 1918. After
the armistice they were replaced by a chain of depots,
extending from Lille to the eastern border, from which
supplies were issued to the people returning to the
devastated regions.

To the French Army the American Red Cross lent every
possible form of assistance. It set up spacious rest and
recreation canteens in Paris and at several of the great in-
tersection points along the railway lines, where thousands of
French soldiers were made comfortable; it established rolling canteens behind the lines; and in conjunction with the
French Government, after it got under way, it furnished
hot meals to almost a million soldiers every month in huge
canteens like lumber-camp barracks, where the weary *poilu*
could not only eat and sing and forget his troubles, but
bid good-by to his cooties, treat himself to a shower bath,
a clean bunk and go away a happier human and once
more fit to associate with his family.

The story of the work of the American Red Cross in
France for the French people and the French soldiers can
never be correctly told without acknowledgment to the
French Government and French officials everywhere for the
hearty and never-failing coöperation in every endeavor.
The Paris *Temps*, commenting on the Red Cross gifts and
on Red Cross accomplishments in France, in December of
1917 said: "We find proof in it that the German does not
wholly monopolize, as he pretends, the secret of organiza-

M

tion; and that other nations can demonstrate, with ours, their energy in work and at the same time their powers of methodical application and disciplined labor."

Such was the beginning of the Red Cross accomplishment in France.

CHAPTER XIII

THE CHILDREN OF FRANCE

The France of To-morrow — The Army of Refugee Children — Methods
of Work — The Call from Toul — The Work Reaches Dinard —
Help in French Schools — Health Centers in Munition Districts —
Children's Wards in Tuberculosis Hospitals — The Red Cross Flag
at Nesle — A Traveling Dispensary — Evian — "The Gateway of
a Hundred Sorrows" — Hospitals and Refuges — Child Welfare
Exhibit at Lyons — German Policy in the Discharge of Refugees
through Evian — French System in the Care of Refugees — Par-
ticulars of American Red Cross Assistance.

IF the old adage holds true that the boy is father to the
man then one need have little fear for the future of
France. It is to this France of the future, the new generation that is growing up in a sense of comradeship with the
millions of our own, that my thoughts now turn. And how
near we of America are to these children of France is best
told in the following letter from a fourteen-year-old school-
girl to the American Red Cross: —

"It was only a little river — almost a brook — it was called the Yser.
One could talk from one side to the other without raising one's voice, and
the birds could fly over it with one sweep of their wings. And on the two
banks there were millions of men, the one turned toward the other, eye
to eye. But the distance which separates them was greater than the
stars in the sky — it was the distance which separates right from injustice.

"The ocean is so vast that the sea-gulls do not dare to cross it. During
seven days and seven nights the great steamships of America, going at
full speed, drive through the deep waters before the lighthouses of France
come into view — but from one side to the other hearts are touching."

It was the effort of the Red Cross to still the cries of the
children that went straight to the heart of France. If all

the rest had been beyond our power, this one thing would have won for us undying gratitude. For France, the saving of the children meant their future and their world.

"There can be no real victory," said a Marseilles newspaper, "unless we can successfully combat child mortality. If we consider the enormous adult death rate for the war period, we can only conclude that after the war nothing will be left of France but a glorious skeleton — glorious in name but depleted in substance. The American Red Cross has come to aid us in the fight for our children. Because of this, if for no other reason, we owe the Society a debt of unbounded gratitude and affection."

"If the Germans," wrote Alphonse Seche, "have changed the idea of war, the Americans are in process of changing the idea of alliance. The war being everywhere, menacing the race, our Allies have decided to be everywhere, in the front and in the rear; shoulder to shoulder with our soldiers, standing side by side with our mothers over the cradles, for the preservation of our race."

The pictures of Toul and Evian, of Nesle and Lyons, of Dinard and Dieppe, of Caudebec and Barenton and Issy-le-Molineaux, are etched into the very soul of France. They are a sage and cautious people these, who do not wear their hearts upon the sleeve. The vivacity which is their form of expression, the politeness which is their philosophy, the good manners which a wise man has said the French invented, — these are not France. They are merely the habiliment of its civilization.

In America not all the children are clean; not all have enough to eat. The great East side finds some occupation still for the welfare worker, but I do not believe America has yet any conception of the magnitude of the child problem that existed in France. The condition was far worse than even the French people or its government had time in the tumult and stress of war to know. And it was growing even worse as the war progressed. There was the awful accumulation of refugee children from all the departments of the north and from Belgium and the shifting fortunes of war; the pitiless rush of the Huns; the increasing destruc-

air and the hungry shells, always ranging
aving more and more little ones orphaned or
med or shaken in understanding and memory. This
was the greater company, the orphaned and the destitute,
those whose fathers were dead or at the front, whose mothers
were gone, and who had none to care for them.

Added to all these was the army of repatriated children —
including a host from Belgium — who, like the adults who
came over the border, were suffering from the varied ills of
malnutrition, if from nothing worse. That was not the
whole story. Even the health of the children who had
homes was running down. Epidemics of local character
could not be checked. The average of doctors in America
is one to 500 people; in France, where the call for nurses
and physicians at the front had been incessant for three
years, the ratio in 1917 was one to several thousand. That
should tell its own story to people who have children of their
own. The necessary lack of care and the scarcity of proper
food made easy the progress of disease. With all the other
crying needs that confronted the Red Cross at that moment,
this peril to the child life loomed high. Much of the misery
and disease was only too obvious, but there was a tremendous
number of children needing treatment whom it was hard to
reach or even to discover. And, to begin with, it was found
necessary to rid the French people of the fixed idea that the
American had come to deal solely with the soldier. It took
time to do that, yet every moment of delay was courting
more and more danger.

To accomplish results, the Red Cross had to provide
suitable places for operation and get the children together
to examine and sort out the tuberculous and contagious
cases, to provide nurses, labor, and medical supplies, dentists and attendants and artisans to make requisite repairs
at a time and in a land where every man who could carry
a rifle was needed at the front. What all of this child army

needed first was to get clean and to be fe...
majority of them were hungry, and food of any ki...
plentiful, — much less the kind of food they needed. ...
devastated regions, the Germans left nothing! They had
destroyed even stoves and water systems, so that in the
districts back of portions of the lines the first desiderata
of sanitary or medical activity were lacking.

Numberless little charities, organized by nuns or by
kindly women who were heartsick at the spectacle of so
much misery, were trying in the cities to do something to
stem the tide. To these, the Red Cross made haste to lend
aid. Many of them, such for example as the refuge founded
at the *Hotel Biron* by Madame Viviani, wife of the former
premier of France, developed into a stronghold of good.
In Moufettard, Paris, Mlle. de Rose conducted another
charity, which was founded by Mlle. de Perignan, a
granddaughter of Lafayette, comprising a social center,
a home for working girls, a model tenement, a vacation
home in the environs of Paris, and agricultural schools in
the country. It lacked a health center, which the Red Cross
supplied together with a dispensary and clinics for children and mothers; it helped every Governmental effort
to cope with the problem. These charities were chiefly in
the cities. But along the highways and in the little towns
there was great need and no ray of hope. Then out of
obscurity rose the virile personality of the Préfet Mirman,
who, when he shall have died and gone to the glory that
is his due, will be the patron saint of the department of the
Meurthe et Moselle. Without Préfet Mirman, Toul would
have been as it has been for centuries, ever since Roman
times, merely the rock-bound gate that has barred the
invaders of many wars from the rich and industrious town
of Nancy. But the Préfet, having faith added to hope and
charity, believed the Americans meant what they said,
and he gave to Toul a fame that will never die.

tion from the was under fire, life there was not worth a
farther, low the artisans of the town had to stay at their
ma---- or France needed them. They are a rugged folk,
these workers of Nancy. In 1917, when the gas shells
exploded they had been trained to gas masks and worked
on, although the children, in panic, smothered and died
in agony. They had no guard against that ghastly death.
On July 26, the Préfet sent a classic telegram to the Committee of the American Fund for French Wounded, begging
for nurses and doctors. They went to the Red Cross
offices just opened; that night the chairman of the *Secours
aux Blessés* left the Red Cross station in Paris with three
camion loads of supplies and eleven doctors and nurses.

As they rumbled into Toul in the gray of the dawn, there
were five hundred women and children swarming the
barracks which the French soldiers had abandoned. All
was confusion; dirt and vermin were over everything. In
the *Caserne de Luxembourg*, — a group of barnlike structures
on the sheltered plateau over Toul, — these women and
doctors swept and scrubbed and scoured, installed beds
and chairs and tables, and business began.

It was slow work luring the confidence of the Lorrainers,
but the ice was broken; and until the spring of 1918, when
the Huns pushed forward again, Toul was a lighthouse of
mercy and health and happiness to the children of the
north. From that the work was established until it reached
Dinard. It would have made the old-time spendthrifts
who dined and wined and danced and flirted in the great
Hotel Royal open their eyes to see the swarm of refugee
children who, in charge of the Red Cross doctors, took up
life there in the wake of the soldiery that had used it as a
barracks. They were doctored and brought back by care
and nourishment to sturdy health; they went on with
the schooling that is the reigning passion of the French
child. The waifs, — the fatherless and motherless from

the crowded wards of Paris, and the wasted *repatriés* from the receiving station at Evian were sent to find in the salt air and water healing a cure from the curse of bone tuberculosis. There was clean, pure life there, a sowing of kindness that will some day yield a perpetual harvest of understanding and good will.

Once having set out on children's relief, there was no turning back. More doctors and more nurses, more teachers and welfare workers kept coming from America. The Red Cross saw the necessity for help in some of the French schools, so work was begun in them. "Unless we can start a canteen up here," wrote the doctor who conducted the children's clinic, "in the Nineteenth *arrondissement* of Paris and give these children some food, this children's work is not going to get anywhere, because what these children need is nourishment and I can't do much till I can put something in their stomachs."

The school luncheons had been cut down, but the Red Cross dietitians figured out the calories in what was left and found that there was need for wheat and sugar, so they built a Red Cross cake and added it to the ration.

Rapidly the child welfare problem grew into one of the most extensive branches of Red Cross work. Health centers were opened in two munition districts just outside Paris, with welfare workers, Red Cross doctors, clinics, and visiting nurses who reached within a very short time three hundred families. It was very sorely needed. The population of the district had increased greatly; two hundred munition factories had risen like mushrooms overnight, with 110 new buildings erected for the workmen to live in. The congestion was terrible and the spread of disease likewise menacing when the Red Cross came to the rescue.

A large area of Paris was covered in the same way. There was so much tuberculosis among the children, that child

REPATRIATED HOSPITAL CHILDREN IN FRANCE.

An American Red Cross cap makes a commanding officer of the small boy who leads the drill.

welfare was combined with the tuberculosis service, and children's wards were established in all the tuberculosis hospitals. In high, healthy country districts, the Director had farm schools established where weak children could be built up and taught to make things grow. The cardinal test of any project was what it promised for the future of the children and of France. Boys were taught trades and girls were taught sewing; and among the denizens of the poorer quarters were promulgated the magic of the toothbrush and the rules of health — for which dentists came overseas with all their tools.

Nesle was another of the northern towns in the track of war which, after the "strategic retirement" of the Germans, suffered bitterly. In four towns about it not a house or building of any nature had been left with one stone on another. When the Germans moved away, they destroyed everything that could be of service in any act of life. When the Red Cross doctors arrived in the old Hôtel de Nesle it was stripped bare. From the outlying country, the children began drifting in, sullen, dazed, stunned by the horrors they had seen and suffered. And none smiled. A Red Cross woman, who worked at Nesle, said that the far horror in the eyes of the children was as if they were looking beyond the things of this earth and into the gates of Judgment.

Here again was a work for Hercules, and it practically wore them out. Throughout the first week all the patients of the clinic were Red Cross workers. There was no heat, and for a day or two no gauze or bandages or dressings; but there were twelve hundred children who needed care and the Red Cross toiled away to give it. It goes without saying that it cost much hardship to raise the Red Cross flag at Nesle!

The Red Cross designed, and built in Paris, a traveling dispensary — an automobile hospital, with drugs and supplies of all sorts and an outside seat on which a nurse could transport a sick child to the hospital. With this mercy wagon, the workers went from town to town about the district. Through the countryside, the children were afflicted with skin diseases and with strange forms of blood ailment, caused largely by malnutrition.

This working for the children of France was a day to day and an all day and all night dealing with the plain animal facts of sick and ill-nourished bodies. There were women fighting the good fight of the Red Cross against the miseries of Europe who, perhaps, have never found the glory that they longed for; but they found what was better — their own mother hearts that they had never known.

Someone has called Evian les Bains the "Gateway of a Hundred Sorrows." It was here, as the war wore on and the food supply began to dwindle, that Germany, balancing up her efficiency schedules, turned back into hungry France the sorry army of French and Belgian civilians who had been taken from the devastated country in the north in the first onrush of 1914, and since held in bondage. In the summer of 1917, this wretched jetsam of the German war was herded over the frontier at the rate of a thousand or more a day. Daily, for a long time, two trains, morning and night, rolled in from the German border. A woman who watched their debarkation day after day said in a letter at that time: "The curtain never falls at Evian." It was so. In the drama that France lived behind her roaring battle lines, there was no more somber scene than Evian. Here, again, as at Dinard, and other one-time resorts on the northern coasts, was a gruesome contrast with the ancient atmosphere of fashion, wealth, and idleness. Nestling on the hills above exquisite Lake Geneva, Evian was the last setting to be chosen for so woeful a spectacle.

From forty to sixty per cent of these cast-offs were children, by far the greater part of them under twelve years of age. A great number were dying from tuberculosis, many far advanced; but all were unutterably dirty, half clad, worn to emaciation with sorrow and hunger and slavery. They were moribund. Germany could wring no more unpaid labor from them. They had given to the uttermost pfennig's worth. The people beyond the Rhine picked out those who seemed past hope and sent them to France to be cared for. They were a multitude, — and these children were not riffraff. Many of them had known luxury and the tenderest care.

It was all one wretched, miserable story after another; and yet, from the gray monotony of it, two cases seem to stand out in the memory of those who saw them for the reason that they proclaim more clearly than others, perhaps, two salient phases of German brutality: one was a wisp of a girl, just turned fourteen, who bore in her arms a year old boche baby; and the second, only a little older and marked with tuberculosis, had for three years worked twelve hours a day in a German coal mine. It is manifestly impossible to tell all the stories of the unfortunates of Evian; but thousands of them are recorded in the files there against the day when the world may know the depth of German iniquity.

When the train wound its way up the grades into the famous old watering place there was a band playing the Marseillaise, and the French and Belgian flags were waving. There was the Mayor and half the town crying welcome to them — welcome back to France — and still they did not smile. French and American stretcher-bearers boarded the trains to take out those that were too crippled or too weak to help themselves, and there were Red Cross ambulances there to carry these helpless ones away to the old Casino, which had been converted into a hospital. There were these heart-breaking processions every day, at morning and evening, hundreds of children and aged people at a time, ambling on toward rest and kindly care, with faces haggard and drawn but singing out of numb hearts their homeland songs ; and men and women with hearts torn at the picture, stood in crowds by the wayside with tears raining down their faces at the misery and the glory of it, and were not ashamed.

"The scene," says the Chief of the Children's Relief, in his professional report, "is indescribably emotional."

The story of Evian cannot be told. Mothers and children met there who had been lost to each other ever since the Germans surged over Belgium. It was a great, overpowering drama of mingled sorrow and happiness, of death — yes, and of resurrection. These children were marked for death, but they were caught in the very nick of time. And even so, there were sad little funerals now and then wending through the village streets. But as an institution it went with a mathematical precision, by every means that science or sentiment could devise, bringing health to sick and exhausted bodies ; and smiles to faces that one might have thought could never smile again. There were children who came to Evian, marked for death in a thousand ways, but who, through the ministrations of mercy there, will go singing their way on to the end of their poor little blasted lives.

From all the touching records of the station which are held in the archives of the Red Cross, I take almost at random this paragraph which, like a ray of sunlight, reveals the other side of the picture : —

"He was crippled, horribly crippled. Only his hands and his eyes seemed to be alive, but he said proudly that the Germans would never have let him through if they had known how many pairs of stockings he could make in a day on his knitting machine, which we have given him to make him forget."

Among the many hospitals and refuges which were established all over France to receive this wreckage, there are several in the vicinity of Lyons, chief of which is the Château des Halles, built by Mangini, the great French railroad builder, whose widow gave it to the French government for use during the war. Lyons is a child town; and the Red Cross, with a broad idea of starting in France a general movement for child hygiene, selected it for the scene of its first child welfare exhibits. The timid said it wouldn't go. It was early in April, 1918, the great drive was on and two hundred miles to the north men were dying under the German guns. Who could think of expositions? But in the week that it was in progress more than 100,000 persons between eight in the morning and ten at night crowded into the hall. There is no doubt it was an American show; but by the same token it had at its opening session twelve hundred doctors, lawyers, government officials, founders of hospitals, and the best citizens of Lyons. For the first time in the memory of man there sat on the same platform the Cardinal Archbishop of Lyons, the Préfet of the Rhone, the Military Governor, and the Mayor of the town. Neither Church nor State could shut its eyes to the patent fact that here was the path to the salvation of France. And it was a great show! It was a veritable field day for the toothbrush, and an American dentist operated while his assistant preached the gospel of dentifrice.

There was, also, a great demonstration of the sterilization of milk; and outside, in the square, there was a playground with equipment for basketball, swings, slides, sandboxes for babies, and all such means of outdoor exercise for the making of strong, sturdy children.

In a glass "greenhouse" in the center of the hall at regular intervals each day, Red Cross nurses washed French babies; the Lyons mothers watched the whole process down to the sanitary and scientific disposition of the last towel.

On the last day of the show, a *poilu* was found by one of the nurses copying the dietaries from a poster.

"I can fight no more," he said; "when I went to the front I had a wife and seven children. My wife was killed by an air bomb, and the children had no one to care for them — so four of them died. I am *reformé*, but I can work for them, and now I know what to feed them to make them grow strong. That is the main thing."

These are simple, homely things. They seemed small in the vast tumult and upheaval of a world at war, but out of the sum total of them, and the French know it well enough, is coming that second army which, now that the cannon are silent, is to win for France the battle for her place among the nations and so complete the victory over the Hun.

By January 1st, over fifty thousand of these people had passed through the little station, and Evian had become not only a tragedy but a real menace to the health and future of France.

Analyzed from the German standpoint, there were three great primary purposes served in the holding and the final discharge of these people: First, the labor which they contributed was of a cheapness which, otherwise, would have been impossible. They cost nothing but the bare food to keep them alive, and, as their condition showed, received far less than they needed. They were driven by every form of terrorization and abuse to do all their wrecked bodies could endure; second, when by reason of inevitable exhaustion and disease their labor no longer showed in the German accounting a balance of profit, the efficiency experts of Berlin converted them into an active military force.

This is not purely figurative. The plaintive picture of these broken people at Evian does not at first blush suggest anything of military value; they could not operate artillery or machine guns nor charge trenches, but there were deadly injuries which, properly utilized, they might inflict upon their own country. Germany figured that the unloading of

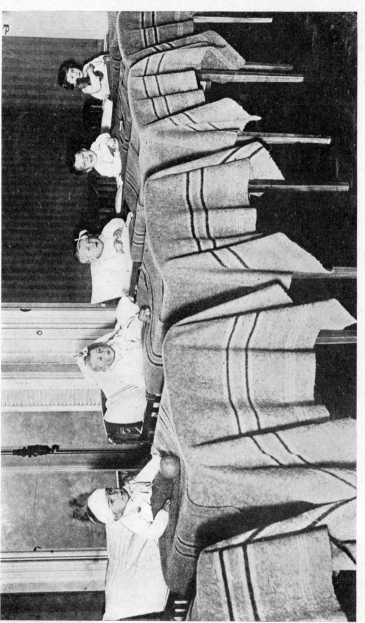

FIVE LITTLE YOUNGSTERS ALL TUCKED IN BED.

This scene is in an American Red Cross home for repatriated children.

these people on France would make a serious draft upon physicians and nurses, money, hospital supplies, clothing, and transportation. In all of these France was seriously reduced; third, and far the more serious purpose, was to undermine for all future time the strength of France by weakening her child population and distributing throughout her borders the carriers of disease.

France could not know the extent of Germany's supply of this deadly ammunition. The number of military prisoners taken by the Germans was passably well established in the Allied countries, by the army records; but of the great population of Belgium and northern France that had simply vanished into the tempest — there was no means of estimating how many of these had died, how many remained to be used as an instrument against the welfare of France. And the reserve forces for meeting it at this time were in the worst possible condition.

What the Germans did not reckon on was the assistance which in this crisis came to France from the American people. The American Red Cross was the x quantity in the equation; and it was here that with the short vision which in the crucial things has seemed to be a German failing, the plans of the Prussian strategists went awry.

Before the coming of the American Red Cross, the French government, realizing its danger, had made well-planned efforts to offset it.

The French government, the Comité de Service des Repatriés d'Evian de Thonon d'Annemasse, and the Comité de Secours aux Repatriés de Lyon had worked out a system of caring for the repatriates, which was prosecuted with what vigor and thoroughness was possible. A physician boarded each convoy train at St. Jingolph, on the Swiss border, to single out such of the company as were too ill to be taken from the station to the Casino. Upon the arrival of the train these were removed at once to the hospital, those badly exhausted to the rest-house, and the remainder were taken either on foot or in ambulances to the Casino. The first effort at Evian was to restore the repatriates to a mental state which would facilitate the work of their handling and distribution. After being fed and cheered up, they were arranged in the great hall in alphabetical groups, and full personal details taken. An elaborate system of card indexes was established for the purpose of fixing the identity of each man, woman, and child, residence, remaining family, so far as known, and their whereabouts.

Telegraphic inquiries were instituted to ascertain if the repatriate had friends or relatives remaining to whom he could be sent. If there were none, he was forwarded to some *préfecture* in the center, west, southwest, or southeast, to be located permanently by the *préfet*. Houses vacated by the war were used for this purpose, as well as for housing of refugees, the government making an allowance for maintenance. A system of colored tags such as is used in America for immigrants, was employed to facilitate distribution. Only in some such way could these swarms be handled. The sick were housed according to the nature of their illness, and on recovery the children whose friends could not be found were sent to institutions, chiefly those near Lyons. Old persons, not claimed, were dispatched to formations created by the Ministry of the Interior.

It was obvious, however, that with the continuance of these deliveries, the facilities for their disposal would soon be overtaxed, and the repatriates would become what Germany had intended — an unbearable burden and a menace both to France and to our army.

So the Red Cross set about assisting the French in the development of further hospital facilities and transportation for patients, and the provision of dispensary service at the Evian Casino, so that every repatriate could receive prompt medical inspection and care; also, of the establishment of convalescent hospitals for those recovering after treatment. A large hotel was converted into a hospital, and then the beautiful Château des Halles was taken over from the city of Lyons, to which it had been given by its owner for use as a children's convalescent hospital.

The dispatch of the tuberculous was attended with some difficulty but was soon satisfactorily adjusted. Meantime, largely through the aid of the Lyons' committees, the expansion of the convalescent system was continued. The people of Evian objected to any permanent hospitals in their neighborhood, particularly for the tuberculous. Evian was, and remained, a clearing house in which the whole solution of the repatriate problem of France had its center.

For what reason the German government chose to make its deliveries of repatriates intermittently has never been disclosed; but there were intervals when for a fortnight these deliveries were wholly discontinued. These were of the greatest importance, as in every instance they chanced to coincide with the requirements of the Red Cross organizers for time to get their equipment in order, and gave the French Committee breathing space to enlarge its facilities for handling the repatriates both at Evian and at the second stage in the orphanages and hospitals at Lyons. In the interval from October 15th to November 5th, the staff of Red Cross nurses from Paris and new supplies of hospital equipment and materials were taken to Evian, and the hospitals received a large number of cases and were in good running order before convoys were resumed.

With the advent of the Red Cross forces came a great increase in the speed and efficacy of the work at Evian. The medical service was combined with social welfare work, and repatriate mothers, who awaited children under treatment, were organized into a working force. What impressed

N

the French was not alone the rapidity and thoroughness of the American staff in handling their cases, which quickly ran into thousands, but the range of their efforts. When a sick repatriate child went out of Evian, he had not only been far advanced toward cure of his ailment, but every physical tendency had been charted, his teeth fixed up, his dietary and exercise prescribed, and his mother instructed in the essentials of hygiene and sanitation and provided with a manual of simple instruction. The new and, obviously, vital factor in all this work, as shown in the French Committee's report, was the tact and sympathy of the American workers, from the doctors down, but the system was severely thorough. At the request of the French authorities, parents were permitted to visit children in isolation hospitals, but they were supplied with caps and gowns, and were compelled to wash their hands and faces in antiseptic solutions before leaving.

If there be any doubt concerning the contribution that the American people has made through its commission to the Red Cross, Evian with its correlated hospitals and rest places, its competent medical work and its correlated demonstration of the value of hygienic methods among the French working people, would be sufficient to dispel it.

CHAPTER XIV

SWITZERLAND THE CENTRAL STATION

International Committee at Geneva — International Agency for Prisoners of War — Swiss Activities in the Interest of Prisoners — Reports on Prison Camps — Great Scarcity of Food and Supplies in Switzerland — Gift of the American Red Cross to the Swiss — Food for American Prisoners Sent through the Red Cross — Receipt Cards — Communication Service Enlarged through the Committee at Berne — Red Cross Commission to Switzerland — Hospital for Tuberculous Serbian Officers — The Swiss Evacuée Problem — Italian Problems in Switzerland — Help for Belgian Children — Number and Isolation of Prison Camps — Process of Locating Prisoners and Providing for Them Thoroughly Systematized — Money Sent Prisoners Paid in German Prison Script.

NOTWITHSTANDING that our experience in the past war, with its imperious demands for big things to be done in a hurry, for unheard-of production both of men and materials, has given us an accurate measure of what we can accomplish when our brains and hands are fairly put to the test, I am not at all sure that it would not be a good thing for some millions of self-satisfied Americans to discover that there are some remarkable people in the world besides themselves. Take the Swiss people, for instance : Switzerland, as we all know, was the parent of the Red Cross throughout the world, and when the storm broke the International Committee at Geneva, with no resources other than its own, struggled bravely with a problem which was great at best but the magnitude of which was doubled by its nearness.

For Switzerland entertained no doubts regarding her

position in the war. There was, to be sure, the great natural barrier of the Alps, but living as she did in the very middle of the war, with cannon echoing on all her borders, it was absolutely necessary that she keep an army of half a million men in a high state of preparedness, a compulsory service that cost her not a few million francs.

None the less, there was no phase of Red Cross activity in which the Swiss were not engaged with all the determination and foresight that they possess to so great a degree. It is not possible, of course, to discuss all their efforts. Lest, however, our Red Cross should be inclined to boast of the successful attempt we made to care for our prisoners of war in Germany, it will be salutary to know that the Swiss Red Cross began the formulation of the system and laid its groundwork in 1914. Its own view of its achievement has been modestly recorded thus: 1914, improvisation; 1915–1916, organization; 1917, coördination. Consequently, when the United States finally came into the war, the International Agency for Prisoners of War was a well-run and well-equipped organization. And that same year the Prix de Vertu Charrau and the Nobel Peace Prize were awarded to the International Committee in recognition of its work in the cause of humanity and charity.

Despite the obstacles that stood in the way, a complete file was kept — always open for consultation — of evacuated, repatriated, and deceased prisoners. There was an Entente Department with a section for Greece which forwarded correspondence to prisoners at Gorlitz; a section for France concerning itself chiefly with search for the dead and the missing; another for Russia working through the German Red Cross into Poland; and still another for Great Britain which sent money to British prisoners in enemy countries. Besides these, there was correspondence with occupied Serbia, not to mention a department for the Central Empires.

At the same period, the Bureau International de la Paix

was handling some 350 letters a day to and from prison camps and all parts of the field of war, seeking the missing, finding the burial places of the dead, and sending to sorrowing people the only small comfort they could ever hope for.

Here is a paragraph from a report of one of their members : —

"I cannot refrain from adding an optimistic note to this account of our efforts to mitigate so much sadness and suffering. And having opened hundreds of letters from German families, after filing thousands of letters from French, English, and Belgian families, I arrive at the conclusion that the mentality of the great masses who are passing through the anguish of doubt and despair is of moral quality much more elevated than one could have believed. It goes without saying that we have strange revelations, to say no more, about the private life of certain families. It remains none the less true that in the uncouth letters of ignorant women, peasants and working women, whether they come from the mountains of Bavaria or those of Auvergne, from the coast of Flanders or that of Scotland, one often finds expressions of gratitude, of serenity, of confidence, which moisten the eyelids, even though they are the eyelids of an old practitioner. It is still among the humble and the disinherited of this world that the Carpenter of Nazareth has disciples after his own heart."

As far back as 1917 delegates from Switzerland had been sent to Germany, Austria, Belgium, France, Spain, Denmark, England, Sweden, Egypt, and India to inspect and report on the prison camps. Arrangements were made for correspondence with the occupied regions of France, Alsace, Belgium, and Rumania and for the repatriation of women, children, the aged, and the sick, that they should no longer be repatriated in groups, but that each case must be taken up individually.

The International Committee overlooked nothing for which warrant existed in the articles of the convention or the rules of war in its care for the interests of imprisoned men ; and, as a result of many complaints, following the visits of its delegates to the prison camps, it made insistent demand upon the belligerents for recognition of the right of imprisoned men to a decent allotment of space and adequate measure of exercise to maintain health. Moreover, it urged upon all the countries at war the wisdom of permitting their officers, when imprisoned, to give their parole as justification for freedom of movement. And that the attitude of the Swiss throughout the trying period of the war was most admirable and ideally neutral, is shown in the statement from the "General Catalogue covering the Benevolent Work of Switzerland during the Present War": "Switzerland gave to French prisoners 250,000 kilos of bread, while nearly 4,000,000 letters for prisoners of war were handled in August, 1916. . . ." (The Swiss post-office had become a benevolent institution.)

A fairly accurate idea of the extent of Swiss activities follows: for the forwarding of letters and the transfer of money to prisoners, they went to not a little pains to perfect their system; they fought for changes in the postal regulations of warring countries which should simplify and expedite the process of transfer; they placed freely at the disposition of the belligerents every service that Switzerland's government or its civilian population, for that matter, could render looking to prisoners' relief; in conjunction with the Danish Red Cross, — which early in 1918 sent a delegate to Geneva, — the International Society moved for the establishment at Paris of a bureau analogous to that founded by the Danish Red Cross at Berlin. Its object was to provide mental relief to prisoners by means of books, games, and sports; to secure admission to personal relation with the prisoners; to look after the food supplies and the inspection of camps; and it secured the promise of this arrangement in behalf of German prisoners on condition of complete reciprocity by Germany.

The reports on the prison camps were thorough and enlightening.

In January, 1918, the Society had been obliged to abolish the delivery of food packages to the section camps because the expenses were growing with the increase of prisoners. Assistance was lacking; food was scarce; and the reserves had been used up. Moreover, there were more and more French arriving and they did not receive the packages sent — in many cases not even so much as one a month. Complaint was made that the sanitary condition of the camps was bad. There was plaintive cry for help to enable the Society to render assistance to sick prisoners. Away back in 1917, the Committee had been fighting against the growing meagerness of the food supply. The reflection of conditions in the German and Austrian camps, from the Committee's reports, was not cheerful. A fund was urged to secure food with reasons as follows: —

"The prisoners suffer more and more from hunger. The food they receive from Germany and Austria is insufficient. Their rations are the same as those allowed the civil population but do not equal those of the armies. Some of the causes for increased mortality among prisoners might be successfully combated if it were possible to get food. In Rumania the mortality has increased three hundred and forty-five fold above normal."

Everywhere war and war makers were consuming the supplies. The civilian populations were taking in their belts. Societies of women in every country in Europe were scraping little supplies of food together, but daily these dwindled. The French and English prisoners lived almost exclusively on food sent from France and overburdened little Switzerland, and prayed that it might not fail. Supplies were sent from Switzerland to the Belgians; the internal Italians had little save the Swiss donations; while great numbers of Russian prisoners — held in the part of France occupied by the Germans — were slowly starving to death, although Switzerland was sending them a share of its victuals.

Imprisoned Rumanians had fifty kilos of food a month from Sweden and there were 79,000 of them, — all of which distribution resolved itself into a mathematical problem of no small proportion.

"It is absolutely impossible," said the Swiss Committee, "to get the necessary food in Europe. In Asia and China it is equally impossible. It is, therefore, necessary that the supplies for the prisoners of war must come from either North or South America; it is also of equal importance that the question be settled before the coming winter, when new restrictions governing the work of neutrals shall be in force and whereby the prisoners will receive less and less from the Austro-Germans."

To say the least no more dismal outlook is conceivable than that which Switzerland, the innocent bystander, faced with pockets and granaries alike empty. She was fairly mothering the multitudinous waifs of Serbia, whose sufferings under the bitter Austrian onslaught had passed all power of description. In Geneva and Berne there were bureaus organized to give the Serbians help, but the transportation was hard and uncertain, and the Serbs went on dying. The Swiss cities were full, as was France, of Serbian officers and men who were sick and penniless and dying of tuberculosis; but, for all that, they were happy in their estate when contrasted with the wretched remnants elsewhere. The cantons were overrun with the sick and homeless of all the world. The cities were crowded with representatives of every country till in Berne and Geneva there was not a house to be had for love or money.

The picture that had been painted of prisoners' life in the German and Austrian prison camps had made them more than a thing of dread than even the cannons or the gas. The subterfuge of food, which Kultur spat upon before it was proffered, the filth, the crowding, the merciless labor, the cold and the brutal usage — these were the softest forms of vengeance that the repatriate prisoners of Allied nations reported when they came back from their confinement.

Facing such possibilities, the heavily handicapped Swiss organization for prisoners' relief was as the shadow of a great rock in a weary land. The American Red Cross gave the Swiss $125,000, to assist in work among their own destitute Swiss population and the Allied troops and civilians in transit from Germany and Austria. There were at the opening of the war only about 75 Americans interned in Germany, chiefly the members of merchant crews from American vessels. But as the American soldier began to take his place in the French battle line the number slowly grew. In the spring of 1918 the Red Cross, through the International Committee in Berne, was supplying food, clothing, and other needed things — for account of the Government — to 230 Americans scattered among the detention pens of Germany. The Red Cross box weighed ten pounds, — four of which went to every man each fortnight, — and contained two and one half pounds of corned beef, two pounds of bread, one pound of biscuits, one pound of sugar, three quarters of a pound of pork and beans, one fifth of a pound of cocoa, one pound of coffee, a pound of oleomargarine, half a pound of soap, and fifty cigarettes. While this list was standard it was varied from time to time.

The Swiss Committee had devised a system of receipt cards upon which the prisoner himself acknowledged receipt of the delivery. If the card did not return, investigation was started through the German and Swiss Red Cross or through the Spanish embassy at Berlin. There was also space on the card for the recipient to indicate any articles of which he might stand in need. Letters received from the prison camps showed that American prisoners lived wholly on the food sent by the Red Cross and turned over their prison rations to the unfortunates of other countries. In a year the Red Cross had sent to the stores in Berne for distribution to American prisoners tons upon tons of supplies which included food, clothing, tobacco, soap, mending outfits, toilet cases, stationery, pencils, shoe laces, brushes, and other useful things too numerous to mention.

Incidentally, the Quartermaster's Department was unable to help as much as was expected. Upon our entry into the war it was prepared to furnish supplies of food to last 10,000 men six months; but the burden of ocean traffic was so great in the transport of men and military materials that only in the spring of 1918 were these supplies beginning to arrive in Switzerland.

It was early in the year that the Red Cross decided to increase the scope of its communication service. Organized, primarily, to maintain a source of dependable information for relatives concerning men in army service, to search for the missing, to find in the haystack of war's confusion the needles of fact for which anxious families at home were waiting regarding their men at the front, the service was now expanded to furnish information, through the Committee at Berne, concerning American prisoners and to establish, where possible, communication between them and their families. The Bureau was also licensed as the sole agency for the transmission of money to American prisoners in Germany. It undertook to maintain communication between persons in this country and their relatives or friends in every territory. But it was not until June, 1918, that the United States Government arranged through the Swiss Government and the Spanish Embassy in Berlin to intern American invalid prisoners in Switzerland.

As easily as can be imagined, the rapidly growing numbers of American soldiers in Europe made it necessary to provide fully for the care of such as might be taken prisoners; and with this purpose in view the Red Cross in June of 1918 appointed a Commission to Switzerland to superintend all relief work for both American and Allied prisoners, and citizens of Allied powers resident in Switzerland, and to aid the Swiss in their efforts to relieve the universal suffering. The budget of the Commission for this work to December 31st, called for a total of $1,972,323.75. Up to that time the Red Cross expenditure had been only $200,000, of which $75,000 was for the care of the interned Russians.

I have already said that the position of Switzerland was desperate. Stripped of food by the flood of people that either passed through her territory or were quartered upon her, she was between the upper and nether millstones: Germany was in a position to shut off her supply of fuel, and France could forbid her food. Meantime, the tourists, who were her chief source of revenue, were absent and in their stead came a tremendous inflow of hungry, half-clothed people from everywhere, — a vast army of mouths for which, in the name of common humanity, food must be found.

To relieve Switzerland herself was part of the task of the American Red Cross Commission, which proceeded to adjust the supply and storage system for prisoners by the establishment of houses at a small town, near Lausanne, and at Bümpliz in the outskirts of Berne, where new buildings were erected; the Commission, also, made a review of the difficulties besetting the Swiss organization, which resulted in a contribution of 500,000 francs to be used solely for the Swiss Red Cross work among the Swiss population and for the relief of Allied troops or Allied civilians in transit from Germany and Austria. This action, suspending as it did the drain on the Swiss organization, caused great happiness among the Swiss people, while there was strong disapproval in Berlin. Definite arrangements were also made for distribution of relief to the destitute Russians.

At Leysin, the Commission found a concrete house containing seventy-five rooms, each having an outside sleeping-porch, which it proceeded to take over and prepare for a hospital for tuberculous Serbian officers. Medical attendance was provided by the Swiss and the Red Cross made a per diem allowance for each patient. This work, I wish to add, was planned with the coöperation of the Serbian minister.

Switzerland, too, had its repatriate problem, or rather *évacués* problem. The poor wretches — women, young children, and old men, whom the Germans had taken from their homes in northern France — were coming into Swiss territory at the rate of 1200 a day. Many of them had walked miles to the train, and their feet were bruised and swollen. All had ridden for two or three days, unfed, unwashed, uncared for. With only brief notice Germany had begun unloading these sorry folk at Basle in November of 1917. A local committee had provided 225,000 francs toward caring for them, which began with facilities for washing in the railway station and a small infirmary such as the Red Cross maintains at its canteen stations in America. There was a room for feeding the wanderers, a special car for bathing and dressing babies, and a storeroom for clothing and necessities. The Swiss Government fed them, while other necessities, including clothing, were provided by charity. As at Evian in France, an elaborate card index system of information was maintained by volunteer women for the purpose of securing information which might assist in reuniting families. It was the same old picture of sickness, dirt and misery that we have seen in France, repellant but heartbreaking in its appeal.

From Bouveret these wayfarers were distributed through southern France, and 10,000 of them passed weekly through the confines of Switzerland on their way to homes that were far away and that would only be accessible when the Germans' should be beaten back.

There was an Italian problem, too. Indeed, there was no problem that Switzerland did not have! At Buchs, where 2500 Italian soldiers poured through each month on their way back into Italy, the American Red Cross established a canteen. These returning Italians were sorry pilgrims, — many of whom were badly wounded while others were tuberculous, lacking in underclothing, stockings and, in many cases, were without shoes. Moreover, most of them were half starved, or worse, since almost every train had its quota of those who had been unable to stand the ordeal of the journey and had died on the way.

In addition there was a great army of interned soldiers in Switzerland who were looked after by the officers of the Swiss army. The minds of many of them had been shaken by the shocks of war and the deprivations and maltreatment of the Teuton prison camps, and with nothing to occupy their minds or engross their attention they were a great and growing menace. Various societies were formed to furnish them with employment in workrooms, in the manufacture of leather goods, glassware, beadwork, portable houses, furniture, and various other things. In many instances these men were barely fit to work; while others had been idle so long that they had lost the faculty of working. The output of these *ateliers* was sent to America and found immediate sale. The first problem was raw material, for the Swiss resources were no longer able to provide for them or to pay the freight of the products to the American market. The Red Cross devoted 750,000 francs to the establishment of these workrooms and training-schools for soldiers interned in Switzerland and founded a bureau for the sale of their products in America. Over $40,000 worth of these things were sold within a year.

Two workrooms for making hospital and relief supplies were added by the Red Cross. The places were reconstructed and re-equipped for extended production of regular standard Red Cross supplies, needy women being employed in their manufacture. Much of the product, such as underwear for women and children, was used immediately at Basle.

In Geneva there was an American Red Cross Chapter conducting workrooms at the Palais Eynard. The Commission planned to establish units of Americans at Zurich, St. Gaul, and Lucerne who might be relied upon for assistance when American soldiers should come to be interned in Switzerland.

But it did not end there: at Fribourg there were 2000 Belgian children who had been under the protection of the American Red Cross Commission of Belgium, and their numbers grew steadily with successive evacuations; Switzerland was full of tuberculous, of all ages and races and degrees of helplessness. Swarms of civilian Serbs were crying for help from desolate Serbia whose sufferings at that time were terrible! The Red Cross proposed the sending of a Swiss-American relief force to Belgrade to establish a dispensary and distribute relief. There was trouble over the Italian prisoners in Austria for whom Italy could not care. Italian societies were ready to relieve them, but food and clothing were unobtainable. There was no doubt of their appalling condition. Those who passed through Buchs gave proof enough that all the harrowing tales were true. Innumerable packages, sent by friends from Italy and from the two Americas, never found their destination or were worthless from bad packing. There was undoubtedly an improvement in the whole prison camp situation in the German and Austrian territory — more prompt and certain delivery of food shipments. Upon packages sent to American prisoners from Berne the record showed that the system functioned perfectly. Ninety-five per cent of these were delivered without interference, and the condition of the camps where Americans were detained was reported as good. Food conditions in Germany were stringent. Returning prisoners said that where the packages were received the prisoners fared better than their keepers.

There were in Germany twenty-seven prison camps, of which Tuchel near Danzig was selected to be the chief place

of detention of Americans.   In nearly all the twenty-seven
centers, among them Tuchel, Berlin, Havelberg, Parchim,
Brandenburg, Cassel, Langensalza, Cologne, Siegburg,
Aachen, Limburg, Mainz, Giessen, Darmstadt, Heidelberg,
Karlsruhe, Villingen, Rastatt, Bayreuth, and Landshut,
there were American captives in June, 1918, either captured
soldiers or seafarers who had been collected from submarined
ships.   There were reports from 231 men, and to all of them
packages were being sent from the warehouses at Berne by
the Red Cross, acting as distributing agent for the Army or
Navy which provided the supplies.   Villingen was the camp
for the officers.

Data obtainable in midsummer indicated that there were
about 200 more captured Americans who had not yet been
located permanently.   There was food enough then stored
up in Berne to last 22,000 prisoners for half a year if required.
Three American prisoners in Tuchel had been appointed a
Red Cross Relief Committee, — custodians of liberal supplies sent there for the use of prisoners when they should
arrive, — and similar supplies were ready for immediate
distribution to other camps.   When it became apparent
that the Germans were slow to give notice of the transfer of
prisoners from one camp to another, heads of the French
Relief at Berne and the Prisoners' Depots at Paris and Lyons
issued orders to French Committees in all the German camps
to supply new American arrivals with whatever they
required.

Arrangements had been made that all, or nearly all, of the
German prison camps should be stocked with similar emergency supplies, in anticipation of the wants of those who
were unfortunate enough to fall into the hands of the enemy.
There were approximately 200 main prison camps in Germany and some 10,000 prison groups, counting the small
detachments of prisoners sent out to do farm labor.   The
American Red Cross laid plans to supply all these work

camps with the regulation food parcels as well as others where American prisoners were held.

The process of locating prisoners and providing for their comfort was thoroughly systematized. Immediately on receipt of the German lists the Central Prisoners of War Committee in Berne wired them to General Headquarters of the American Expeditionary Force in France, which in turn cabled them to Red Cross Headquarters in Washington. Food packages were immediately dispatched, every item of which was accounted for on the receipt card. Shoes, hats, and clothing could be ordered. Officers' uniforms were made to measure in Berne from cloth stored there for the purpose, and the rank insignia accompanied them when shipped. The Red Cross notified a prisoner's relatives of his capture, and letters could be sent either direct or through the central bureau at Berne.

The prompt provision of clothing is important, since a man captured in battle is apt to be pretty badly disarranged before he is taken. Individual packages shipped by friends and relatives at home were also forwarded, as well as money remittances. The practice of sending food and clothing from America had been discouraged, but there is a human side to it which was considered in the framing of the program and its regulations. With customary Teutonic caution, the German authorities paid over moneys sent to the prisoners not in German currency but in prison script, which was good at the prison-camp canteens but outside of which would purchase nothing. From the communications received from American prisoners it was indicated that the cruelties of the early years, reported to have been permitted and even encouraged in the Austro-German camps, were not practiced so largely in the treatment of American captives.

CHAPTER XV

BELGIUM

Belgian Refugees in Other Countries — Work in Belgium, a Department of the French Commission — Housing Problem — Coördination of Scattered Relief Agencies — The Plight of the Belgian Army — Recreation and Eating Hut Provided by the Red Cross — Canteen and Other Comforts for the Soldiers — The Red Cross Supplemented the Work of the Belgian Government — Plans for a Possible Catastrophe — Barrack Houses Erected — Work of Belgium's Queen — Private Enterprises of Relief — *Colonies Scolaires.*

IT is one of the psychological phenomena of the war that the longest mark in the Belgian's score against his assailant is that the villain, not content with destroying his agriculture, also took away all the industrial machinery of the busy Belgian cities to his own shops across the Rhine. That one item of vandalism left in the Belgian soul a scar that time cannot obliterate.

By ill fortune Belgium was the first horrible example which Germany depended on to awe the rest of Europe into submission. The brutality of the blow, delivered when German strength, long held in check, was at its bestial maximum, staggered civilization. When the first numbing impact was past, Belgium struggled to her feet. If, in her agony, however, she was an object for pity, in the longer and more trying struggle for self-maintenance she gained universal admiration. A helpless and vicarious sacrifice to humanity's salvation, she rose from her altar a giant in courage and a model for faint hearts the world around.

And so although Belgium ran the whole gamut of suffer-

o   193

ing from the first hour of war down to the present minute, and although she still suffers, her stalwart courage and conspicuous practicality, her sturdy sense and simple dignity have long since lifted her above the lime-light zone of hysterical pity.

In September, 1917, however, there were 275,000 Belgian refugees in France; 150,000 in England; 50,000 in Holland; and many thousands more in Switzerland. It was estimated that in free Belgium, — the 500 or less square miles which still remained free from invasion, though all within easy reach of the German lines had been swept every day and hour by missiles from the German guns, — there were 90,000 more stubborn ones to whom the soil of home was dearer than life. There were fewer than 250,000 left of the Army, who had gathered about the stalwart figure of the King and settled down in the trenches of the coast sectors in a grim determination to see it through.

The rest of the teeming population, which had made Belgium the leader of the world in productive agriculture, and, for her size, foremost as well in industrial output, Germany or the grave had swallowed them all. Belgium had nothing save what she could borrow — no land, no industries, no food, and no clothing. She was down, helpless, stripped, and with Winter not far away.

Into this situation came the Red Cross, in the person of a deputy dispatched by the Commissioner for Europe to visit what was left of Belgium along the British front. "This strip," the deputy wrote back, "is only about thirty-five miles long and fifteen miles wide and there is no foot of it that cannot be reached by German shells or air bombs."

Of the 90,000 people still clinging to this target that they called home, more than 10,000 were children, and from this district the Belgian government, circumscribed as it was, had already taken away six thousand imperiled children and placed them in homes in Switzerland and France, viz.

A SOURCE OF MALARIA AND OTHER DISEASE REMOVED BY THE RED CROSS.

The upper picture shows the swamp before the Red Cross engineers tackled it; the lower picture the result of their labor: one thousand acres drained.

in Paris and in the *Colonies Scolaires* north of Paris, and others in the departments along the coast of the English Channel. At this time, however, burdened as they were with a multiplicity of problems, they had come to the vanishing point of their resources; so they asked if the American Red Cross would not help to remove and furnish shelter for some six hundred more who were in the area of greater danger.

The world has never seen a more pathetic lot than were those children! For "coolness under fire," as the phrase runs, commend me now and evermore to those little children in the lost corner of Belgium who, day by day, they tell me, went trudging fearlessly and cheerfully from shell-shattered homes to half-ruined schoolhouses, along roads where the deep shell holes yawned like giants' graves! In all the great panorama of danger and desperation and death that made up the battlefront, I venture to say there were no stouter hearts than these. To mark their unconcern, as the missiles came and went, was to understand a little more of the spirit that kept their fathers on the firing line through four years of hardship and misery, and their mothers guarding the home fires and holding the families together as best they could, with hideous death forever at their elbows. These toddlers had seen their mothers, fathers, brothers, and sisters blotted from the earth beside them in a whirl of sand and not gone mad. They were the soul of Belgium!

At first, the Red Cross work in Belgium was organized as a department of the French Commission; but later, as it expanded, there was established a separate commission with headquarters at Havre. And when once the start was made in Belgium the labor did not lag. The territory that remained accessible, of what was Belgium, was so small as to be easily canvassed and planned for; only the refugee problem was distributed over a large area. But in it all the work was simplified, first by the keen organizing sense and the intense devotion of the leading people, both men and women, among the Belgians, and second by the habitual industry of the working folk. It was speedily found that a great number of these were nearly or almost self-supporting. After the Belgian fashion they had sought service at the trades in which they were skilled. The Flemish refugees from Belgium in the year 1917 tilled 60,000 acres of land in France, and helped to feed the Belgian Army at the front. The Red Cross and the Belgian organizations made systematic effort to place the refugees; and lace makers, jewelers, machinists, and men and women proficient in many lines were soon permanently and profitably established. Most of them, to be sure, were old, but a Belgian is seldom too old to work. When he is he dies. The French government, likewise, with all the multitudinous loads of its own to carry, was giving to a great many of these Belgian wanderers a small allocation or allowance to guard them against want.

A most perplexing need, however, was for living quarters for the refugees. Naturally, in the cities of France, — Paris and Havre, — to which most of the refugees made their way, no proper provision had been or could be made to care for such a horde and under such stress of circumstances; as a result, respectable Belgian families were compelled to take lodgment in the lowest quarters of the city, sometimes in wretched old houses, sometimes in sheds or outbuildings where there were no conveniences, no comfort, and no sanitary safety.

When the Red Cross first came to Belgium, it entered into close and practical coöperation with the government officials and, together, they attacked at once the troublesome housing problem. In Havre, — where the population had increased by sixty thousand and never a new house had been built, — the situation was most acute. Here the Red Cross and the Belgians took over and equipped a group of vacant barracks and also leased a number of apartment houses, thus providing shelter for several hundred families. With the *Famille Belge* the Red Cross organized a chain of coöperative stores, such as are in vogue in Belgium, and cut down the high cost of living to the refugee families.

To assist in maintaining the health of the Havre colony a 250-bed hospital was presented to it, which was managed by the Minister of the Interior and included in its personnel the Red Cross staff of doctors and nurses. Health centers were established at Havre and Rouen with infant clinics and *pouponnières* for the care of abandoned babies. The operation of these shelters was taken in charge by a group of prominent Belgian women.

Here, as in France and Italy, it was the aim of the Red Cross in all its work of relief to coördinate by means of needed assistance, monetary or otherwise, all the scattered agencies and enterprises that were trying to cope with the situation, organizing them all into sections under the direction of a government official. There was a host of them, too, for clothing, for layettes, for the families of Belgian soldiers, for emergency relief, for mothers and children, for housing, for hospital service, and for tuberculosis. By means of monthly conferences with delegates from each section, however, all the work was correlated and widely extended, and coöperation was maintained through a system of weekly inspection with all governmental and private agencies of relief, both French and Belgian.

Meanwhile, the refugee problem was never quiescent: always the stream of the newly homeless kept drifting down the long road from the zone of war. To relieve the situation in Havre the Red Cross gave $600,000 for the construction of a village of temporary cottages. The site was prepared by the Albert Fund, with paved streets, water supply, and electric lights. Each of the hundred cottages soon boasted a laundry-shed at the rear and a garden neatly fenced in.

There were two schoolhouses with Belgian teachers, a church with a Belgian priest, and the inevitable coöperative store, without which the Belgian would not feel at home even in Brussels. There was also a town-hall for meetings and administration use. The rents were nominal. As a matter of fact the whole project was characteristically Belgian.

After its entrance into Belgium, the first important contribution of the Red Cross was 500,000 francs to the Belgian Red Cross toward its great military hospital at Wulveringhem. La Panne, which had been the hospital center, had become a barrack town; and the great hotel where the hospital was installed was a pet-mark for the German gunners and air-men. At Wulveringhem the work on the splendid new hospital with its wide range of barrack wards was lagging for lack of means, but the Red Cross gift hurried it to usefulness. When it was finished the plant and the patients from La Panne were moved there and, once more, the Belgian Army doctors could operate without the perpetual interference of German shells.

It was a needy army, in those days, that Belgian Army which helped the English to hold the Channel front, and it lived the life of a hunted animal! There were the *abris* and dugouts in the first line, wet and overcrowded; on the second line, about seven or eight miles back, some shelters and ruined buildings; and in the rear some new brick barracks where at intervals good Belgian soldiers went when they did not die. When they did die — and their casualty roll mounted into the thousands each month — there was the endless graveyard near at hand. It was a somber place, all in all. "It is not the bombs that we are afraid of," said a Belgian soldier, who had once been an *attaché* of the Rockefeller Foundation, — "it is not the bombs, or even the shell when they have the location of our quarters; it is the bitter cold and the wet feet, and no place to go."

Indeed, they had no place to go. All the way by Merck-hem and Bixschoote and up to the edge of the Houthulst forest trench lines were blotted out; in their mad plunges for the mastery of the Channel coast the Germans had torn the whole land to tatters. The entire front was a wilderness of shell-holes, cratered and furrowed to the limit of desolation! The defenses were not lines at all — merely advance posts, machine-gun emplacements and batteries, and always under fire. In the second line retreats there were no lights of any nature. In the tumbledown barns the soldiers on *repose* slept on soggy straw, or ran back and forth all night to keep warm because of the lack of blankets. Many a Belgian hero took his "day off" sleeping in a pig-sty; and where there was a stove the men were brought in to get warm beside it in detachments.

It became evident, therefore, that the Red Cross must do something towards removing this situation. A million francs was appropriated; and together with the Belgian Minister of War, and other Belgian representatives, a project was set on foot for the erection in the Army zone of recreation and eating huts and of double tents, equipping them with dishes, baths, moving pictures, and reading rooms. The men themselves undertook to manufacture the furniture.

In addition, the Red Cross gave a fund to the *Livres des Soldats Belges*, which sent out books to soldiers in the field. There was a great demand for technical books of the professions by soldiers who had left engineering and law offices and scientific schools to take their places against the invader and who did not wish to die intellectually. All these demands the Red Cross supplied. It contributed to societies whose object it was to furnish small comforts to the soldiers; it helped in the expansion of the canteen system; and it gave money for the erection and equipment of new canteens. It also gave money liberally to the *Foyer du Soldat Belge* — and if there ever was a *soldat* who was entitled to a *Foyer*

it surely was the *soldat Belge*. There were thousands of
them who had not known a day away from the cheerless
expanse of mud and shell-holes and ice since the war began,
for the very simple reason that they had no place in
the world to go nor a *sou* to take them anywhere. In
the Army, where the wages of the soldiers ran as low as
seven cents a day, where the baths were few and far between, and the clothing dilapidated, one did not travel for
pleasure. So, when the Red Cross took detachments
of these poor fellows and cleaned them up and with money
in their pockets to spend sent them for a ten days' stay
in Paris for a look at the bright lights and a change of diet,
it brought these men back to a realization that there were
still people in the world who were not dirty and unshorn,
unshaven and scarred, and it made a distinct contribution
to the cause of democracy.

There was a Red Cross canteen at the *Gare du Nord* which
had been supported by English donors, and which the Red
Cross helped to enlarge and supply. This was for Belgian
soldiers coming to Paris, or passing through, and it did anything and everything to make them comfortable. The Red
Cross also made substantial contributions to the *Congé du
Soldat Belge*, which had been supported by the Belgian,
French, and Italian trades unionists. The *Congé* was different : its plan was to take a small number of the Belgian
soldiers and treat them like country cousins who had come
on a visit. The old number was ten at a time. The Red
Cross increased it to fifty or more.

But for the most part, as I have said, the "leave" of the
Belgian soldier was not burdensome to his hosts. As soon
as he was cleaned up and well fed he went out and got his
pay check, which there was no trouble about his doing, and
when he went back to his dugout he had money in his pocket.
The Belgian Minister of Agriculture supplied employment
for a multitude of the Flemish farmers on leave. The Red

Cross started a fund for wounded men who, on account of their injuries, had been released from the Army, to provide them with civilian clothing to take the place of the uniforms — which they must surrender when discharged — and to help them make a fresh start.

Altogether, there were half a dozen hospitals in Belgium and three in France accommodating about 5000 persons, which the Red Cross assisted. It contributed to a mess at Sainte Adresse, near Havre, which supplied 300 meals a day to workers in munition factories; it furnished money to the soldiers' club at Fécamp, and another at Dieppe; and a great deal of work was done at Calais in connection with the School of Gunnery. For the canteens and barracks for *permissionaires* at Ouvre, Ile de Cezambre, La Panne, Isenberghe, Bulscamp, Hoogstaade, Hondschoote, and other places, maintenance funds were provided. Libraries, games, and moving pictures were furnished to keep the soldiers cheerful and mentally fit. The library equipment was extensive. Actors and singers were secured to give entertainments. A valuable work was done in the support of educational courses, in which thousands of students were enrolled; individual gifts were distributed to all soldiers who were decorated or cited in Army orders for bravery.

In all these undertakings — the providing of comfort for the soldiers at the front, recreation for soldiers on leave, hospitals, hospital equipment, medicines, instruments, looking after the families of soldiers and stiffening all along the line the Belgian military morale — the Red Cross was helping a government which had only a temporary abiding place, and was carrying on national business under a tremendous burden of difficulty. But throughout all the Red Cross work in Belgium it held merely the position of a contributor. The Belgian government had a thoroughly competent system for the handling of its problems; what it lacked was the means to carry its plans into execution. This the Red

Cross furnished. It was a very vital contribution, for not only did it lighten the load of an overtaxed governmental machine, but it put new life into the Army of 200,000 men.

In planning its work for the territory back of the lines, the Red Cross had a more perplexing problem, which resolved itself into a species of speculation on the fortunes of war. There had been no moment since the line adjusted itself in the north that was free from the possibility of swift and imperative demand. Any day some change in conditions along those northern sectors, held jointly by English, French, and Belgian troops, might send a final stream of refugees rolling down into France, calling for shelter and for instant supplies of food and clothing; or, a German retreat might release new areas whose inhabitants wretched after long periods of German rule would create an even more stringent condition. There would be a great and instant tax on the Army supplies, the Red Cross stores and the foodstuffs gathered for the remaining occupants of free Belgium. With an impossible condition of transportation and a paucity of food to begin with, it was plain that any diversion in the Belgian sector of the front would make trouble, and failure to meet it would be fatal.

It was here perhaps that the Red Cross performed its most important task in the Belgian field, although the crisis which it was devised to meet never arrived. In the fall of 1917, twenty barrack-houses, each twenty by one hundred feet, were contracted for near Adinkerke. Nine of them were first erected by Army labor on sites convenient to railway lines, highways, and canals, in order to provide prompt distribution. Arrangements were made with the Friends' Ambulance Unit and the British Red Cross for the use of their trucks in case of need. In addition, Paris Red Cross Headquarters agreed to place from twenty-five to fifty loaded cars in the Belgian region on demand, within twenty-four hours. Canal boats were placed under charter, in order to make use of the network of canals running all through the districts. With these provisions made, the Red Cross Commission set about the purchase of $2,000,000 worth of emergency supplies, such as food, clothing, blankets, to supplement the great stocks in the Red Cross warehouses in Paris, which could be drawn upon at short notice.

An idea of the nature of the food supplies laid up in these warehouses against the day of need may be got from this list of goods shipped in for the first of the buildings that was completed : —

> 500 cases condensed milk
> 310 sacks of rice (50 kilos)
> 40 sacks of rice (100 kilos)
> 7 sacks of macaroni (100 kilos)
> 60 sacks of dried peas (100 kilos)
> 190 sacks of lentils (100 kilos)
> 914 cases of salmon (50 lb. to case)
> 913 cases of corned beef (50 lb. to case)
> 120 sacks white beans (100 kilos)
> 600 boxes biscuits ($4\frac{1}{2}$ lb. each)

All this was simply a gamble on the chances of war, an insurance against the horrible possibilities which the lack of these supplies might cause. What happened in Italy, what happened in Belgium itself at the beginning of the war might easily be repeated, and in the depleted condition of the country after four years of war the possibilities were awful to contemplate.

"The danger from the beginning has been recognized," observed the Red Cross Commissioner at that time, "and we have resolved to take no chances. We prefer to lose part of our goods rather than to be caught napping. We realize that none of this food put in the warehouse at the front may ever be needed, that the lines may not change, and there is a possibility, even, of their changing in the wrong direction. But if the lines should change both railroad and highways will be filled and there will be delay in

getting food up there from Paris. There have been pro-
tests against putting the food there on account of the danger
of its being shelled. A high officer of the British Army
told me that he had been in command of troops which took
possession of a sector of French territory, and that if his
soldiers had not been double-rationed the civilians would
have starved to death before any help could have reached
them. The world will never forgive," he emphasized,
"the American Red Cross if it does not run the risk of losing
some property for the sake of saving lives."

It was wonderful tenacity that the Belgian folk displayed
in clinging to this vestige of land called "free Belgium."
Their infatuation for home soil stands out as the most
graphic feature of the war situation in Belgium. After
the fighting around Nieuport in the spring of 1917, and the
stubborn battle for Paeschendaele Ridge in the fall, this
country became not only an armed camp but a battle
ground wherein these peasants went about their homely
tasks with their lives eternally at hazard. Many of them
paid the last price, but that did not frighten away their
neighbors; and the Belgian government, knowing its own
people, encouraged them to stay on. They farmed away
in utter disregard of German marksmanship, of danger and
of horrible death, and in the words of an American writer who
visited the section, "their ditches and hop-poles and stacked
wheat, quite beyond the needed crops for which they stand,
are so many markers of Belgium's claim to her own. . . ."
Some of the most serious fighting of the war has been carried
on here, from shell crater to shell crater. But to the civilian
Belgian these stretches of ground and the civilian country
that lies between them and the sea are alike and the same.
They are his native soil. They are free Belgium, heritage
of the past and earnest of the future.

At this time the Red Cross came in touch with the
splendid work done by Belgian's Queen, who, as all the

world knows, was an indefatigable worker for the children and the aged, and who lived in such constant peril and distress. La Panne, where the hospital had been, was at first the center for relief operations, but when the vicious attacks of 1917 began to make it untenable, the refugees there had to be gotten out and away to safer places. At first out of one hundred and eighty old men and women in the *Repos d'Élizabeth*, her Majesty's charity, only twenty-six answered yes when all were asked if they wanted to be taken out of danger. But when the houses all around them began going there was no longer any room for home love, and the Red Cross furnished the money to transport the whole company to a comfortable and safe place in France. Gradually the Society joined in, more or less as a silent partner, with all the organized forces of relief in the district. It gave money to the *commissaries* of the *arrondissements* and to the *Service de Santé* conducted by English and French women. Clothing and milk were supplied for the babies, of which, in Belgium, even in normal times, there are plenty; a portable barrack was found for a baby hospital at La Panne, and a Red Cross woman was sent from America for the clinical work. In areas where it was impossible to buy milk the Red Cross furnished it; it also bought supplies of eggs for tubercular patients.

In all the story of the war's miseries there are probably no more pathetic chapters than those of some of the private enterprises of relief in Belgium. In the heart of the British war zone the Countess Van Steen, herself a nurse, had a hospital. Her home, which she had in the beginning turned into a hospital, fell into German hands and, like a soldier, she withdrew and began work in free Belgium where she was made directress of the Elizabeth Hospital at Poperingue. Again the bombardment forced retirement, and in the next station at Proven the shells were still falling all about her and the highways resounded to all the clamors of war. On every hand the rough military buildings sprang up. To her little station there was always a procession of wounded, soldiers and civilians alike — wounded horribly. There were children, sick and injured and blinded with gas. The record of horrors in that neighborhood is not pleasant reading. In one evening twenty-eight cases were brought in from one little neighboring village. The wards, the tents, were all full, always full, and the means were very scanty. Then the Red Cross came and supplied what was lacking, and the work went on without hindrance.

It was so with the *Colonies* of the Belgian Abbé Delaere at Wisques and Wizernes, which had grown out of an earlier work at Ypres. The Abbé Delaere had been the last of civilians to leave Ypres. There were others of these *Colonies Scolaires*, too, — nearly sixty of them, — scattered all over northern France in all sorts of available buildings, filled with thin-faced children brought from places within range of the never silent cannon, broken in nerves and full of fear. To all these schools the Red Cross made gifts, supplying everything from buildings to buttons. The Queen's school at Vinckem was a thriving establishment, with playgrounds, infirmary, and splendid gardens. But it was well in the danger zone, for the King and Queen refused to leave the soil of the Kingdom, and to be in Belgium meant to be under fire. The Red Cross assisted the Queen to expand the school's facilities by the erection of a babies' pavilion so as to take in younger children; it established school buildings at Cayeux-sur-Mer in France to accommodate children from the abandoned establishments until the new permanent institutions could be completed at Leysele on the French frontier; and it transferred whole colonies of children, at the suggestion of the Queen, through Switzerland to many retreats in France. Victory, indeed, found the Red Cross more than a helper in things Belgian, — it found it a friend.

CHAPTER XVI

THE STORY OF ITALY

The Red Cross Uniform in Italy — The Disaster of Caporetto — Emergency Commission from France — Refutation of Propaganda to Discredit America — Coöperation with Italian Authorities — Arrival of the Permanent Red Cross Commission — Ambulance Sections at the Front — Rolling Kitchens — Aiding Soldiers' Families — First Anniversary of America's Entering the War — Epidemic of Influenza — Aid for American Soldiers — Establishment of the Red Cross Hospital — Red Cross Welcome to Our Soldiers — Forward with the Victorious Army — Care for the Starving Civilian Population — The Problem of Italian Prisoners of War — Opening of the Department of Tuberculosis — Activities Turned Over to Italian Authorities.

THE many millions of Americans, whose support made possible the work of the Red Cross abroad, can have no adequate conception of what the presence of Americans of the Red Cross, in the uniform of their country, meant to the people of Italy in the fall of 1917, and the year following.

It was not until July, 1918, that American fighting troops were sent to Italy. Then one regiment was dispatched from France, receiving a welcome that will never be forgotten. They had been preceded in the last week of June by about 1600 officers and men of the United States Army Ambulance Service, but before that time the only uniformed American force in Italy had been a few student aviators at training camps and the personnel of the Red Cross.

It came about, therefore, that at a critical period in Italy's history and in the progress of the war, workers of the Red Cross, conducting their work from one end of Italy to the other, from the front lines to the tip of Sicily, brought to hundreds of thousands of Italian soldiers and to millions of Italian people in civil life their first sight of an American in the uniform of his native land.

The American Red Cross came to Italy just three weeks after the disaster of Caporetto, when thousands had been slain, hundreds of thousands taken prisoners, vast quantities of munitions captured, and a half million or more old men, women, and children had been driven from their homes by the invading enemy. Such a disaster has had few parallels in history and it is, perhaps, the greatest tribute possible to the power of resistance of Italy's people and the courage of her soldiers that on the slender stream of the Piave,— almost negligible as a military barrier, — her retreating troops reformed and repulsed a numerically superior foe, advancing with all the *élan* that a great victory gives; while behind the lines the people of Italy, who had suffered the hardships of war for two years, rallied to the support of her heroic Army, and stood firm.

It was into these darkest days of the war in Italy — when no one knew how long the Piave line could hold and no one could tell when the burden placed upon the people would become greater than they could bear — that the Red Cross found its greatest opportunity for service there. Upon a telegraphic request from our Ambassador in Rome, an Emergency Commission was sent from France, and Italy had her first widespread opportunity of welcoming officers and men in the uniform of the United States Army. The Red Cross men appeared as the first visible evidence of the sincerity of America's pledge that she would devote every man and every resource to winning the war. German propaganda had been extremely active in Italy; one of its endeavors had been to discredit America's sincerity by the assertion that the United States was growing rich out of the war, that she was willing to prolong it by supplying

THE CEREMONY IN THE COLISEUM HELD UPON THE ANNIVERSARY OF THE UNITED STATES' ENTRY INTO THE WAR IN HONOR OF THE WORK OF THE AMERICAN RED CROSS.

the Allies with money and munitions but that she would never send her men. The men and women of the American Red Cross in Italy served as living refutations of that German lie; moreover, it soon became known to the Italians that these men and women were not merely the advance guard but that they had come to Italy as volunteers, leaving behind homes and positions in order to share the lot of the Italians and side by side work with them in the great common cause. Everywhere that I went in Italy, I heard from the Italians, from their statesmen, and from their women and little children, expressions of gratitude, friendship, and admiration for the spirit of the American people, as represented by these workers in the Red Cross, who came to them first in their hour of greatest suffering.

The immediate problem to be dealt with was the feeding and housing of the hundreds of thousands of refugees from the invaded districts. Few nations in modern history have been called upon to face a more serious problem than that with which Italy was confronted: from the two northernmost provinces the civilian population had come in a great flood that overflowed the roads and swept on over the fields toward the south; the barrier of steel which had held back the Austrian and German troops at the border had given way without warning, and women and children and old men, knowing only too well the cruelty of their foes, had left everything they possessed in an effort to escape. Women trudged along with children in their arms; the bedridden were carried in wheelbarrows and on stretchers. Fleeing civilians were inextricably mixed in with the retreating soldiery: abandoned guns, trucks, ammunition wagons, ambulances, and automobiles clogged the roads. Daughters were separated from mothers; little children were swept away from their parents — some of them to be united months later in American Red Cross homes, others never to be together again. Women trudging along barefoot in

P

nightdresses; many walked until they fell, weak with hunger. In the midst of this great military disaster and the future of the Kingdom at stake, Italy, already suffering from privations, with every resource strained for the transportation of fresh supplies of munitions to her troops, was thus called upon to transport a civilian army of half a million or more souls, to find new homes for them, to feed them immediately, and to supply them with clothing and food for their journeys to other already burdened localities.

The way in which she met the problem and solved it won the admiration of every American in the Red Cross who saw the conditions at close range. The American Red Cross coöperated with the Italian authorities and Italian Relief Societies, bringing carloads of foodstuffs and clothing from our storehouses in France, buying other necessaries in the open market, distributing food to the refugees in trains who journeyed often for days, establishing homes and, as the destitute homeless women reached the destinations assigned to them, providing work for them that would occupy their time and afford a small remuneration. Asylums were opened for the children where these war orphans could be taught, fed, and clothed. Soup kitchens were inaugurated to give simple, sustaining food to those who, still laboring under the influence of that nightmare of panic-stricken flight, were trying to adjust themselves to their new environment. In this practical way the Red Cross went about its mission of relieving the wounds that war had caused to innocent women and children. The Italians accepted it as an earnest pledge of America to share a part of the great war's burden, and the morale of the people was strengthened as the morale of any one who is suffering is strengthened by the presence of a friend.

Adding to the mental distress induced by her reverses and to the physical deprivation consequent upon the loss of two rich provinces, the winter of 1917–1918 fell upon Italy

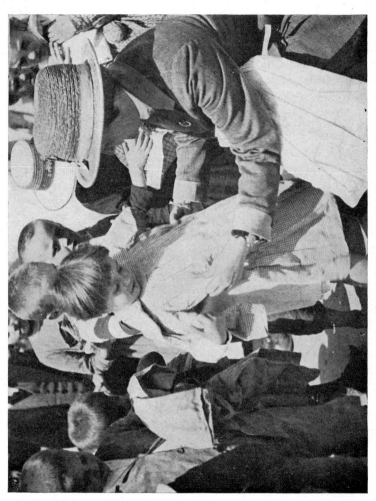

CHILDREN AT PERUGIA RECEIVING AMERICAN RED CROSS CLOTHING.

with unusual severity. There was snow in the streets of
Rome and on the mountains, and in the plains the soldiers
suffered from the intense, penetrating cold. It was a fore-
gone conclusion that when the weather permitted in the
spring the Austrians would resume their drive, for all
through that dismal winter the invaders boasted confidently to the unhappy inhabitants left behind in the
conquered district that they would go on to Rome before
the trees were green again. The forces of the Austrians
were numerically superior by twenty-three divisions
and military commanders awaited with anxiety that
threatened attack. Would their soldiers, their morale
inevitably weakened by a great defeat, be able to hold the
Piave and the mountain passes, or would the enemy break
through and invade the Lombardy plains? No human
intelligence could answer those questions; and yet upon
the answer Italy's fate depended.

These were the conditions in Italy when the permanent
Red Cross Commission arrived. Immediately, ener-
getically, devotedly, they took up the work begun by the
Emergency Commission, extending it until it had reached
all parts of Italy — all of which was accomplished in
almost an incredibly brief time. There is a map, repro-
duced on another page, showing graphically by means of
dots and symbols the extent and variety of the work in
Italy. A large majority of dots and symbols were placed
upon the map in the three or four active months after
the arrival of the Permanent Commission when every
hour was filled with the work of organization and of actual
relief.

Multiform as were the activities and urgent as was the
need for haste, — for with the enemy threatening always
in the north not a moment was to be lost, — a clear, consistent purpose ran through it all. Everything that was
done became the expression of the spirit of the American

people in their consecration to the common cause for which Italy had suffered. To Italians, whose deep love for their children is a national characteristic, the American Red Cross became in a very real sense the great mother. Many thousands of children whose fathers were fighting for liberty were taken under the shelter of the American Red Cross schools, homes, and day nurseries. Nearly all of these children were suffering from undernourishment, the slow starvation that renders the young an easy prey to disease. They were supplied with milk and wholesome food from America. Some of the older girls were taught lace making; the boys were taught the rudiments of carpentry and shoe-making. To mothers, whose husbands or sons were soldiers, the opportunity was afforded to supplement their meager pensions by work in shops where garments were made out of cloth from America, and these garments, together with the contents of the Chapter boxes that came in great quantities from the United States, were used to clothe the children of the soldiers at the front.

Those whom war had deprived of their natural means of support were enabled to become self-supporting by work that went toward the winning of the war, and the spirit on the part of Americans and Italians engaged in the work was the spirit of coöperation, of mutual helpfulness, of sympathetic understanding, and of fraternal friendship. Without the effective, complete, and cordial coöperation of the Italians, indeed, the work could not have achieved the measure of success which it did.

The result of this widespread activity became evident very quickly in the changed spirit of the troops. In the records of the American Red Cross at Rome are many post-cards glowing with thanks from soldiers and letters from commanding officers, and in the minds of our men and women workers are the memories of innumerable spoken tributes, all eloquently indicative of the change which came

YARN SUPPLIED BY THE AMERICAN RED CROSS BEING WEIGHED BEFORE DISTRIBUTION TO THE REFUGEES AT TIVOLI, ITALY.

about in the morale of the Army, of its renewed hope and determination to resist, now that America had come to its support.

There was much that was done, too, which affected the soldiers even more directly than this care of their families. Hospital supplies, drugs, medicines, surgical instruments, bandages, hospital furniture had been lost in vast quantities after the defeat of Caporetto, and it was almost impossible to replace them in Italy.

Red Cross Medical Warehouses were established in Rome and other centers, particularly in the war zone; from these warehouses many Italian military and not a few civilian general hospitals were supplied with the things they lacked. In all between 1500 and 1800 hospitals were aided, many of them two and three times.

In other ways less obviously urgent, perhaps, but having scarcely less effect upon the morale of the troops, the Red Cross came into close contact with the soldiers. Ambulance sections were established at the front with advanced posts near the lines. The ambulances were manned by young American volunteers, many of whom had seen service in France. These ambulances did effective work in transporting the occasional casualties and the many sick from the front lines and from distributing hospitals to base hospitals or evacuating base hospitals to the rail-heads.

To bring some degree of comfort to the men in the stormy trenches of the Alps and the icy, mud-caked trenches along the Piave, the Red Cross established "Rolling Kitchens" where the soldiers returning from the trenches could always have hot coffee, jam for their dry bread, cigarettes, and the friendship and encouragement of the Americans in charge, and which, undoubtedly, counted far more than the food. There were a score or so of these posts, through which, it is said, a half million or more Italian soldiers passed in the course of a month. Men who had stood for hours in the cold under arms went away from these little kitchens where the Italian and American flags flew side by side, revived by the hot coffee and cheered by the greeting of a fellow soldier from another land. Of Lieutenant Edward McKey, who took out the first "Rolling Kitchen" and who lost his life in the work, it has been said that to the Italian Divisions who held the key-positions of the Brenta passes, "he was the entire American Army."

From time to time, as the winter wore on, upon the occasion of a feast day such as Christmas or New Year's or upon days significant to Italian patriotism, gifts were made to the soldiers of packages containing useful articles, generally a cake of soap, warm socks, a cake of chocolate, and a package of cigarettes, with post-cards bearing a symbol of the union of Italy and America in the cause of liberty.

As the spring advanced every effort was made by the American Red Cross, always coöperating closely with the Italians, to carry the practical message of the American people to every soldier and to every city, town, and hamlet. During part of the months of March and April, American Red Cross agents, traveling in automobiles by day and night, actually visited more than two thousand towns and villages. They sought out the destitute or needy families of soldiers, families that lacked medicines or food or clothing, and supplied their wants immediately by leaving in the hands of duly constituted authorities sufficient funds to meet the local emergency. In this work the Red Cross had the efficient coöperation of departmental prefects, mayors, and community committees. The Italian Premier, Signor Orlando, advised the prefects of the coming of Red Cross representatives; with the result that when our agents arrived they found the lists of the needy prepared and crowds of women and children waiting to receive this visit of men from America. Then, by means of speeches and of placards posted upon the walls, the purpose of the visit

IN FRONT OF THE AMERICAN RED CROSS *RECREATORIO* AT FIESOLE.

AMERICAN RED CROSS WAREHOUSES AT MILAN.

was explained. In all more than 300,000 families were aided in this way in the short space of a month; and from these 300,000 families word went at once to their men at the front that America was actually and actively in the war, for they had seen with their own eyes and had received with their own hands the pledge of America's faith.

On the occasion of the first anniversary of America's entrance into the war with Germany, I was in Rome and was present at the impressive ceremony held in the Coliseum in honor of the day. No one could have doubted the sincerity of the words there spoken, words of gratitude on the part of Italy's representatives, addressed to the President and people of the United States and the American Red Cross; nor could any one have failed to be touched by the spontaneous applause from the soldiers and the men and women who, in a downpour of rain, stood in that great ruined open amphitheater to do honor to our country. Later, I went to other chief cities of Italy, and everywhere there were the same cordial, fervent demonstrations of friendship and appreciation. The message of America had been well carried to the Italian people.

The Austrians had boasted, as I have said before, that they would be in Rome before the summer; but when in June they began their delayed offensive they found opposed to them men confident in victory. By weight of superior numbers they forced their way across the Piave in several places only to be beaten back with severe losses; the passes of the Brenta and the Grappa had become walls of granite which they beat at in vain. The failure of that offensive marked the salvation of Italy.

In the time of actual fighting the American Red Cross concentrated its forces in the war zone, aiding the hospitals with supplies to care for the increased demand upon them. Our rolling kitchens, supplemented in number, continued their work, and all our ambulances were in action, many of the men receiving the War Cross for their service under fire.

During the summer the work of the Red Cross throughout Italy went on with unabated energy. The main attempt of the Austrians to break through was followed by a lull in the fighting, but another affliction came upon the people of Italy: An epidemic of influenza or "Spanish fever" of great severity ravaged the entire kingdom, claiming many victims. In helping to check the spread of this plague the American nurses of the Red Cross and our men did heroic service. Milk was greatly needed to nourish the victims of the disease and to fortify children against attack. So while the nurses were visiting stricken communities, making house to house visits, our men distributed large quantities of condensed milk received from America. In every way possible our organization coöperated with the Italian authorities in combating the epidemic, even though our hospitals were filled with patients from our Army and Navy, from our diplomatic corps, the Young Men's Christian Association, and our own personnel.

With the arrival of American troops the work of the Red Cross in Italy took on another phase. The scope of this work was, necessarily, limited by the small number of American troops, but the Red Cross was able to do many comparatively small things, and stood ready at all times to meet any demand upon it by our few thousand soldiers actually in Italy, or by larger contingents, if they had been sent. In the summer the Army Ambulance Service that had been in camp at Allentown arrived in Genoa. The Red Cross at once undertook the establishment of a hospital, and in the short space of two weeks a suitable building was found near the encampment and equipped as a thoroughly modern hospital. Later this hospital was given by the Red Cross to our Navy for the use of our sailors and soldiers.

A few weeks later when an American regiment of the

line, the 332d, arrived in Italy from France, the Red Cross made our soldiers welcome, provided coffee for them at the stations through which they passed on the long journey overland; at the place of detraining in the war zone they were met with something hot to drink, something to smoke, and a temporary hospital. Likewise, when these men took their place in the line, Red Cross Home Service men went with them, following them across the Piave in the victorious advance against the Austrians.

The story of Italy's complete and brilliant victory over Austria in the closing days of October, and the rapid forward march into and beyond the reconquered, devastated districts, forms the culmination of the story of our Red Cross work in Italy. It was a victory upon which every hope had centered, toward which all of the long effort of Italy and those associated with her brave soldiers and her patient, enduring people had been devoted, but when it came it was so much greater than any reasonable anticipation could have foreseen, so much more complete and rapid, that its immediate effects were well-nigh overwhelming.

After a stubborn resistance, the Austrian line in the mountains and on the plain broke, and then followed the utter rout of the enemy. Our ambulances and rolling kitchens with our officers and men swept forward with the Italian troops. It was difficult to keep up with the advance, so difficult, for instance, that our American regiment outstripped its commissary and for three days practically subsisted, contented, happy, and victorious, on the light stores that the Red Cross with its more mobile transportation was able to bring up across the crowded pontoon bridges and over the shell-torn roads.

In the year that the Austrian, German, and Hungarian troops had held the northern provinces of Italy, they had systematically despoiled the remaining inhabitants of their possessions. It had been a year of slow starvation for those who, unfortunately, had been unable to escape, with food growing more and more scarce. When the final rout came the enemy took all that was left. It became a case of general loot : shoes were taken from the feet of citizens ; women were robbed of their clothing ; all of the supplies of food were commandeered, and what had been slow starvation changed to acute suffering and death from want of something to eat.

The Italian Army of fifty-three divisions, the French and English with three divisions each, and the 332d American Regiment pursued the rapidly fleeing enemy. All the railroads were torn up and the bridges destroyed, so that all supplies had to pass through the narrow neck of the bottle represented by the temporary pontoon bridges over the Piave and then be transported by camion over roads which were choked with moving troops and guns — wretched roads neglected by the enemy and filled with pits from heavy artillery fire. There was small opportunity at that moment of vital military emergency for Italy to take care of the starving, shivering civilian population ; and it is probably no exaggeration to say that the opportunity for service which then came to the American Red Cross was the greatest and most urgent it had during all its Italian experience.

In some places the trucks of the American Red Cross laden with provisions entered a town within a few hours after the Austrians had quitted it ; rarely did more than forty-eight hours elapse between the departure of the enemy and the establishment of a Red Cross center for distributing food — condensed milk, soups, beans, peas, sugar, and often, salted beef. Pitiful stories of cruelty, oppression, and long privation were told by these unfortunate people, day after day, as they stood in line before the Red Cross distributing stations, and many and fervent were the blessings upon America as they received the life-giving

AMERICAN RED CROSS WORKROOM AT RIMINI.

food from the hands of men and women in the uniform of the Red Cross.

With the signing of the Armistice following upon Austria's utter defeat there was thrust upon Italy a new problem of large proportions — the problem of feeding, clothing, and transporting Italian prisoners of war released by the cessation of hostilities. Austria — anxious to be freed of the burden of their care — turned these men loose without direction, without system, and without preliminary arrangements. They came from prison camps by tens of thousands, making their way south, as best they could, on trains as far as the trains would go, then on foot by road and field and mountain pass, a hungry, half-clad, ragged army, weak from long confinement and insufficient food. Over the Alps and down upon Trieste at the head of the Adriatic and upon the devastated, suffering redeemed districts they poured, straggling into the cities and towns.

The city of Trieste, which more than five hundred years before had fallen into Austrian hands but had remained, through many vicissitudes, Italian at heart and in speech, was the objective of many of these released prisoners. A few thousand came the first day, more the next day, and still more each succeeding day until, finally, they stood shoulder to shoulder a vast unorganized hungry army of many thousands, crowded into the only space where they could be put, — the public shipping docks. At the time Trieste was cut off by railroad ; there were almost no ships available ; and the mere problem of feeding the liberated city, rejoicing in its new freedom, was taxing every resource without the added burden of this army of men who had suffered many hardships, who could not be moved, and whose number constantly increased.

As fortune would have it, however, a Red Cross "rolling kitchen" with two Americans had followed the troops from the Piave far to the east, and in the first hours of the Armistice pushed on through the Austrian lines and, skirting the sea, reached Trieste overland with a stock sufficient for, perhaps, 2000 rations of soup. These men at once took up their station in the concentration camp, and while one of them served the soup the other got on board a torpedo boat and went to Venice for more Red Cross supplies. Our Venice representative with a deputy commissioner from Rome arrived in Trieste the same day and made arrangements immediately to coöperate with the military authorities. From that time on until the men were reformed and disposed of, — a period of about one month, — the Red Cross, working always with the approbation of the Italian authorities and aided for a time by a committee of Trieste ladies, relieved the situation. By camion overland and by sea provisions were sent from our warehouse; other provisions were brought by the British Red Cross. Clothing was brought and the army of the repatriated, crowded, sick, and hungry, in that provisional concentration camp by the sea, began to emerge from its long nightmare of Austrian prison camps and to experience once more the joy of liberty and life among people of their own nation and its allies who, in spite of the urgent need among themselves, had the spirit and willingness to provide for these soldier sons of Italy who had come back home again in the hour of victory.

In the reconquered districts, meanwhile, and in the land of Italia Redenta, upon which for centuries Italy had looked as provinces lost to her that would some day be restored, foodstuffs were supplied, hospitals refurnished, and the sick visited. The progress of events ever carrying the work into the towns of the Dalmatian Coast across the Adriatic.

The work in all this newly opened territory, with normal means of transportation utterly lacking, gave to the American Red Cross an opportunity to show again its effectiveness as an organization for emergency relief and, by the very nature of its organization, the relief was forthcoming more quickly than could have been possible through the more complex governmental or military machinery. The result, seen so often in the war, was typical not alone of Red Cross activity in Italy, but in all countries.

While attention was centered on the territories liberated by the victorious armies and while effort was concentrated there, the work went on throughout all Italy of caring for the women and children who were sufferers from the war. New activities were added. One entire new department began its work during this period: the Department of Tuberculosis, consisting of experts sent from America by the Red Cross to coöperate with the Italians in combating the ravages of the disease which, through conditions attributable directly to the war, has become of even greater menace.

The cessation of hostilities brought about a change in Italy, as elsewhere in Red Cross work, as there was no longer need for many of our military activities. Wherever possible and advisable the activities of the Red Cross were turned over to the Italian authorities and to duly constituted Italian societies — a process made easy of fulfillment by reason of the close association in the work between Italians and Americans; moreover, nearly all of the children's institutions established by the Red Cross were being carried on by Italians, as wherever it was necessary, provision was made for these institutions during the period of adjustment. In all cases the American Red Cross fulfilled its obligations, express or implied; and even though our personnel are to-day no longer on the ground mingling with those who had come to be their friends, nevertheless the spirit of the work is going on, providing a lasting bond between our two countries — a result in which not only the devoted workers of the Red Cross in Italy but every supporter of the Red Cross in America may, with just pride, claim his or her share.

CHAPTER XVII

GREAT BRITAIN

HOWEVER much I may have taken advantage of the rather exceptional opportunities that I had of observing the manifold sacrifices — be it financial, moral, or military — that Great Britain made to strengthen her support of her Allies, my good friends the British would prefer, I know, that I should not enumerate them. But for all their modesty the soldiers of the American Army know what the British did in France; the men of the American Navy know full well what the British did for us in the transportation of our Armies and in the moving of our supplies; and the Red Cross knows, as neither the Army and the Navy can know, how ungrudging was the measure of British achievements in labors of Mercy at a time when her own resources in man-power and money were taxed to the breaking point.

There was no scene of suffering, whether near by or distant, in Belgium or Baikalia, France or Mesopotamia, Italy or Palestine, wherein Great Britain did not bear the largest part of the burden of relief. From the early days of the

AN AMERICAN RED CROSS CANTEEN IN ENGLAND.

War the members of the British Red Cross, never ruffled or flurried, went about performing their difficult task in that unostentatious manner that is so characteristic of their race. And no matter whether the Americans pitched their tents along the northern shores of the White Sea or beside the southern waters of the Black Sea or anywhere else, they were sure to find that an encampment of the British Red Cross had preceded them.

Whatever disagreements, to put it mildly, may have been fated to the two great English-speaking nations in the past, there can be no question that Great Britain, from the King to his last stout soldier, has been our close friend and good Ally all through the Armageddon that has now ended. Quite naturally, therefore, it was our appreciation of this friendship, together with the knowledge of the magnitude of the British efforts, that had so much to do with the spirit in which the work of the American Red Cross was begun in Great Britain. For some time British activities had enjoyed our intelligent help in England, not a few of our men having foreseen our eventual entry into the war. Indeed, it is a well-known fact that more or less definite plans were made for the establishment of our work in England — chiefly through the organization of a London Chapter — before the declaration of war in April, 1917. So that when the tide of American soldiers began to flow through England, it was clear that we had in that country a great natural center for our work on behalf of our troops, even though it offered little protection against the bombing planes. And, in time, as we all know, this center became a great distribution depot for our men until we had established adequate facilities on the French coast.

In October, 1917, the War Council appointed the Commission for Great Britain. Scarcely had it arrived at its post before its Commissioner made a large donation to the British Red Cross. It was nothing more than an act of civility, and the War Council proceeded to vote three more appropriations in rapid succession, amounting to $4,750,000, to enable the British Red Cross to expand its work still further. Nevertheless, it is not difficult to imagine that a people, who had given for one war purpose and another until giving was very hard, should have shown, as indeed they did, a lively appreciation of our gift.

It was not long, however, before the wisdom of our promptly setting up the American Red Cross organization in England was made manifest when it was suddenly decided to brigade American troops with the English in Northern France. Thousands and tens of thousands of American soldiers thereafter went to England, and nobody at that time could foretell how many of those who reached France would be borne back on hospital ships to Dover and Folkestone and Southampton, — towns which, as every Englishman will tell you, had had more than their share of that sort of thing.

In the midst of these preparations there suddenly came the news that the *Tuscania* had been sunk by a submarine, off the Irish Coast. No sooner had the first tidings of this disaster reached London than a little company of Red Cross men were rushed to the scene. In true American fashion they went strenuously to work, helping to equip the survivors, supplying money for needful things, talking with the men, and writing letters home for them; in short, doing everything that was necessary and helpful to relieve their anxieties until the last train-load had left the little Irish village. Obviously, since this was a new experience for us, most of the troops who came through safely were quartered at five British Military Camps in the North of Ireland, where all their needs for clothing and other things were supplied from the British Red Cross stores under an American Red Cross guarantee. Necessities were purchased wherever they could be obtained, and each man was not only fully supplied but had an extra bag of good things when he boarded the boat

AMERICAN SOLDIERS SEEING LONDON FROM AN AMERICAN RED CROSS OMNIBUS.

at Belfast to complete his journey to his camp in England. When it was learned that nearly all of the 107 officers on the *Tuscania* lost their outfits, the Red Cross at once advanced $17,000 to enable them to reëquip.

Nor must it be supposed that this disaster did not teach us anything; far from it. From that time on there were provisions at half a dozen Irish stations for six thousand men in case the submarines should score another hit off those difficult coasts. Arrangements were also made for prompt billeting of any number of men, and squads of Red Cross motor cars were kept in readiness for the transport of workers and emergency supplies. And that the American Red Cross had certainly taken time by the forelock in establishing these Irish Emergency Stations and preparing for every possible contingency — not only in Ireland but along the shores of England and Scotland — was soon shown by the terrible *Otranto* disaster that followed. It was after this tragedy that the Army gracefully acknowledged its obligation to the Red Cross through the Commander of the American Forces in Great Britain. "The first thing we did," said General Biddle, "was to go to the Red Cross for material and supplies . . . we in the army feel a gratitude to the Red Cross which is hard for me to express in words." And praise from the Army, to paraphrase the well-known saying, is praise indeed.

But it must not be thought that the other departments were not at work in the camps and along the lines of communication. Effort was concentrated in an attempt to bring an atmosphere of home into the life of every American soldier and, particularly, to surround the sick and wounded with it. The hospitals for American wounded had to have a thoroughly American personnel, and the patients back from Northern France found themselves in the sympathetic hands of American doctors, surgeons, and nurses, to say nothing of the smiling Red Cross women "Visitors."

Q

In regard to hospital work of the American Red Cross, it is necessary for me to go back to the time of the arrival of the Commission in England. This was, of course, work that would brook no delay and the Commission opened its first hospital within a few weeks at Mossley Hill, Liverpool. From the very first day of its installment there it was filled with Americans who had been taken ill on board the incoming transports. In more ways than one it was a distinct achievement on the part of our people; for otherwise our soldiers and sailors would have had to be taken to the British hospitals in the vicinity.

Another hospital was early established at Paignton in sunny South Devon, which was taken over in January, 1918, from an American Committee which had established it as far back as 1914 for the use of British privates. Like many similar enterprises in England and France, this hospital was in danger of being discontinued from lack of funds. After assuming responsibility for it, we arranged to leave it to be used by British privates until it was needed for American soldiers a few months later. There was a similar institution at Lancaster gate in London for officers which was taken over with the same understanding.

In this connection, it would be a mistake not to include St. Catherine's Lodge in London. This house had been given by an American for the duration of the war, together with a gift of fifty thousand dollars for equipment, and was occupied by British officers until the American began coming back from the hard fighting of the late summer. It was conducted in conjunction with the famous British Orthopedic hospital at Shephard's Bush.

By all odds the most impressive American Red Cross hospital in England was located at Salisbury Court, not far from Southampton. It was opened with about 400 beds, but had facilities for about three thousand more. It was in the park of one of the most beautiful country estates in

CENTRAL BUILDING OF THE AMERICAN RED CROSS HOSPITAL AT SALISBURY, ENGLAND.

England, and had a mile of waterfront along the Hamble. Around the Manor House our Red Cross began building acres of hut wards, a separate isolation hospital, and large buildings for the medical and surgical staff. And, as often is the case in England, there were trees of the great-grand-father type on this 186-acre estate, and from which, by the way, much of the heavy timber was taken for the hospital buildings. Well might a wounded soldier feel that he had the best chance in the world of convalescing successfully in a hospital situated in the loveliest of the English picture coun-try, with boating, fishing, fresh milk and eggs, and the prod-ucts of a 10-acre vegetable garden to tempt him back to hunger and health!

In some ways, perhaps, the most pretentious of all the American institutions in England was the Naval hospital in Park Lane in London. Built by a South African dia-mond king, this big marble mansion occupied an entire block, and was used during the first years of the war as a hospital for British officers before it was taken over by the Red Cross to provide a place for the officers and men from our warships.

Another London hospital was that in Kensington Palace Gardens, the former residence of an Indian prince; and a little way out of London was the magnificent Lingfield rest house for convalescent officers. It gives me pleasure to recall that among other kind thoughts on the part of the British Red Cross, it offered to build for us a model war hospital in the Royal Park at Richmond, which work of construction was just starting when the Armistice made its continuance unnecessary. In summing up I must not neg-lect to say that our Commission also established tent hos-pitals to accommodate men suffering from minor ailments in about fifty small American cantonments in England.

While the needs of the sick and wounded were being thus provided for, another large section of Red Cross personnel in England was devoting its attention to the soldiers who were not ill. These were pouring into England by the thousand, shipload after shipload, in never ending streams. Needless to say these men had no aches and no pains; they needed no bandages, no sphagnum moss, and no ether; but what they did want was the old comfortable familiar things which they had seen the Red Cross doing along the line of communication in the States, and the Red Cross saw to it that they got it likewise in England. As a matter of fact, our whole Camp Service, with every familiar feature, was transplanted from America to England by a Red Cross man who knew it backwards and forwards. He saw to it that a homelike Red Cross headquarters was set up in every camp; and that we had the same familiar type of Field Director from New York or Boston or Chicago or Ohio, ready to do anything or get anything. Let me take a few figures from the record to let you know how prodigiously this Camp Service figured in the life of the American Army. The record shows that in one month there went out from the Red Cross storehouses to the American fighting men on their way to the front the following supplies: 30,000 sweaters; 2000 blankets; 10,000 razor-blades; 500,000 paper napkins; 5,000,000 cigarettes; 3000 pairs of socks; 10,000 pairs of gloves; 300,000 boxes of matches; 8000 pounds of soap; 2000 pounds of chocolate; 50,000 sticks of chewing gum; 10,000 tubes of tooth paste; and other things ad infinitum.

As for the canteens — they were along the railways and in the camps and always had the best British war bread and the toothsome "Chicago ham" and "lamb-chop" and chocolate and all the rest of the innumerable other things at hand. Our supplies, of course, required considerable storage space, although nothing like that in Paris. Nevertheless there were three large warehouses in London, two in Liverpool, and more in Glasgow and in Edinburgh and various

AT WORK IN THE LABORATORY OF A BRITISH BASE HOSPITAL.

It will be noticed that every possible known contrivance is used for easing the pain of the wounded and hastening their recovery.

English and Irish cities, and their contents all went to our soldiers.

On the whole our Red Cross in England had every right to feel that they took as good care of the soldier on their side of the water as we did on our side, if allowance is made for the fact that in England, however hospitable and considerate her people, facilities there were not comparable with those at home.

Nor did an American soldier ever have to lose sight of the Red Cross on his journey to the continent. Just as the Red Cross had been the first to meet him when he landed in England and last to bid him good-by when he embarked for France, just so it again welcomed him on the French dock and took him in charge.

On each succeeding visit I made to England during the war I was impressed with the fact that the Red Cross in England was really a good deal like, if not precisely a replica of, our Red Cross at home : the Chapter was there, the work-rooms, the busy fingers, the flying needles, and the gauze for bandages. The London workrooms were a modest affair at first, but in a few months they grew to 30 vigorous branches with 2000 workers turning out 300,000 articles a month. When a call came for 2,250,000 surgical dressings of a special type, they were turned out at the rate of 150,000 a week, and the whole order was finished long before the time set by the Army.

With branches everywhere throughout England, the London Chapter had what was called a "Care Committee," composed of American women who were notified as soon as an American soldier arrived at any hospital in England, and the members of this Committee, I am told, looked after 10,000 American soldiers on an average in a month, estab-lishing communication with their families and providing all the little things that go to make life in a hospital more bearable.

Communication Service also was maintained at a high level of effectiveness. Home Service — which somebody dubbed the "Trouble Bureau" — was as busy in England as it was everywhere else, and everyone knows how busy this Department can be. Moreover, a large staff of searchers was enrolled by our Home Communication Service in England, and in one single day they secured complete records of more than a thousand American soldiers in British hospitals; and what is more it did not fail to gather detailed information concerning each and every one of them.

As may be easily seen there were all sorts of odds and ends of kindly work for the Red Cross to do. The schedule was never exhausted. Those whom it served, British as well as American, included not only officers and men but war workers, soldiers' families, and slum babies. Eight maternity centers were opened, and the Red Cross maintained a considerable amount of health and welfare work among the children of half a dozen crowded cities. Working in conjunction with local associations in London, it dealt with 500 cases of aggravated shell-shock among children after the German air raids; and it provided money to send those most in need of quiet to homes in remote rural districts.

Then there was our Library Committee in London, first organized by the London Chapter. It dispensed from its headquarters upwards of ten thousand books monthly to soldiers. This feat may be said to have aroused the interest, if not envy, of His Majesty King George V whenever he visited an American camp or hospital. He is represented as being unable to understand how our convalescents received the American papers so promptly. I do not know, of course, what explanation was given to him, but all Americans will understand, I think, when I say that the Red Cross saw to it.

Grosvenor Gardens was the center of Red Cross war activities. The organization occupied five or six buildings

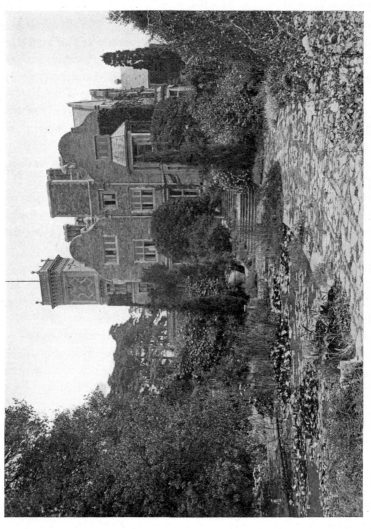

AMERICAN RED CROSS CONVALESCENT HOSPITAL FOR OFFICERS AT LINGFIELD, ENGLAND.

close to the American Army and Navy Headquarters as well as the Embassy. And how busy these Red Cross buildings were during the height of their activity may be judged from the fact that their total budget reached nearly a million dollars a month. It is almost a pity that I have not space for the items of this budget, for they reflect clearly the tremendous increase in the number of men sent over during the latter months and the corresponding increase in Red Cross activity which spread rapidly to the remotest corners of the British Isles. Thus the canteen service installed large canteens at Southampton, Edinburgh, Birmingham, Cardiff, Glasgow, Winchester, Leicester, Derby, Romsey, and Chester, as well as hospital exchange canteens in fifteen places. The items in the general budget included provision not only for hospitals and camps but such things as officers' clubs, camp warehouses, shower-bath buildings, garages, portable houses for infirmaries, hospital theaters, and so on.

On October 25 the indefatigable British Red Cross had what is called "Our Day," which is the date set apart for its annual drive for funds. It was our good fortune to start it off with a rush the night before when the Commissioner of the American Red Cross for Great Britain, at a Red Cross dinner given in their honor, handed to the Treasurer of the British organization a check for five hundred thousand pounds — two million, three hundred and eighty-five thousand dollars at the then current rate of exchange — as a subscription from the American Red Cross. Many distinguished British and Americans attended the dinner. Towards its close our Commissioner, in a few happy words, told his attentive hosts how grateful we Americans were for the great and generous service of the British Red Cross in placing at his disposal almost their entire organization. "I can cite countless instances," he went on to say, "of your valuable assistance . . . and we should be sadly lacking in appreciation if we did not make some effort to show our gratitude."

The remarks of the Commissioner — as all who were present have testified — expressed so succinctly the appreciation of our people for the stupendous and ever increasing effort during four years of war on the part of the indomitable men and women of Great Britain, that there is no need for me to give here the contents of the letter which I sent with the check on behalf of the American people to the representatives of the British Red Cross and the Order of St. John. In conclusion, suffice it to say that no American could have been in England or the War Zone without a realization that no words could adequately express his admiration for the glorious part that England played towards bringing victory to her Allies and to herself.

CHAPTER XVIII

RUMANIA

IN the chapters of unhappiness which German-made war has written, there is none, to my mind, more pathetic than that of Rumania. Geographically, that country is a part of the Balkans whose mountain passes, since the days of the Cæsars, have resounded without ceasing to the clash of arms. Battered by Romans, Turks, and Austrians, traded upon by Greeks, Russians, and Prussians, she has held fast to her place on the Danube, to her oil fields and her salt mines, her honesty of purpose and her faith in God.

Here is a nation skilled in arms but which has no need for capital punishment. Here is a people which, even amid the horrors of destructive war and in the clutches of starvation, maintained and expanded its system of compulsory education; a country where there are petty misdemeanors but no crime. Subject for divers periods to the Moslem, it remains a Christian nation. Surrounded by Slav, Goth, Vandal, and Turk and, although invaded times without number, it has still in its veins the blood of Trajan's soldiers. It remains a Latin race.

To understand the dislike and rancor of the Teuton powers towards Rumania, one has merely to recall to mind that Rumania has a Hohenzollern king and that it was the people of Rumania who indorsed the Allied cause. In justice to the King, however, it must be said that once the decision was made, he loyally acquiesced and won the respect of his people and those of the Allied countries by his courageous leadership in the midst of disaster. The ambition of the Rumanians was to recover their ancient province of Transylvania and restore to their own household the populations suffering under notorious Austrian misrule. With this prime purpose in view at their first entry into war, they drove their armies through the Austrian opposition into Transylvania in the autumn of 1916, and with the remainder held watch upon the Danube against the Bulgarians, who were massed to the south. But the Rumanian armament at the opening of the war was of German manufacture and, obviously, could not be replaced. Again, their third province, Dobrudga, was by the terms of alliance to be defended by Russia, who, as we all know, failed in her compact. And Russia's failure in her part of the task spelled disaster to the Rumanian contingents on the west. German forces were added to the Austrians, and together they drove the Rumanian armies back into Wallachia; they bombarded Bucharest, and with its fall and the removal of the court to Jassy there began the Rumanian exodus into the northwest.

Moldavia is a little province no larger than the state of Connecticut, and it was at once filled with millions of people who had little or nothing to eat or to wear. This was in the beginning of December, 1916, — and Rumania has a climate, it is well to note, that is not unlike that of middle and lower Canada.

When in 1917 the American Red Cross went into Rumania, its army was holding with grim tenacity the Moldavia boundaries, but machine guns could not block the progress of the invisible legions of disease. Every condition in the overcrowded, underfed remnant of Rumania, that still was free, was a standing invitation to this most deadly of the forces of war. At first came pneumonia, then typhus with a toll alone of 1000 lives, which was followed by recurrent fever and smallpox, all traveling with fatal swiftness through the crowded thoroughfares of Jassy and other towns, and along the country roads where the little villages joined one another. The uncomplaining, half-clad refugees, huddled like animals in their dugouts, struggled to keep the cold from pinching their lives out. They were consumed by vermin, the chief and efficient distributors of pestilence. In these wretched retreats the dead lay with the living, and hunger, the last executioner, waited at the doorway for such as might by miracle escape. There were two feet of ice and snow through that awful winter, and children, whose covering consisted only of a single cotton garment, went up and down crying for food until the clutch of the cold at last strangled their crying and put an end to their hunger. The dead were everywhere in the Jassy streets; in the wards of civil hospitals patients were frozen to death. This was the price the Rumanian people paid for casting their strength into a cause that seemed to promise a united nation, living its simple life with work in a place of freedom.

When the Red Cross went to lend what help it could to

Rumania and its army at the front, the soldiers were well-ordered and intent upon their purpose, but the Russians were yielding to the spirit of disorder which followed the revolution. Wherever they were quartered, there was filth. The manure piles from their horses littered the streets of the villages. The Russians drove the people out of their houses and took up residence in their stead; they invaded the hospitals and slept beside patients who were ill with contagion, and they consumed eternally the food supply, while the Rumanian peasantry starved and died. The people in the villages back of the lines had no shoes and no stockings; the refugees slept in the fields, exposed to the pitiless winds.

There was little left to sustain life nor medical care to sustain what there was of it, for the doctors were in the army or had succumbed to disease. A fortunate hamlet here and there had bread twice a week, while others had none at all. There were people in these miserable districts who subsisted like the beasts, by gnawing the grass and roots of the fields.

In Beltiu, a village in the district of Putna, our Red Cross visitors reported the most gruesome conditions. They found in one house three children whose father was at the front and the mother had died from typhus. A girl of ten was trying to care for the other two, one of whom lay dying on the floor of starvation. The third had only a ragged shirt, which partly covered her and whose little body was no more than a framework. There was no one to help them — three little souls flickering out.

"It was a tragic picture," our representative wrote, "of famine and disease from which even the Rumanian officer was forced to turn away."

Another report told of a dilapidated house with the roof full of shell-holes and the glass all shattered from the windows, and in which ten persons were crowded in squalor and misery. There was no bedding except some bags. The tenant was an old woman whose husband had just died, but she had three sons in the army. She was a mere specter. There was not even a handful of cornmeal in the house. One child of three lay under the stove in which there lingered dying embers of a little fire; the other nine were strewn about the place. Hunger-stricken, horror-stricken, waiting the death-stroke from shell-fire or pestilence, trusting in the bravery of the Rumanian Army to guard them from harm, complaining not at all, burying at night their poor little possessions to save them from the Germans — these were the wretched people for whom Marie of Rumania, granddaughter of Queen Victoria, sacrificed earthly riches and gave gladly the best years of a gifted and beautiful life.

In the first crowded months when the Red Cross War Council faced its problem of carrying relief to a world overwhelmed with suffering, the word that came out of Rumania had been sorry enough; but by the time the Red Cross Mission which was dispatched in August had traversed the long way to the scene of its labors, Rumania had become a tragedy, the more heartbreaking because it was played out in stoical silence and with unwavering faith. All know that in our devotion to the niceties of surgical science we demand the perfection of sterilization; but the wounds of soldiers in Rumania, torn by German missiles, were being dressed with whatever was available. Rumanian children swarmed the streets with stomachs and feet swollen from dropsy; pellagra claimed its victims by thousands.

To reach Rumania, the Red Cross Mission was compelled to journey by Vladivostok and cross the long reaches of Siberia. It was met with every courtesy by the Russian government, but underneath the visible surface of its wartime life, Russia, like every other Allied country, was honeycombed with German intrigue and peopled with German agents gnawing like rats at the underpinning of the state.

Russian railroads, for the most part in the secret control of Germany, lagged and miscarried in their labor of supplying the Russian troops. On the wharves of Vladivostok were lying millions of dollars' worth of supplies for the Russian soldiery which should have been delivered three years before. Already, the great clumsy body which had been Russia, was tottering to its fall; and in the midst of the unrest there came to the surface the ancient hatred of Rumania, which had been put away when the Rumanians entered into the Entente.

Assiduously nourished by the German agents, this hoary grudge wrought itself out in the studied delay of Rumanian supplies, the failure of the Russian officials to ship, even, into Rumania, the food for maintenance of their own troops. As a result, Russia, a well-nigh inexhaustible granary, was herself starving, and with munitions awaiting them somewhere, the Russian peasant soldiers confronted with bare hands the merciless artillery of the Huns.

In this light, it is not difficult for me to understand why the Red Cross Mission was ushered with all politeness and the greatest possible expedition into Rumania but thereafter could secure almost no transport for the material of relief. There was no access to the suffering Rumanians after the reverses of 1916, save over the endless roads of Russia, with the invisible German clutch upon them all.

Slowly, but surely, the patriotic people of a brave little country were being starved into the arms of the Central Powers. Behind them Turkey, Bulgaria, and the Sea; on the north a Russia which had played them false and was even now on the brink of a German peace; and to the west, the Hun, taking fuel from the Rumanian oil wells, feeding on the Rumanian harvest, harrying the devoted army, and through its Russian agents stopping the supply of the simplest necessities. Seemingly, the doom of Rumania was written, even then, in letters so large that no man could fail to read them. On the black horizon shone no ray of hope save that at last the Allied Arms might triumph and the dream of centuries come true.

It had been the purpose of the Red Cross to perform a great labor of relief in Rumania, to care for her refugees and her fighting men, to supply nurses and doctors and food and clothing in abundance, to restore her strength and to uphold her courage, to help her stand firm as the pillar of Allied strength in southeastern Europe. But Germany had planned too well. From the time when the German divisions, fighting every step of the way, drove down into the rich plains of Wallachia, the days of Rumanian resistance were numbered. This fact was all too evident. Indeed, the Director of the Red Cross Mission has since informed us that he had had no illusions about the truth of this statement from the moment of his arrival at Jassy. It was the program, however, of this first Mission, to make rapid and thorough canvass of Rumanian needs, and after a few weeks to return and outline a broad general plan of action. When it came to Jassy, the Mission brought with it only the smallest of supplies. In that land of desolation and want they vanished in a day. It was not a question of studying the needs of Rumania; the need of Rumania was a nightmare. Its voices were never silent. It stared in the streets; it prayed from the cadaverous faces of that misery-marked populace; the sick, the naked, and the starving were on every hand and winter was at the door.

In all the tragic panorama of the War, there appears, perhaps, no sadder and nobler figure than Marie of Rumania, a Queen, to paraphrase, who is every inch a woman and who had been trying at the cost of every conceivable sacrifice, with a courage equaled only by her devotion, to stem the tide of suffering. Utterly fearless, she had gone among her starved and scourge-ridden people like an angel, carrying such food and clothing and medicine as she could gather among those who themselves had nothing. Into the typhus hospitals where hundreds lay dying of smallpox; into the horrible dugouts of the refugees; into every place where there was a mouth that she could feed or a soul that she could cheer, day by day went the Queen of Rumania, and yet, by some strange dispensation, she lived. But, although passing scathless herself, her youngest son, unfortunately, fell a victim to the typhoid in the early days of his struggle; yet far from giving up from this new grief in her heart, she plunged all the deeper into her work of mercy.

To our Red Cross Commissioner this unhappy Queen told in detail the story of her country's misfortune, which had been crowded into one brief year.

"The retreat from Wallachia," her Majesty said, "the sorrow and depression of a vanquished Army is a story filled with tragic grief; the winter was one of darkest horror, thousands of our soldiers died of sheer want. We could neither feed, clothe, warm, nor house them. Disease in its worst form fell upon us; and being cut off from all aid, we struggled against odds we had no means of overcoming. Row upon row of graves and uncounted numbers of rough wooden crosses throughout the land stand as mute witness of a tale too sad to relate. Thousands of little children, left without father or mother, died before help could reach them, and I, the Queen, heard each cry of anguish, shared each terror, and divided each fear. Then spring came — and as by a miracle, our armies seemed to have a rebirth. The specters that had haunted our streets in winter became soldiers once more. Our thinned ranks were filled up. A new desire for vengeance and intense longing for homes taken away by the enemy steeled every heart for a new effort. But our newborn hopes were destined to wither away. The Russian revolution had sown discord and disorganization in the hearts of our nearest allies, and when the great hour for action came — the hour which our army had hungered for, and into which our troops had thrown themselves with a bravery that justified our dearest hopes — our neighbors failed us."

In the files of the Red Cross, there are many declarations in various languages of gratitude for the great and the timely aid of the American people. It is doubtful, however, if ever there came a deeper note of thankfulness than that of

the Rumanian Queen and her suffering people for our work of
relief during the winter of 1917.

"But there was only one thing to do," wrote the chairman
of the Commission. "To get food, medicine, and clothing
from any source and in whatever quantity possible, in order
to save what lives we could before disease and starvation
and the winter should outstrip the German armies in the
ruin of the land. . . ." Fortunately the Commissioner
had some funds which had been placed in his hands for
such casual use as might be required, and he requisitioned
this for obtaining food.

It was not, of course, a dietetic question. The need was
for food, — anything that would sustain life. And the report shows that with all possible haste agents were dispatched
to every corner of Russia, where starvation had already set in,
to pry out from its hiding place whatever food the magic
of money might discover. To Moscow, to Petrograd, to
Odessa, and even distant Archangel, to every place that
might afford a chance of victualment, they hurried at post
haste. In Moscow they found flour and beans; in Odessa
they bought tons of dried vegetables; in the North they
found five thousand barrels of herrings, and all these and
other things they drove forward over the congested and dis-
organized Russian railways through districts whose populations were even then on the verge of civil war, with guards
riding the "wagons" to fend off the hungry mobs in towns
through which they passed.

So at last when the food train rolled into Jassy, there was a
storage house ready for its cargo, and in the heart of the city
adjoining the national theater, a canteen was opened and
equipped. All that were there unite in saying that it was
indeed a sorry coterie — some five hundred and odd persons
who came on the first day merely to satisfy their curiosity.
For the Rumanian, near neighbor to the hard trading East,
had little faith in the story that these strange Americans

R

would give away food for nothing. If it were true, they told themselves, then such people must be seen anyway, for such a phenomenon would never happen again. On the second and third days, however, the number increased until on the fourth day the American canteen was feeding two thousand people who without it would have died of starvation. In this connection I am sure that an excerpt from a Rumanian newpaper would be of interest. It read as follows : —

"The hungry poor from the outskirts of the town, especially the women and children, began to assemble early in the morning in front of the shed, in which were also the kitchen and the store full of food brought from beyond the ocean, from the country of friendly deeds, not of words, empty and illusive as the dust of the road. Every day the number of those who came from the borders of the town, the naked and hungry, increased. The distribution of the food begins at ten o'clock and lasts until three. Around the two tables there is room for a hundred and twenty people. All of these are in rags, and with faces emaciated to the bones. In one hour, about nine hundred can eat. The greater number were children between six and twelve years of age. I have even seen mites only three or four years old, with shaggy hair, bare feet, and clothed in rags, out of which their thin little bodies protruded. Some came from as far away as the windmill where on the Tatarasi hill the white belfry of the church in the Eternitatia cemetery stands. Early in the morning they leave their shanties, half dug into the earth, and drag their rags through the dust or mud of the numberless little alleys toward the shed out of which daily flows the aroma of hot food. It seems as though the American mission had spoken the Biblical words of the Savior, 'Suffer little children to come unto Me.' And the children, with thin faces and naked feet, descend every morning from all the suburbs toward the foreign Pity, which rises like a white Christ out of the midst of human evil."

Was there ever an article that appealed more to the heart? And what is more those present declared that this motley throng cheered the American flag, kissed the hands of the workers, threw things into the air, and wept and prayed and carried home morsels of food to their brothers and sisters, who were too weak to undertake the journey, while, almost

THE KING AND QUEEN OF RUMANIA RETURNING FROM A VISIT TO A RED CROSS HOSPITAL AT THE FRONT.

simultaneously, I may say, the Commissioner was cabling us in Washington for supplies of every sort.

Although hampered by the almost total lack of transportation, the relief of the refugees was already under way and advancing day by day. There was a crying need, of course, for some means of supplying hospital accommodations for the multitude of wounded and sick. Without these, it was plain, disaster would overtake the army, which was almost entirely bereft of any means of caring for its wounded men. Besides, the defection of Russia has brought a heavier blow than the military reverse: The hospitals, maintained by the Rumanian Red Cross on the front, had been swept away in the German deluge, and at best they had little enough of equipment. Moreover, Moldavia was so far from the original front that no possibility of retreat to it had ever been entertained, and no preparation made there for the establishment of hospitals. And when the retreat did come with its great lists of wounded, every school and other large building was utilized, but there was no equipment. For beds, they had coarse sacking stuffed with straw and only one sheet and one blanket to each bed. There was no adequate supply of fuel and the transport service, what there was of it, was all employed in army supply. It must not be forgotten, also, that Rumania had few railways. The highways were good but there were few cars, and the oil supply was in the hands of the enemy. Many of the oxen which did most of the heavy hauling of the country had been taken by the army and lost. Three million of them, along with proportionate numbers of horses and sheep, had been sold to Russia and Germany at the beginning of the war by men whose greed obscured their vision. In almost everything Rumania was beyond the possibility of self-help. She had no trained nurses — only willing women — and of her twelve hundred doctors, two hundred had died from typhus, and a great number, not definitely known, had met death in battle.

Indeed, so obvious and so vast was the lack of hospital accommodation that almost immediately upon the arrival of the Mission in September, the Director cabled a requisition to us in Washington for a comprehensive list of hospital supplies, which in condensed cable form covered nearly two closely typewritten pages. The list began with 250,000 yards of mattress cloth, ran through the entire range of simple drugs and essential instruments, and ended with spaghetti sufficient for 20,000 patients for six months. This list was the minimum. Two days later, the following supplementary cable was filed : —

Civil population worse condition. Three million in territory inhabited by one million. No clothing, shoes, or material for same obtainable any price. Plainest food bought in Russia limited amount. Transport uncertain. No nourishing foods available for sick or wounded. Eighteen thousand orphans registered; probably many more. All without clothes or shoes of any kind for winter. Unless warm clothing, shoes, or materials with needle, thread, and accessories make same, sent immediately, these and many additional civilians must die this winter. Much sickness now. Some typhus. Severe epidemics inevitable this winter unless can obtain supplies and take prompt measures required prevent far-reaching disaster. Useless try handle situation without some one with authority and access to Government on ground with proper organization similar to Belgium look after transport, receive, and distribute supplies and spend what money can be advantageously used here and in Russia. Can probably secure coöperation of representatives of Allies here. Deem situation so serious am willing to remain all winter, organize, and handle matter if desired, provided can be assured substantial support. Will probably require several million dollars for effective work. Large part would be spent in America, remainder here. Details be sent later. Must have regular transport for definite supplies. Think we can arrange this in Russia if you can arrange ocean tonnage. Announcement of definite policy and appropriations would have most beneficial effect now.

Spurred on by this revelation of the imperative need of Rumania, we of the War Council made haste to ship from

New York such hospital supplies and food as could be obtained. Shortly after this five of the members of the Commission, following the original program, returned to America; but the Chairman together with the remaining members stayed on as did the eleven doctors and twelve nurses. And this little force set out to cope with the disheartening task of Rumanian relief despite the fact that everything seemed against their success.

But they did not have to struggle with this forlorn hope all alone : the British Red Cross fought side by side with them. This organization had undertaken a brave work of relief, but like the Rumanian Red Cross had been swamped by the conditions. Their doctors had made a canvass of all the districts in the little provinces and learned the sorrows of Rumania first hand ; they had traversed the front from Delli to the Carpathians and studied the needs of the makeshift hospitals where even bedding and food and hospital clothes were wholly lacking and the patients undernourished, and where used bandages and blood-stained garments were put back after the soldier's wounds were dressed. But for the betterment of these dire conditions, there was no hope save in shipments from the United States. All western Europe was struggling under a need of them which it could not supply. There was nothing left for them but to wait and to hope, while the poison of German intrigue and treachery increased from day to day the uncertainty of all dependence upon Russia.

Meanwhile, the labor of civilian relief went on. By the New Year our Red Cross, in coöperation with the British Red Cross and Queen Marie, was feeding ten thousand people in Moldavia, and awaiting with such patience as it could the arrival of supplies which we had shipped to them. By good fortune the Director of the British Red Cross had in storage a quantity of condensed milk which he contributed for the feeding of infants; while on our part attention was given to the alleviation of the misery of the soldiers at the front. At Roman in the hospital the Red Cross gave something the patients had never dreamed of seeing — an American Christmas. Evergreens were brought down from the mountains, and candles were found in all sorts of places for their illumination. There were little gifts, such things as the workers of the Commission could find or manufacture; there was food and songs to sing, and as if in despite of the misery that hung like a pall everywhere, there was the spirit of the Christmas over it all. To brighten the sky for a multitude of unhappy refugees, the Chairman of the Commission cabled us that he had given to the Queen just before Christmas for distribution the sum of 250,000 lei (about $20,000). Food of every sort and in lots both large and small was purchased wherever obtainable.

There was a distribution two days before Christmas in Sascut of dried fish, sunflower oil, and cornmeal. Two hundred and sixty-eight families carried away supplies of food and plans were made for further dispensation through a committee of the Commune, the Notar, the village priest, the schoolmaster, and the chief of police, who were to furnish lists of the needy. A Belgian sugar refiner in the district and his wife attached themselves to the Red Cross and gathered every available scrap of old clothing and other supplies; they established a Red Cross sub-depot in their house and visited the people of the surrounding country three or four days each week. They organized a company of young Rumanian women as relief workers, and when the first of March came, they were ready on the coming of spring to carry on the work on a larger scale. Through January the Red Cross had started to lend a hand to the government work for orphans. These constituted a large problem in themselves. The casualties of war and the ravages of disease had raised this menace to a terrifying proportion. Schoolhouses were secured which, formerly, had been used as Army hospitals and in which during the preceding year hundreds of men had died from typhus. The slow process of cleaning and equipping these places had gone on steadily. The relief work in Jassy and many of the outlying districts was well organized though hampered by the fatal lack of supplies. The hospitals at Roman and in Jassy with their 500 beds were doing a distinguished work with the limited facilities available. The Red Cross, in the face of almost insurmountable obstacles, had brought comfort and healing to the thousands of sufferers (and even dying people). In a land where there was no food it was feeding 40,000 people and turning out from its relief station clothing that saved unnumbered lives. It had reached through a sea of difficulties the firm ground of organization where it was ready to handle a great work of relief.

From America, in November, there had come two carloads of hospital supplies and one of food; and with these and what remained of the British equipment, the Red Cross took over the British hospital at Roman, 60 miles from Jassy and 30 miles from the front. This single shipment was all that ever reached Rumania of the supplies which were sent forward by orders of the War Council in Washington. But even with such materials as these limited sources could supply all accounts agree that the Commission made of the Roman hospital by far the best institution of its kind in all Rumania. The British had turned it into a good establishment, heated by steam and lighted by electricity. Its function was that of a base hospital to which soldiers were removed after first treatment at the front. A number of civil cases were also taken. In the rear of the hospital were erected wooden barracks with sleeping accommodations for upward of a hundred orderlies. There were also a carpenter's shop, shoemaker's shop, machine shop, an outside swimming pool, a disinfector, a large laundry, two motor ambulances, two operating rooms, an X-ray laboratory, and ocular and dental departments. The Thanksgiving Day celebration at the hospital, which the Queen attended, was an occasion long to be remembered.

Once having got the Roman hospital into thorough operation, the Red Cross undertook to establish a civilian hospital in an old palace in Jassy, a work which was well on the way to completion when the concentration of troops in Jassy made it necessary to take the building as barracks.

The winter was now at its height, but the clothing problem had in a measure been relieved. From various places in Russia the Commission had secured some 400,000 yards of cloth, 100,000 spools of thread, 50,000 needles, half a carload of buttons, and 50 sewing machines. The Red Cross Canteen at Jassy was operated in connection with a public *triage* — a bathhouse and disinfector; and having cleaned and fed and restored to animate interest in life some thousands of starving women, the Red Cross opened in conjunction with the canteen a clothing department. There women, as soon as supplies were obtained, were set to work in the hurried manufacture of simple clothing to save threatened lives. Thousands of garments were manufactured, the Queen herself distributed many of them in the small country villages and, in addition, the utter lack of shoes was overcome by making simple moccasins from canvas and burlap, which proved a most satisfactory substitute. There were, at least, fewer frozen, bleeding feet in the streets and highways of Moldavia. The records show that at the relief station in Jassy where now food, clothing, disinfection, and medical attention were dispensed, 1200 persons were cared for daily from the date of its opening on February 25 up to March 9, when the Commission was forced to leave Rumania by the imposition of the German peace.

Now that the suffering had, in a measure, been modified, every hand in Rumania was called into service. Widows and orphans and crippled soldiers joined in the work, carrying Red Cross assistance to the needy when their own government was powerless. The American flag and the Red Cross emblem in every district were the signboards pointing the way to help. The heroic Queen traveled Rumanian roads in good and bad weather. There was no such thing in all Moldavia as public charity, for no one had anything to give away. They had lost it all. Charitable organizations, which had been amply endowed for whatever relief was necessary in peace times, were hopelessly crippled by the terrific strain of war. Commercial stocks of food and clothing had vanished and there was no hope of replacement. The greater part of the factory installation in Wallachia had been left behind in the retreat; those in Moldavia were destroyed to save them from German hands. There was no oil for machinery, no cows to furnish milk for babies, no Russian ally.

It was a people dying for a principle, no more, no less. With all their suffering, they made no complaint. The Army must have the best — all, if need be. In the desolate villages behind the front it was counted good fortune for a peasant family to get the entrails of an animal that had been slaughtered for the Army. The wretched people boiled this offal and made soup to keep the breath of life in them. The Army was in good order and would fight to its last soldier. It had no other purpose. But if Russia fell, everything fell.

And then, indeed, the bell rang for the curtain. On the 9th of March, to save herself from the utter annihilation which Germany had promised for the little Balkan country's portion, Rumania gave up the struggle. It left her hemmed in by revengeful enemies and with the knowledge that Russia, her former protector, had played her false in practically the last political act before she herself went down into an abyss of revolution and Bolshevism.

The Allied world laid no charge of bad faith at the door of

Rumania. Her necessity was too obvious. She had tried and failed. In the trial she had stripped herself bare of every possession, and had lost by slaughter and disease about ten per cent of her population. With us such a payment would mean ten millions of our people! It is indeed to be hoped that Rumania's sacrifices be not wholly forgotten even in these days of short memories.

Scarcely had Rumania yielded than the Germans ordered the immediate dismissal of all French, British, and American agents of relief from the country. It was folly, of course, to expect any reversal of this order. At the time of the Mission's departure Rumania's Queen cabled to Washington as follows: —

"At this hour when tragic events leave my country defenseless in the hands of a revengeful and relentless enemy, my thoughts turn with grati- tude towards those who in anxious days, but when there was still hope, came to my aid. I wish once more to thank the American Red Cross for the splendid way in which it answered my appeal of a few months ago. The work the American Red Cross Commission did amongst our wounded and amongst the suffering population is unforgetable to me and my people. Now that my country has to remain alone and forsaken, sur- rounded by foes, I wish once more to raise my voice and to thank all those who helped me, and to ask that we and our nation should not be forgotten, although a dreadful and humiliating peace has been forced upon us. I ask of the great heart of America to remember Rumania, if even for a while. Strangulated, her cries will not reach it, and her tears will have to be wept in secret."

There is little more of this sad story to be told. To the thoughtless, or those who think in numerals and have not the larger view of what the Red Cross purpose really is, it might appear that its mission in Rumania was a failure. But even these persons, I think, would not say so had they been among the fortunate ones who were present when Marie of Rumania conferred decorations on the members of our Mission. All of them have since said that they knew that the decorations were the only proofs of her gratitude that the Queen had left to give, but it was easy to see that she exulted in the giving. On our part, the Commission put into the Queen's hands an order for food sufficient to feed several thousand persons for six months. And when the Commission took up the perilous road to the North through Russia, thousands of these people, who for centuries have forgotten no kindness and no injury, crowded the public square to say Godspeed to those who were leaving their unhappy country. It was a demonstration of a Nation's affection and an assurance that the memory of our efforts, however pitiful when contrasted with the need, will never fade as long as the Danube flows to the sea.

CHAPTER XIX

THE TRAGEDY OF THE EAST

IN telling the story of the Red Cross in the East the discomforting thought is ever present in my mind that I may not dwell as long as I should like upon a scene as touching as that which concluded the report from Rumania. No sooner have I visualized the little station at Jassy and rejoiced, however vicariously, with the departing mission in their consciousness of a deed well done than I am called upon by the very nature of this book to depict scenes of suffering in Serbia and Greece, Palestine, and the Near East that would appear to be more poignant than anywhere else in Europe.

Until our own entry into the struggle the Balkans, if the truth must be told, had been merely a name, a far-off place associated with rugged hills and beautiful embroideries; and, in a relief way, our only touch with it had been in the special Typhus Commission that went to Serbia in 1914.

Serbia's rôle in the war may be fixed by events before and after the Great Retreat in the fall of 1915 — when the Serbian Army, hopelessly outnumbered, commenced its retirement with the snow three feet deep and the cold in the bleak Albanian hills almost unbearable. Soldiers were little better clad than the wretched civilians who dropped in the snow and lay where they fell. The historic retreat of Napoleon's armies across the snowbound Russian plains from Moscow was less fearful. Of the Serb Army of 250,000 that had opposed the enemy at the frontiers, less than 100,000 reached the ultimate haven — Corfu, that lies like a fairy isle in the Ionian Sea. Fifty per cent of the civilians who fled out of Serbia died of starvation, disease, and exposure before help could reach them; while of the remaining half, 20,000 found sanctuary in foreign lands, Corsica, Switzerland, France, and Italy, and along the African coast. During the following year, great effort was made by the British and French governments, and sympathetic individuals everywhere, to mitigate the sufferings of these homeless people who had been driven from their firesides to the ends of the earth.

But I must not forget that it is of the Serbians in Serbia of whom I would write, the singing Serbs of the gentle hearts and genial firesides who, in the midst of a turbulent land, under a wise and generous government, have managed to preserve the autonomy of the Serbian States as well as its customs and traditions.

In June and July, 1916, the beaten army began to struggle out of Corfu, bolstered by allied support, reëquipped and reclothed by allied funds. Many still suffered the effects of the retreat, and their physical stamina was not of the strongest; but there were 30,000 Serbs at the front with the allied forces that drove the Austrians from Monastir!

By April, 1917, there were 50,000 civilian refugees in the little recaptured area, crowded chiefly into the shell-raked city and the wretched outlying villages; and there were 200,000 more scattered through the bleak plains of Macedonia all the way to Saloniki. It was here in this region that the Red Cross found them in the summer of 1917, living in cellars, barns, churches, and mosques, subsisting as best they could, menaced by cold, hunger, and disease. The enemy had stripped the countryside of its grain, horses, cattle, food, and metals; there was nothing, they say, not even a match with which to start a fire. Dearth, indeed! To go into such desolation was like going into a wilderness. It was like making the world over again.

The base of the Red Cross activity was, perforce, the Greek port of Saloniki that was having troubles enough of its own — with half of the city homeless after the great fire — without 10,000 additional refugees. Here the Red Cross established soup kitchens; the sight of hot, appetizing food apparently conjured out of empty air seemed a mysterious feat to the natives; barracks, sewing rooms, hospitals, and dispensaries were set up in accordance with the regular prescribed formula for the building up of civilian relief. Chaos enough there was in the city of Saloniki, more cosmopolitan than ever now with its narrow, hilly streets filled with strange, surging throngs; with strange ships in its harbors and Turkish guns trained at its heart; with strange soldiers in its streets and cafés and bazaars and always the crying, hungry masses that the Red Cross had come to feed and comfort. A dismal, endless, hopeless task it seemed and more wretched, somehow, than a similar task had seemed in other places. There was so little on which to build, either materially or spiritually.

In the harbor of Alexandria, Egypt, lay the collier *Cæsar*, loaded with food, clothing, and medicine, which had been sent by the American Committee for Armenian and Syrian relief. Its destination had been Beirut on the Syrian coast, but operations in the Mediterranean had checked its departure. Of this the Red Cross took immediate advantage, buying the shipload of supplies outright and bringing them at once to the distribution point. This was more than timely; it was like manna from Heaven in this remote region which, inaccessible enough to the western world in normal times, was now struggling with the additional difficulties of Turkish gunboats, Austrian submarines, and British mines.

At this point, I take the liberty of making a slight digression in order to extend the gratitude of the Red Cross to the American Committee for Armenian and Syrian Relief for its splendid coöperation in the Near East. This had been one of the first relief agencies in the field endeavoring to salvage the thousands of starving and homeless people along the coast of Palestine and ancient Judea. After our coming we were glad in many instances to profit by their experiences and to follow their example. What the Red Cross could not do the Armenian and Syrian Committee did; territory untouched by the Red Cross was covered by them, and throughout there was the spirit of friendly understanding and coöperation and a happy dovetailing of enterprise at all points where they met on a common platform. It is therefore timely that due thanks be extended to this capable organization that contributed so largely to the relief so vitally needed in this desolate region.

In Serbia proper the Red Cross centered its refugee work

in Vodena, a city half-way between Saloniki and Monastir, in which about 5000 refugees had found shelter. The first act of the Red Cross was the setting up of a fifty-bed hospital in a building supplied by the Greek Government; later, a second one of twice the capacity was established at Banitza, sixty-five miles from Saloniki.

The villages about Monastir were crowded with homeless people who would not be dragged from their shattered firesides. To pamper this home-clinging spirit the Red Cross constructed a number of adobe houses on frameworks of wattles, a type of dwelling peculiar to all the Mediterranean countries and the Near East. In Saloniki, forests of tents were laid in the suburbs to shelter the fire victims, and milk was distributed regularly to the children. Clothing, shoes, and staple foodstuffs which they could not give to the penniless strangers within their gates, were purchased from the local shops ; and, in this way, the hungry were fed, the naked clothed, and the Red Cross became the wonder-worker of the East.

For the troops, rolling canteens like those in use on other battlefronts were dispatched to the Serbian front; motor trucks were ordered from Italy; and quantities of canvas for beds and hospital stretchers were purchased and made up. An artificial limb factory was started in Saloniki, while a staff of American dentists with ten fully equipped dental ambulances was sent from New York for service with the Serb armies. A sum of $50,000 was given to the Serbian Red Cross, which had moved its headquarters to Corfu, with a branch in Geneva.

I have not yet mentioned the Serbian prisoners of war in Austria and Bulgaria. These, also, became the wards of the Red Cross, and theirs is yet another chapter in the story of terror and cruelty. There were 154,000 of them in captivity, facing the Austrian winter without proper food or clothing. The Red Cross made an appropriation of $70,000 to take care of their most vital needs, and tons of supplies soon began to move through Berne to Serbs in enemy prison camps. The story of these prisoners is an old one, and it were trite to dwell anew on prison camp life with its attendant horrors of pestilence, death, starvation, cruelty, and cold in a strange and friendless land. Many a Serb in his ransomed home to-day owes his life to the food sent by the Red Cross. In addition, generous appropriation was made for the sustenance and medical care of tubercular Serbs in France, Switzerland, and Italy.

Thus the Red Cross intrenched itself in the hearts and hearths of Serbia. With the grand rally of the Serbian Army in the autumn of 1918, when all events moved towards the great climax, the Red Cross was still there with its rolling canteens and its comforts, although it was desolate enough at that, and sounds far more encouraging in printed words than it actually was, for the whole situation was hopeless and lacking in all those essentials that are absolute necessities to the efficiency of the spoiled and pampered westerner. It was a last, grand desperate effort, backed up by allied aid, against a staggering foe. The last bitter campaign was marked by great suffering among the troops. There were no women nurses, no anæsthetics, no surgical dressings save the pitifully small amount the Red Cross was able to supply, for the transportation problem was always an uncertain factor, one on which wagers could not safely be laid at any time. Tonnage was more precious than the jewels of a Rajah, and when it came to the loading of a relief ship there was always a debate as to which should be given preference — food, clothing, medical supplies, or surgical dressings, each item being needed as badly as the other. If some were clothed, wounds were neglected; if wounds were dressed, backs went bare or stomachs empty. Over $600,000 was spent for relief supplies in Serbia, and even then, the Red Cross task was only half done.

s

Looking down the long vista of her history, Serbia will find no page that is illumined with more valorous deeds and superhuman courage in the face of titanic odds than that which fills her rôle in the Great War — "Serbia that fights only for freedom and surrenders only to God."

. . . .

Of all the strange, incongruous settings that had to do with the transplanting of the Red Cross and its modern trappings, there have been none to compare with Greece — that cradle of art and classic antiquity, whose finger-prints are visible through the ages wherever men have tried to live greatly. Strange, indeed, it must have seemed to see the all too familiar bread lines and soup kitchens and dispensaries within the shadow of the towering Acropolis, white against the Athenian sky under the frown of Olympus or in the Daphne haunted glades of Tempe.

The rôle of the Red Cross in ancient Hellas was confined almost entirely to civilian relief work, although this does not mean that its field there was a narrow one or in any way circumscribed. The hordes of destitute Greeks could not have been greater nor more forlorn had there been a wholesale enemy invasion of the Hellenic peninsula. Thousands of Greeks, living outside of Greece in Bulgaria and Turkey, became the objects of cruelest oppression and persecution when, at the beginning of the war, it was decreed that every Christian should be driven from Islam at the point of the sword. The Twentieth Century reverted overnight to the Seventh, the shoddy cloak of tolerance fell from the shoulders of Turkey, and the Holy War was on as if there had been no surcease. Saladin rode again in defense of Acre.

In 1914 Greece had just emerged from the Balkan struggle of 1912–1913 and had acquired by the treaty of Bucharest a portion of Eastern Macedonia, an indifferent land, unproductive, peopled with refugees driven out of Bulgaria, or residents whose homes had been laid waste during the campaigns of the Balkan wars of those years. It was a barren countryside filled with a hungry, clamorous people. So Greece already had her refugee problem when the holocaust of Europe took flame; Belgium, France, and Serbia were old stories to her, and the war but served to enhance her difficulties.

The political position of Greece was a peculiar one. We are all familiar with the circumstances that led up to the abdication of King Constantine and the final decision of Greece to enter the war as an allied power in June, 1917. These civil disturbances had not served to heighten the morale of the people, and at the time of the appeal to the American Red Cross, Greece was a sad, tottering, hungry land, with swarms of her own people knocking at her gates for admittance, demanding shelter and food that she could not give.

Countless stories have come from out of the East in regard to Bulgarian and Turkish atrocities, of hordes of women and children driven naked across the land, forced to march without food, clothing, or shelter under the pitiless desert skies — of young girls carried off into slavery, of massacres in the silent depths of Asia Minor, of Greek children kidnapped by the Bulgars and forcibly denationalized, and of countless other cruelties too numerous and too terrible to relate. Our task there was to salvage the unhappy remainder that knocked at our doors, faint with hunger, burning with fever, or driven insane by their experiences.

When, at the close of the year 1917, the Greek Red Cross appealed for aid, an American Red Cross representative was sent from Saloniki to Athens to consult with the Greek Government and the Red Cross, while only a small commission was sent through the interior to look over the field. Of course the usual quota of relief supplies was in order : food, clothing, surgical dressings, and medical needs, as well as hospital equipment, sewing machines, and uncut materials, hospital bedding, towels, linen, and ambulances.

There were 50,000 Greek refugees in the islands of the Ægean Sea — those beautiful storied islands, lying like jewels on the bosom of the bright water, past which the Greek fleet had sailed on its way to Illium, past which the adventurous Argosy had run, whose shores are cloudy with almond blossoms in the spring ! These wanderers were utterly destitute, having been driven out of Turkey with only the few poor rags that covered them.

In the homeland, the mobilization of the forces had left the same economic problems behind as it did in other lands. After the Saloniki fire, still more homeless ones thronged the streets, while the civilian hospitals were being emptied to take care of the wounded.

But the Red Cross had done so much it could do more. In the early emergency, fifty tons of general supplies were purchased from the Serbian Commission for use in Macedonia, and at the end of September, 1918, the special Commission for Greece set out with a personnel of seventy. By that time, the whole situation in the Balkans had changed for the better : Bulgaria had capitulated; the flag of the Christian had been raised over Jerusalem ; the Red Cross found itself in a more cheerful spiritual atmosphere when the new Commission arrived at Saloniki. This, of course, was very close to the end of the war. With the obligations of the army removed, the way became at once easier and the Red Cross has since been steadily helping Greece back to her hearthfires. A good-sized appropriation was set aside for the rehabilitation of Greek refugees, while arrangements were made for the shipment of 320 tons of foodstuffs monthly for a period of three months, coming from Italian ports to the Piræus and the Island of Mitylene.

In the city of Athens, the children became the special

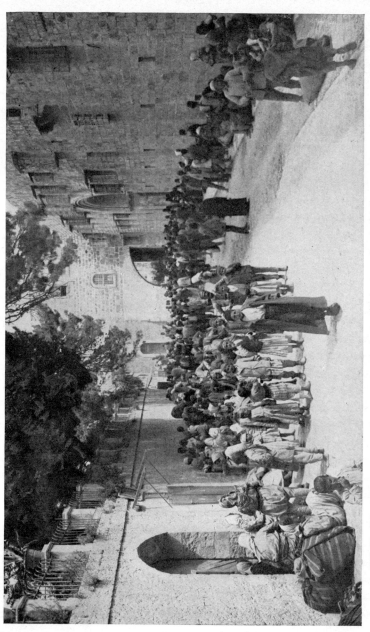

SOME OF THE 1500 ARMENIAN EXILES AS SEEN BY THE RED CROSS COMMISSION.
Many of these children have walked over 600 miles in the deportation ordered by the Turkish military officers.

charge of the Red Cross as they have always been wherever the Red Cross has gone. Centers for the care of children of employed mothers were opened, and a daily milk ration provided for; while sewing rooms were opened not only in Athens but on the islands of Chios, Samos, and Mitylene in the Ægean Sea and in Serres, Kavalla, and Drama, the Macedonian centers of Red Cross work. In addition to this, a number of Greek women were given special training in care of children and home hygiene, — after the manner followed in France, — and by which the trained women in the rôle of visiting practical nurses could take the child welfare idea into the Greek homes. The Red Cross was also able to go into Bulgarian territory and give some comfort to a number of Greek prisoners in internment camps there.

The Red Cross came late to Greece, perhaps, but more than one report says that its presence had a most enlivening and heartening effect upon the people. Certainly, owing to the circumstances of the country, the Greek agencies were unable to handle the sorry situation that confronted them. It was fortunate indeed that the Red Cross was able to step into the emergency and discharge so well its obligations.

. . . .

In April, 1918, the Red Cross War Council received from the American Committee for Syrian and Armenian Relief the following cablegram which gives a fragmentary picture of the conditions which prevailed in Palestine at that time, and supplies the reason for the Red Cross' going into the Holy Land : —

Fifteen hundred Armenians, survivors of many thousands exiled from Adana, Kharne, Marash, Aintab, Ourfa-Kessab, two and a half years ago, to the wilderness east of the Jordan, found trekking to Jericho. For months had been compelled by Turks to break stone on roads. Brought to Jerusalem in British motor trucks. Although weak and hungry, faces lighted up at first glimpse of Mount of Olives.

Six thousand Syrian refugees from Es Salt vicinity expected this week. We will equip expeditions to meet exiles and will provide industrial relief if additional funds can be sent. Five hundred Armenians rescued by Arabs at Tawfile, between Maan and Dead Sea, will be moved to Port Said. For months from twenty to thirty died daily of starvation. Original number ten thousand. Following message has come through from Tawfile : "The price of a life is the price of bread."

Fortunately for us the British Armies had cleared the way. They were at Antioch far to the North, in Jerusalem and in Jericho, and were crossing the river Jordan. The British Relief Fund for Palestine and Syria had already established Medical Units at Gaza, Hebron, Jaffa, and Jerusalem and invited the participation of the Red Cross. Until the coming of the British Committee, relief in Palestine and other near parts of Asia Minor had been in the hands of the American Committee for Armenian and Syrian Relief, which had sent $10,000,000 worth of supplies, $3,000,000 of which had been contributed by the Red Cross prior to our active participation in this field.

So in March, 1918, the special Red Cross Commission for Palestine sailed from New York with hundreds of tons of supplies and complete traveling and camping equipment. The route was long, for travel in the Mediterranean was still hazardous and they went around the African continent, touching at Ceylon and on through the Red Sea, so that it was June before the Mission arrived at the port of Beirut.

The field before them in the Holy Land embraced half the measure of Asia. There was no turning back, once begun. Although housing and sanitary conditions in that part of the world had never been ideal, according to occidental standards, there was, fortunately, a more substantial background on which to build than there had been at other relief points; for one thing, the British engineers were engaged in intensive sanitation work in Jerusalem itself, and after the fresh waters from the hills had been brought

down to the city by means of modern plumbing and pump-
ing, the water-skins, filthy though picturesque, disappeared
from the streets for the first time in two thousand or more
years.   Indeed, permit me to say here, that the work of
the Red Cross in Palestine was made largely possible through
the generous and benevolent attitude manifested by the
British authorities in the occupied enemy territory, and by
their marvelous and rapid organization and control of the
civic functions.   On the part of the officials there was always
present the spirit of the most cordial welcome and a generous
willingness to meet us halfway in all our undertakings.

The Jerusalem that the Red Cross Commission found was
a teaming babel, orderly enough under British Army discipline, of course; but it is doubtful if the ancient city with
so many strange peoples mingling amicably in its streets,
with heavy British cars and Army camions disturbing the
calm of the stolid donkeys, the sleepy camels and the wailing
thousands of refugees — more wretched than those that have
wept before its walls for a thousand years, and more forlorn
than the lepers that used to ask alms at the gate — ever
knew times as stirring or as full of wonderment as these.
On a Palm Sunday long ago, perhaps, the city had been as
crowded with surging throngs; as bewildered and as clamorous, perhaps, as now in the midsummer of the year of our
Lord, 1918; but that was a very long time ago and Jerusalem
has slept and dreamed through nearly two thousand sum-
mers since then, while the world has grown old about it and
the crescent of the Turk has hung over its gates.

Therefore it was an unique atmosphere in which the
Red Cross found itself : the birth-spot of Christ just set
free from the Saracen, spread over with villages that
had been villages when Joshua conquered Canaan, when
Abraham journeyed from the plains of the Jordan down
into Hebron ; and through which David had passed when
he was fleeing into the wilderness from Saul — villages that

looked for all the world like western Indian pueblo villages, clinging old and brown and shapeless to the hills. It would be strange, indeed, if a little time was not given to meditation in a place of such antiquity, surcharged with memories that have so vitally influenced the life of the world. One can stand on one of the rolling Judean hills and watch the shepherds with their flocks in the purple shade of the olive trees; two thousand years ago they might have seen the Star from that very spot, for Bethlehem lay just across the valley.

But the pressing need, according to all accounts, was for action and not meditation. The first relief work undertaken was among the homeless refugees, crowded into the city of Jerusalem, housed in various odd buildings, and tented in the vacant spaces. Strangely enough, among them were a number of Russian women pilgrims, stranded in Jerusalem by the war, although they are not to be classed with the type of refugee that had trudged across the Jordan Valley: these were intelligent, clean, hardworking, devoutly religious women of fine physique and handsome Slav features, who welcomed the advent of the Red Cross sewing rooms that were soon opened.

In the city of Jerusalem fifteen hundred women — Moslem, Jewish, and Christian — were employed in the industrial workrooms instituted by the Red Cross, and engaged in spinning, weaving, knitting, dressmaking, basketry, rug making, mattress making, embroidery, and lace work. The Red Cross custom of helping the refugees to help themselves has always made for contentment and satisfaction in the subjects of our aid, giving work to impatient, idle fingers and, thereby, assuring them of the type and character of clothing they preferred — a factor to be considered if they were to attain any measure of happiness. It was familiar things they wanted, things to which they had been accustomed, things they had known through all their dark narrow lives.

They admire western culture, perhaps, but they do not want it — not much of it; in fact, they are rather afraid of it.

There were ten refugee centers in the city, two of which were on the Mount of Olives; there was an orphanage for boys, conducted by German agencies before the war and which the British desired the Red Cross to take over. Later it became necessary to establish another orphanage for boys and one for girls. Following the opening of the American Red Cross Hospital in the city, there also was established a series of clinics for children and adults in the city and in four outside centers. Six hundred orphans formerly the charges of the British Relief Committee were taken in hand, and a liaison was effected with the Zionist Unit for the relief of suffering Jews.

At Port Said, at the head of the Suez Canal just across that curve of the land towards the west, where Asia Minor ends and Africa begins, a number of Armenian refugees were concentrated under the charge of the Red Cross, assisted by the Armenian Society and the British Relief Fund for Palestine and Syria.

Refugee work along the foregoing lines was conducted in five centers in the Holy Land: in Mejel, where a hospital was established; in Remleh, with a clinic supplementing the work of the Government hospital; in Jaffa, a few miles west of Jerusalem on the coast; at Ram Allah and at Wadi-Surar, in western Palestine, where two thousand or more refugees were gathered under tents on the plain. Here was also a halfway camp for Armenians being taken to Port Said, and a flourishing school of six or seven hundred native children. Also, a small civilian hospital was established in Nazareth. In the agricultural districts, and Palestine is largely a pastoral land, ox-teams were secured for indigent farmers.

Altogether the field in Palestine was most satisfactory, and with the cessation of hostilities and the subsequent opening of the ocean lanes and ports, many problems that had existed as decidedly material barriers to the progress of relief work have disappeared. All the routes to Asia are open now. Supplies can go through and keep on going through without cessation.

For all this work, including food, medical, surgical, and sanitary supplies, salaries and expenses, the War Council of the Red Cross had appropriated by October 1, $558,479. In addition to this, a monthly contribution of $50,000 is made to the Red Cross by the Armenian and Syrian Relief Committee for the work among the civilian population.

The end of the war, however, does not mean the end of want or the end of suffering or disease in the Holy Land. It is a land sunk deep in tradition and superstition and into which the light of modern science or modern thought has not penetrated; it is a land that has long suffered oppression and cruelty and misunderstanding, where the spirit of the peoples has been shrunken and terrified by persecution. But in this land the Red Cross has set a bright lamp, and we hope it will shine forever, bringing light and hope and good will to the old, old lands of the East.

CHAPTER XX

RUSSIA

IT is a bolder pen than mine that essays to write of Russia
to-day, even from the standpoint of relief work carried
on within its borders. Perhaps everything that there is to
be said of Russia that will convey an idea of its present
condition — if there be a present condition in a land that is
constantly changing — has been said. Perhaps everyone
who reads this will have his own idea of Russia, as nearly
every one of us has — each of those ideas different, each of
them short of the truth in varying degrees, for Russia, unconsciously, hides herself from those most anxious to understand her. Those who have been in Russia at any time the
last three years think they have seen Russia; almost believe
that they understand Russia; but they do not. Russia
is as a kaleidoscope. We look upon to-day's picture and
say: "This is Russia!" and scarcely have the words left our
lips than there is a change and we discover that what we
thought was Russia is not Russia at all. It was only a

distorted vision. At that, I am most ready to believe and not a few who have been there agree with me that the workers of the American Red Cross and other relief agencies came closer to that vague, intangible thing that we like to speak of poetically as the soul of Russia, than a host of others who were never in close touch with the people — the common people, the peasants, and the people of the land, those teeming millions of the steppes struggling in the dark to discover just what the demise of the Romanoffs will mean to them.

Russia is more than a country; it is a world in itself. Russia has every imaginable thing that land or water can hold in store for the benefit of mankind, and has it in a measure that is incalculable: there are fertile wheatlands capable of yielding billions of bushels of grain, and mountains that are rich in ore, silver, gold, and precious stones that have slept there through the ages; there are valleys gushing with oil, vineyards heavy with wine, waters teeming with fish, and forests untouched. If ever a land flowed with milk and honey, it is Russia — Russia the virgin.

It was into this country, this Garden of Alladin, shuddering under the suddenness and swiftness of the revolution that the Red Cross went, drawn by the suffering and by the needs of the Allied and American forces there — (albeit the Red Cross was in Russia before foreign troops were sent in). It was an effort to help the affected population to withstand the stress of the times as best they could; often help of this kind, at such a time, is as efficacious as forests of bayonets, although to say so in the Russian situation were an exaggeration. Yet, although Russia is still in a state of flux, like hot metal that has not found its mold, the work of the Red Cross, infinitesimal as it was in comparison with the crying need of Russia, has not been in vain. The Red Cross could not lead Russia to her destiny, but it could hold out a timely flame of hope to the be-

wildered, suffering millions that poured through the steppes
— 12,000,000 they say it was — running away from the
Frankenstein of their own hands' creating; it could show
them that human understanding and human kindness still
existed; it could point the better way, although it could not
command.

When the great army of Russia surged behind the standard
of the Little Father, up and down Petrograd and the Carpathians to the frontiers of Prussia and back, see-sawing across
the land — now driving the foe before them, now giving
ground without resistance — they left the same wake of
suffering as did the armies in Belgium, Serbia, and France.
But it was greater, it was more remote from relief, and it
was voiceless. The Russian is Asiatic in his fatalism.
Centuries of oppression have taught him not to complain.

But overnight, Russia roused from her centuries of
passivity. The Little Father no longer sat on the great
throne in Petrograd. The Czar was a hunted exile in his
own land and Russia was free!

It is impossible to tell of the Red Cross in Russia
without going into the conditions in that country; for
vague and imperfect though it, obviously, must be, the
work and policy of the Red Cross were molded and
limited by the political situation there. Of all theaters
of operation in which the Red Cross was active, that
of ancient Moscow may be said to have been the most
difficult, even if it was the most interesting and, perhaps, the most romantic. To appreciate the difficulties
with which the Red Cross had to contend, the obstacles
that had to be overcome, one must know or, at least, have
an idea of Russia at the time. There, the Red Cross
was confronted by problems heretofore unforeseen, un-
encountered. That its position was a difficult one will be
shown by the brief statement that it was a neutral, non-
combatant relief agency operating in a land whose armies

were still recognized as part of the Allied forces, a land where those who were revolutionists one day were peaceable soil-tilling folk the next, or where the stolid peasant of yesterday became the cutthroat of to-morrow. It was a situation, to say the least, that called for careful diplomacy and great delicacy of action. Contrary to the expectations of the average Russian, to whom "liberty" and "democracy" were but vague terms, the millennium, as we all know, did not come with the dethronement of the Romanoffs. Russia began to wander through an evil dream, while her children cried for food and the enemy menaced her borders; the Army refused to fight; authority was unrecognized; the papers of one faction were worthless in the eyes of the next. Leaders rose and fell, commerce was at a standstill, transportation failed; people cried for that bauble of freedom that they thought was within their grasp and killed each other in the streets, in misled hope of gaining the much-sought prize through bloodshed; children cried for food and ran homeless into the fields. The Brest-Litovsk Treaty went through at last.

Such was Russia — a cauldron, a bedlam, a world of many minds with but few who thought they saw the way, and a huge remainder doubting, suspecting, fearing, longing only for some sort of peace and stability — a few months after the outbreak of the revolution, when the American Red Cross came.

Arriving at the port of Vladivostok, late in the month of July, 1917, the Commission was met by representatives of the Russian Red Cross, which had come through the months of turmoil a sorry wreck. Perhaps a few words about the Red Cross of Russia will not be amiss here, since the remnants of that organization were to form an important liaison between the Russian people and the foreigners who had come to help them. Under the old régime, it had enjoyed fair organization and had ramified the empire from Petrograd to the Bering Sea. At the time of the Russo-Japanese War, it had thoroughly supplemented the medical corps of the armies and had earned the confidence of the people; but its very foundation was autocracy and, for this very reason, it went down with the fall of the autocrats. In February, 1918, the old Central Committee was dissolved by force of arms, and its guiding members found little mercy at the hands of the revolutionists. However, in the summer of 1917, a sincere body of its representatives met the Americans at Vladivostok and assured them of their ready coöperation and assistance wherever it might be needed. In a land as strange to Americans as Russia, the need of such assistance was obvious and the desire for coöperation unquestioned.

The American Red Cross came to Russia with ambulances and $200,000 worth of medical supplies, intending later to order vast shipments of medical and surgical needs that were to find their way into Russian hospitals. One of the most urgent needs was for milk in the cities. The infant mortality in those congested spots was increasing each day. There were 150,000 homeless, destitute children in Petrograd that winter. The food situation was acute, although it was largely a matter of transportation rather than actual scarcity. However, it became necessary to send food to the Russians in the Murmansk district for the reason that hungry Petrograd would permit no food to go into that barren, frozen land. To the south of the Russian capital there were acres and acres of ungarnered grain, while the cities cried and fought for bread. A Red Cross appropriation of $20,000 for the relief of officers' and soldiers' families in Petrograd was made before the political situation became so acute that it was thought best to remove the Mission from the capital, which lay under the menace of possible German occupation. In March, 1918, the Mission left the city, and with the American Ambassador proceeded to Moscow, leaving one man behind to carry on the milk distribution. It became clear that under the existing circumstances, with the old capital and the surrounding country under the menace of invasion, that the work of the Commission was over. The field of action became daily more and more circumscribed, yet they stayed on — in Moscow, Murmansk, and in Archangel, doing what they could. Although the land was in ferment and confusion, somewhere beneath the chaos lay Russia reborn.

There were two utterly unrelated factors that helped Russia through the strain of the last two years, factors that made many things possible that otherwise would have been impossible, one of which gave cause for continued Red Cross activity, and the other which made that activity possible — two factors on which the face of Russia may be said to have depended during that period : the Czecho-Slovaks and the Trans-Siberian railway.

I will speak briefly of the latter first. All through the turmoil of the revolution, the great iron way that traverses Russia from Vladivostok to Petrograd — 6000 miles — was kept going, somehow, and in that fact lies something of the quality of the spirit of the real Russia : the employees of the railroad yielded to the lure of the freebooters and the revolutionists that infested the land less than any other class of workers, and it was their loyalty and steadfastness that kept the interior of Russia open, for they worked in the face of unimaginable difficulties, and enabled supplies to be carried from Vladivostok inland. The life of these men was one of exceptional hazard. Their families were in want and misery ; for months they were unpaid ; yet something made them see that the trains had to move if ever hope was to come out of the situation at all. The psychology of this vision, this urge on the part of these loyal Russian laboring men, will forever remain a mystery. It was something of the real Russia, the Russia that is worth while, the Russia

"IS EVERYBODY HAPPY?"

There can be no doubt about it if smiles mean anything.

that will finally triumph. At that, I do not mean to convey the impression that the Trans-Siberian was a perfectly running, perfectly managed road. Far from it. To begin with, the rolling stock was old and dilapidated, the engines badly in need of repair and fuel was scarce; nor did they run on schedule time, breakdowns being the rule rather than the exception; but they ran, somehow, the trains from Vladivostok inland, and it was through this medium that Red Cross supplies were taken into Russia.

And the Czecho-Slovaks: Czech soldiers had been in Siberia since June, having joined the French and British forces in the field. The care of the wounded became an obligation of the Red Cross, while the American consul at Harbin, in Manchuria, was asking for coöperation with the Russian Red Cross there to take care of the refugees coming in along the routes of the Trans-Siberian Railway. The misery of the tumult was breaking out in a new place. Around the Czecho-Slovaks there was rallying a formidable force of Russians, and the port of Vladivostok, with its vast quantities of supplies which Sukhomlinoff had kept from the Russian armies, was now in Allied control. A crisis was imminent. Russia wanted peace and safety wherever she might find it : she would take it from Germany if the Allies could not produce it the more quickly. In the meantime, suffering increased and the cities, though in the midst of plenty, were still in the grip of famine — the peasants refusing to give up their grain at Government prices, when they could sell it in the open market for its weight in gold. Food commissions, created by the soviet government, were sent into the farming regions, there to wrest the food from the peasants by force, if they could obtain it no other way. Children from the breadless cities were sent into the country, thrown upon the charity of the peasants for their food. Some months later 1200 of these "lost children of the Urals" were corralled by the Red Cross in

T

Tumen and Irbit and brought back from savagery to normal life. The number of children who died in the wilderness will never be known.

And so, as in Italy the previous autumn, the Red Cross went "to war" — it having been decided not to send, at least for the present, an American Army to Russia — to hold the Russians to the cause of right and save her from that greater chaos that wholesale enemy occupation would precipitate; kindness and the relief of pressing needs in the way of food, clothing, and shelter was the means by which she was to be won to the Allies' cause.

Meanwhile, across the German frontiers, Russian prisoners released from bondage in enemy prison camps — in some instances of four years' duration — were pouring by the thousands back into a Russia they did not know, a Russia that had come into being while they were rotting in captivity, a Russia that would flay them and try their hearts anew before granting them the peace for which they had fought. A large proportion of these men were ill and wasted physically. Many of them were tuberculotic.

The needs of the newly released Russian prisoners offered an opportunity to bring home by clear, practical demonstration, the fact that the Red Cross had come there to help them. Fortunately, our men were able to get a Government chartered ship, in which a load of food supplies, medicines, and drugs was soon on its way.

Encouragement, also, came at that time from the fact that the call of the United States Consul at Harbin could be answered and was now going forward for the relief of the refugees there. There were swarms of them — a heterogeneous mass of bewildered folk, ranging from the unkempt mendicant classes to unfortunate families who had known comfort and prosperity — Russians, Tartars, dark, round-eyed children from the Balkans and Armenia, and wailing Serbs, utterly destitute and forlorn.

From the beginning, the purpose of the Red Cross was to help the people of Russia without regard to political situations, and with utter indifference to the policies of the political party that happened to be in power. Its aim was to keep clearly before the Russians the fact that the United States, through the Red Cross, wanted to help them. Yet the picture of Russia is a difficult one to paint, so many vital things were happening simultaneously. It was while the relief ship was preparing for northern Russia that a new and keenly urgent situation arose in the Far East : the Czecho-Slovaks had developed a new theater of war and stubborn fighting was going on along the railway lines in Siberia and along the Volga. Light was beginning to filter through upon a state of things which three months before had been hopelessly black. By July 15, 1918, one year after the Red Cross had come to Russia, United States Marines and regulars were landing at the Russian ports; the Marines at Kola on the Murmansk front; and Infantry from the Philippines at Vladivostok. Allied forces were in that city guarding the stores, and the Czecho-Slovak wounded were moving back over the railway in increasing numbers into hospitals already filled to overflowing. The United States cruiser *Brooklyn*, lying in Vladivostok harbor, was temporarily converted into a floating hospital, aboard which the Czechs were taken. Civilian conditions among the refugees driven back from the fighting zone were growing steadily worse.

However, in the present emergency, as always, the letters from the Navy and State Departments and the cables received by the Red Cross were turned over to the Fourteenth Division, and the ball was rolling before the ink on the letters was fairly dry. The Secretary of the Navy cabled to the Commander of the *Brooklyn* that relief was on the way. It was a day and a week of the swiftest direct action and one in which the Fourteenth Division played one of its most conspicuous parts.

The physician in charge of St. Luke's Hospital in Tokyo was summoned by cable to take charge of the situation in Vladivostok at the head of a relief expedition, while the representative of the Russian Department of Commerce at Vladivostok was requested to oversee all preparations until the expedition should arrive. It was perhaps the most urgent and most vital emergency work that the year had exacted of the Red Cross, in a year filled with vital emergencies. There was fast work, too, in Tokyo and in Vladivostok. The Peking Chapter was accumulating supplies, while money poured in from Americans in Shanghai, Tientsin, and Harbin. In Tokyo, the assembling of the hospital unit was hastened, and in eight days the staff with their supplies landed in Vladivostok ready for work.

Out of all this energy grew the American Red Cross relief base at Vladivostok. On Russian Island — a dot of land two and a half miles out in the harbor, commanding a beautiful view of the busy ship-dotted bay and the broad, blue sweep of the Sea of Japan — the military hospital was located in buildings already there. There grew up, too, in an incredibly short time, refugee barracks at First and Second Rivers, near the city, capable of housing 2000 people, with soup kitchens, sewing rooms, laundries, and clinics. The sewing rooms gave employment to hundreds of refugee women who were able and eager to make garments if the material was provided. Sanitary trains were equipped to accompany the Czech army into the interior and a rolling canteen and a station canteen were set up between Harbin and the forward lines, in which many American women cheerfully volunteered their services.

The Far East, alarmed at having the war suddenly brought so near, was thrilled at the spirit of coöperation that quickly put things into action. The Americans were at last in the great game, and the war and the Red Cross had come three-quarters of the way around the world to them. The great drama was being played on their very doorsteps.

It was August and the beginning of the Siberian winter was but ten weeks away. Refugees were still coming in, especially from the district east of Lake Baikal, pouring across the Siberian steppes to the Pacific coast where the winter was a bit milder. A few well-to-do Russians in Harbin and Vladivostok volunteered financial help and the Russian Red Cross still stood by ready to render what assistance it could. The food and clothing survey held small hope of the possibility of being able to cope with the needs of the coming season, and heavy winter underclothing, overcoats, shoes, and uniforms were needed for 75,000 Czech troops.

There was no agency to meet this demand except the Red Cross, and again the Chapter machinery was set in motion. Within a few days, quantities of knitted garments made by the women of the Mountain and Pacific Divisions were moving out of San Francisco harbor. This shipment included 250,000 pairs of socks and 250,000 sweaters. From New York came a shipment of a quantity of underclothing and mittens and 150,000 pairs of shoes, donated by the Russian Embassy at Washington for distribution by the Red Cross in Russia. An appropriation of $3,500,000 was made by the Red Cross War Council to carry on this momentous work of relief.

Some idea of the speed with which this work went forward may be had when one realizes that, despite the distance from the base of supplies and the broad and diversified program of the Red Cross in Siberia, the refugee work in Vladivostok was well in hand by the middle of August. Red Cross had in its charge 4000 children and 60,000 adults scattered through that corner of Manchuria around the city of Harbin, where the Manchu territory seems to jut up into Siberia. There were fourteen American and seven Japanese doctors in the hospitals, assisted by American, Japanese, and Chinese nurses. Fifty additional nurses and as many physicians were summoned. Altogether, quite a plant was growing up in Vladivostok. It was assuming the aspects of an industry. The whole nature of the old Siberian port had undergone a change — a relief center with its streets now filled with refugees from all points of Russia, soldiers in strange uniforms, and its hospitals filled with the wounded of foreign armies.

Incidentally no one failed to speak of the Japanese in terms of the highest praise. Their coöperation in the relief situation is said to have been magnificent. There was nothing they could do to help that was not eagerly and promptly done.

In time, the tide of war changed. Success followed the sword of the valiant Czechs, and early in September the Red Cross was called upon to furnish incidental equipment for 360,000 Russian and Czech soldiers, while the Czech commander asked the Red Cross to take entire charge of the army medical service, with the request for 100 specialists, nurses, and dentists. From Russian sources came new stories of need beyond Baikal for clothing, farm tools, kerosene, window glass, and general household items, all through the devastated regions, left bare by the retreating revolutionists. It seemed that the Russian situation was no sooner in hand than new situations sprang up. For such circumstances, the Red Cross must always be ready. The success of the Czech forces had great moral effect on the vacillating Russians. Thousands of them rallied around the victorious Czech banner, and in the heart of Russia the world's fortune once more swung in fine balance. Supplies for the use of the American troops were coming in from the United States, and there went into the interior a quantity of Red Cross supplies based on the requirements of 10,000 men and a 500-bed hospital.

AN AMERICAN RED CROSS DENTAL STATION IN SERBIA, THREE
QUARTERS OF A MILE FROM THE FRONT LINE TRENCHES.

In the meantime, chaos was having its fling in Moscow and the city found itself cut off from northern Russia, facing the winter without food, fuel, oil, or wool, and very little clothing. Moscow the luxurious was perishing; people fell in the streets from hunger. Soldiers were breaking into the homes and stripping them of all valuables and metals; telephone service was cut off; street transportation ceased; only blood and tumult from day's end to day's end remained, while in the slow Russian mind the fear that they had been tricked began to dawn.

Hanging on in the midst of all this misgovernment were the Red Cross men of the original commission who had remained despite the fact that spectators in Moscow could see no hope for Russia's regeneration, and irrespective of the orders from the United States Department of State for all Americans, official or otherwise, to leave Soviet Russia. Part of the Mission had drifted through Finland, and thence back to the Archangel district where American troops were in action; others started down the Volga Valley to see what the Czechs were doing; everywhere they found not only a visible lack of necessities at all bases of supply but infinite difficulty to be overcome before supplies could be transported to the needy quarters. While the Red Cross workers in European Russia were doing what little circumstances would permit, and while the high-speed relief work was going on in Vladivostok, a Red Cross ship laden with supplies was making its way to Archangel with food, medicines, and all manner of needs for the soldiers and civilians of north Russia and a new Red Cross Commission was ordered there to operate with the Allied and American troops that were fighting their way south, to effect a junction with the Czechs with the help of the reconstituted Russian forces. So much, at any rate, of the military situation must needs be told, in order to make the picture of Red Cross work in Russia clear. Half the time, it was like working in a bad dream. Unforeseen emergencies constantly arose, apparently insurmountable barriers continually presented themselves. Difficult enough is the work of relief in time of calamity and of war when the affected population is ready and able to coöperate, but in Russia, menaced by the constant threat of invasion from the west and the revolutionists that placed every possible obstacle in the path of law and order, it became a question of helping Russia in spite of herself; and never had the Red Cross endeavored to carry out its purpose in the midst of such adverse circumstances.

By October, the new Commission for north Russia was taking hold of the situation, and the Red Cross supply ship had reached port just in time to relieve the food conditions in Petrograd, where with the Siberian, Volga, and Ukranian food supplies cut off, starvation again threatened — if it had ever been wholly overcome. Fifty-seven per cent of the school children were sick — in some districts as high as eighty-seven per cent; infant mortality had risen to fifty per cent and degeneration, riot, and death were widespread. The city's social welfare society had 70,000 cases on its inadequate hands, many of them homeless school children. Typhus appeared in the city.

With each day bringing winter nearer, the Red Cross, in addition to its regular relief work about the base at Archangel, launched expeditions into hitherto unreached parts of the district. A Russian trawler loaded with food and medical supplies went along the White Sea coast of the Kola peninsula where the inhabitants, in virtual isolation, were facing starvation and suffering with scurvy and other diseases caused by undernourishment. Later, "antityphus" trains financed by the Allied powers, and equipped and managed by the Red Cross, made regular runs through the typhus infested regions.

So the Red Cross knocked at the heart of Russia, working steadfastly through the terrible cold, giving impartially and with largesse. I cannot but feel that the problem faced and solved so well under the most trying circumstances was an unique one, and that in Russia, above all other places, the Red Cross proved its worth in time of need as easily as it demonstrated its ability to organize and act at a moment's notice. Through it all it has kept faith with itself and with those whom it has served, and at all times it has been deeply appreciative of the ready and effective coöperation of other agents in the field — the Red Cross societies of Great Britain and Japan, the Russian and Czech Army Medical Corps, the Allied Prisoners Commission of a somewhat late date; and finally, but not the least, the warm responsive welcome of the Russian Red Cross and the Russian people.

CHAPTER XXI

THE LEAGUE OF RED CROSS SOCIETIES

The Armistice — Demobilization — Conference with President Wilson — Formation of the League of Red Cross Societies — Appointment of Chairman and Other Officers — Conference at Cannes of Medical Experts — Program of the League of Red Cross Societies.

LOOKING back, as I begin my last chapter, I realize that what I have written about the various spheres of Red Cross activities in Europe must seem unsatisfactory if not obscure and meager. Especially is this the case in the chapters which relate to Russia and the Near East where, perhaps, the lack of concrete details is more marked than anywhere else. In fairness to myself it should be said, however, that I have endeavored to refer to every important incident which came to the knowledge of the War Council from those distant countries; and, therefore, the blame, if blame there be, should rest rather on the very nature of the undertaking, which made it inevitable that not a few of the splendid efforts of our relief agencies should fail to attain their rightful place in our annals in Washington.

Thus far, patently, my task has been to deal solely with the activities of the Red Cross in the stress of war; but the time has now come when I have to concern myself with the peace efforts of the Red Cross which, despite any opinion to the contrary, must be regarded as scarcely second in importance if not more difficult than those of war. As a matter of fact, it is becoming every day more and more apparent that our foreign problem, and our home problem as well, not only 'did not end but rather began when the bugles sang truce across the battlefields.

In that infinitesimal second before the guns were suddenly quiet the whole war effort of America was at its height. Of the intense drama of that moment only the soldiers at the scene can tell; and they are strangely silent. To them, however, it brought a laying down of arms and a marching down to rest billets; to the women of the world it brought a prayer; while to the Red Cross it marked an end and a beginning — a visible end, at least, to everything connected with actual warfare, and a beginning of the fulfillment of its obligations to aid the feet of humanity in struggling along the pathway of enduring peace.

There can be no gainsaying the fact, either, that on the day of the armistice the Red Cross was doing its part and extending its efforts to the utmost. The home office at Washington, visioning months of activity ahead of it, was one of the busiest places in the National Capitol; food supplies were going forward to all parts of the world, and production was approaching its crest; the men of our foreign commissions were in action or going into action in all the war-scarred lands; and, specifically and most important of all perhaps, the Red Cross Commission in Paris, having just completed a thorough reorganization of its nine thousand loyal members, was equipped to render maximum service to our own army under whatever conditions the future exigencies of the war might develop.

In view of this great concentration of relief work at the time of the cessation of hostilities, it would be folly to suppose that the Red Cross, like the soldiers, could lay down its arms at once. Far from it. Even if we had desired to follow such a course, attainment was impossible because of the tremendous impetus behind us.

Nevertheless, little by little the thoughts of all mankind began to turn to peace and the reconstruction of the world, and it behooved the Red Cross to adjust itself to the new conditions. As a consequence, therefore, and after consultation with the heads of its European commissions, the War Council proceeded to take up the exceedingly complex question as to how the Red Cross might complete the performance of its war obligations and yet, at the earliest moment, transfer its effort to the peace organization — by no means a small undertaking, when one takes into consideration the fact that the armistice left the great organization intact, with all its energies a-tingle, and all its unspent resources free.

But, be that as it may, consistent with the results aimed at, there followed a cutting-down of production and a gradual diminishing of Red Cross work in the actual war areas; while an appreciable reduction took place in the personnel everywhere, particularly in the ranks of the volunteer war-workers who, naturally, were compelled to return to their vocations as soon as possible. Furthermore, it was decided at a conference between the President and the War Council that they should retire, and March 1 was set as the date on which the Executive Committee would become, as before the war, the permanent directing body of the American Red Cross. In this connection it gives me great pleasure to state that it was most fortunate for all concerned that Dr. Livingston Farrand was, finally, prevailed upon to accept the chairmanship of this committee.

But all the while that this transfer from a war-time to a peace-time basis was taking place, not a few of those who had followed Red Cross effort during the war were deeply impressed with the idea that it was their duty not to suffer the slightest diminution of the humanitarian spirit which the war had aroused in the American people for their fellow-beings throughout the world; that it was nothing more nor less than an obligation on the part of the American Red Cross to make certain that the results of its experience during the war should be placed at the disposal of the other Red Cross societies of the world, and vice versa.

Hence, when I presented the idea of adopting a peace-time program of Red Cross activity to President Wilson, president of the Red Cross, he grasped at once its vast importance and asked me to concentrate my efforts towards formulating some plan which would accomplish the purpose so much to be desired. Accordingly, soon after this interview I went to Europe where I called into conference the Red Cross societies of the more important countries with a view of developing a plan of coördination and coöperation. It did not take them long to recognize how vitally important it was for the future of the world that the Red Cross should have a peace-time function; yet nowhere, I am glad to say, was this more quickly and clearly realized than in the council chamber where President Wilson, M. Clemenceau, and Premiers Lloyd George and Orlando met daily to draw up the final treaty. They saw, as did every student of the situation, that there could be no peace until the peoples were able to enjoy peace of mind as well as peace of body; that no set of men could establish with pencil and paper a peace which could endure unless the distress throughout the world could be relieved. And so it came about that in the revised Covenant of the League of Nations there was inserted the following paragraph as Article XXV:—

"The members of the League agree to encourage and promote the establishment and coöperation of duly authorized, voluntary, national Red Cross organizations having as their purpose the improvement of health, prevention of disease, and mitigation of suffering throughout the world."

And, indeed, as a whole it was a wretched world, a ragged, frightened, helpless world with so little to rebuild with and so little to cling to. Perhaps it thought that the transition to peace would be easy; perhaps it did not fully grasp the extent of the wastage of the last five years; perhaps it did not realize the hunger and pestilence and dearth that war had engendered. On the other hand, nothing but the armed conflict of half the world could have aroused the people to the possibilities of the Red Cross; nothing but the agony caused by the destruction of all the factors of existence — houses and bridges, roads and fields and, in a sense, even life itself — could have shown the need of a universal organization for the promotion of good will wherever human life exists. In a word, these thoughts, far easier to feel than to express, united to form the idea of the League of Red Cross Societies which, with Article XXV of the League of Nations as a sort of international charter, came formally into being in Paris, May 5, 1919. There were present delegates from the Red Cross organizations of the United States, Great Britain, France, Italy, and Japan, whose representatives constitute the board of governors, of which board I was chosen chairman, and by which Sir David Henderson was appointed director-general. At a later date Professor William Rappard, of the University of Geneva, became secretary-general.

Invitations to join the league have been issued to the Red Cross societies of the following countries: Argentina, Australia, Belgium, Brazil, Canada, Chili, China, Cuba, Denmark, Greece, Holland, India, New Zealand, Norway, Peru, Portugal, Rumania, Serbia, South Africa, Spain, Sweden, Switzerland, Uruguay, and Venezuela. Eventually, of course, it is confidently expected that every nation in the world will have a representative in the League of Red Cross Societies which, already, has begun to function at its established headquarters in Geneva. At this point, therefore, if only to avoid any misunderstanding, I think it advisable to state authoritatively that while the relations between the League of Red Cross Societies and the League of Nations will be of an intimate character there will be no statuary

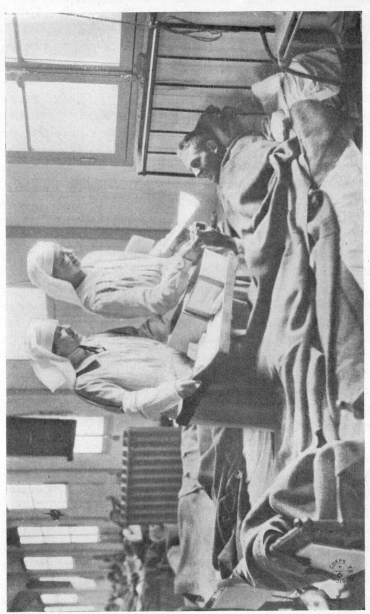

"SECONDARY AID."

With the American Red Cross in the Argonne.

connection, since the League of Red Cross Societies is essentially a voluntary organization, non-political, non-governmental, and non-sectarian.

But even while the League of Red Cross Societies was in process of formation, there was practically no limit to the reports, which came from every quarter of Europe and Asia, that the distress was beyond computation; that the vitality of whole nations had been lowered almost to the death point; that entire populations were without clothing; and that it was certain that there would be a shortage of fuel and food at the approach of winter. At best, it was a situation so appalling that the governments alone could handle it satisfactorily, even if the governments did only the major part of the work, leaving the minor part to the voluntary organizations. And in view of all this it may be pertinent to give here the objects of the League of Red Cross Societies as set forth in the articles of association :—

1. To encourage and promote in every country in the world the establishment and development of duly authorized voluntary national Red Cross organizations, having as their purpose the improvement of health, prevention of disease, and mitigation of suffering throughout the world, and to secure the coöperation of such organizations for these purposes.

2. To promote the welfare of mankind by furnishing the medium for bringing within the reach of all peoples the benefits to be derived from present known facts and new contributions to science and medical knowledge and their application.

3. To furnish the medium for coördinating relief work in case of great national or international calamities.

As will readily be seen the plan as adopted here, taken as a whole, is a conception which involves not merely efforts to relieve human suffering but purposes to prevent it; to relieve not the suffering of one people alone but an attempt to arouse all peoples to a sense of their responsibility for the welfare of their fellow-beings throughout the world. But vast as is the scope of the program of the League of Red Cross Societies, its application, nevertheless, is simple, practical, and scientific. It could hardly be otherwise since it received the unanimous indorsement of an unique gathering of medical experts who at the invitation of the Red Cross met at Cannes, France, in April, 1919. This conference, by the way, was presided over by Professor Roux, the successor in Paris of Pasteur, and Dr. William H. Welch, of Johns Hopkins University, and also included many of the foremost men of America, France, England, Italy, and Japan. All in all it was regarded as one of the most remarkable gatherings of health experts ever held.

These experts adopted at the conference a minute declaring that a great part of the world-wide prevalence of disease and suffering is due to widespread ignorance and lack of application of well-established facts and methods capable either of largely restricting disease or preventing it. "Altogether we have carefully considered," the minute asserts, "the general purpose of the Committee of the Red Cross Societies to spread light of science and warmth of human sympathy into every corner of the world; and we are confident that this movement, assured as it is at the outset of the moral support of civilization, has in it great possibilities of adding immeasurably to the happiness and welfare of mankind." That statement represents the judgment of men who are qualified to speak with the highest authority on the subject of the great scourges of humanity, such as tuberculosis, malaria, venereal diseases, and epidemics; men who are authorities on preventive medicine and who represent the knowledge of the world in the great field of child welfare. It is their belief, based on certain scientific knowledge, acquired by practical experience, that these scourges can be controlled, or even eliminated, by organized, coördinated effort and coöperation. Moreover, regarding the proposed plans, the consensus of these experts was that they should be put into effect and placed at the disposal of the world at the earliest possible moment. They, also, claimed that in no way can the work be done so effectively as through the agency of the Red Cross.

Through its headquarters at Geneva, the League of Red Cross Societies plans to stimulate peace-time activities of all National Red Cross Societies, and to help them to grow and to carry out the program of the Cannes conference for a world-wide public health campaign. It is not the thought that the National Red Cross Societies themselves should have the responsibilities of the actual work of safeguarding and improving public health, but that each society should stimulate and encourage the natural agencies for such work within their respective countries, including the departments of health of their governments; and in cases where such departments do not exist, the societies should endeavor to create public sentiment for the establishment of such departments.

Another point to be noted is that the League of Red Cross Societies will supplement the work of the International Committee of the Red Cross of Geneva, acting in harmony with it; in no way will it supersede, absorb, or conflict with the activities of national societies, but on the contrary it will put at their disposal the latest knowledge and approved practices of experts in public health and preventive medicines throughout the world. In all probability its immediate functions will be to coördinate relief work in combating pestilence such as typhus.

In conclusion, I wish to say that actual experience has demonstrated beyond all doubt that the people of all nations are quick and eager to seize and act upon knowledge that leads to increased happiness. It would seem, therefore, that the far-reaching effects of the program of the League of Red Cross Societies may be measured by the suffering which exists and which it purposes to relieve. Hand in

U

hand with the world campaign for the betterment of public health will go the improvement of social and economic conditions of humanity, and a protective union, as it were, with all working together in a spirit of kindly consideration and coöperation for the common good. Surely this spirit of service among the peoples cannot fail to develop a new fraternity and sympathy to a degree not dreamed of hitherto; surely the League of Red Cross Societies has a glorious future in the field of human kindness ahead of it.

APPENDIX

THE Red Cross War Council was appointed May 10, 1917. It went out of existence on February 28th, 1919.

The First War Fund Drive for $100,000,000 was held in the week June 18 to June 25, 1917, and resulted in reported subscriptions of approximately $114,000,000. The Second War Fund Drive was held in the week May 18 to May 25, 1918, and resulted in reported subscriptions of approximately $170,000,000. Under the financial plan, Chapters were permitted to withdraw 25 per cent of their collections against War Funds, the remaining 75 per cent being at the disposal of the Red Cross War Council.

Up to the conclusion of the administration of the War Council there had been collected against the two War Funds a total of approximately $283,599,000, of which $229,799,000 had been credited to National Headquarters and $53,800,000 withdrawn by Chapters.

As the figures show, the total revenues of National Headquarters and Chapters for the twenty months ending February 28, 1919, were $400,178,000, and during that period the total expenditures amounted to $272,676,000. Thus when the War Council turned over the affairs of the Red Cross to its Executive Committee, the permanent administrative body, the total resources of the National Headquarters amounted to $110,756,000. This money was represented by supplies held in the United States and overseas valued at $48,678,000; cash advances amounting to $12,834,000, and current assets amounting to $52,606,000. Against the foregoing assets there were appropriations, which had not been expended and yet which constituted an obligation, amounting to $16,714,000. Thus the total net resources of National Headquarters were $94,042,000.

On the same date the balance in the hands of Chapters amounted to $33,460,000.

The accounts of the Red Cross are audited by the War Department and the full report is annually submitted to Congress. Details of receipts and expenditures of course are covered by these audited reports, which, however, only cover the period of successive fiscal years. The figures given below cover the finances of the Red Cross for the period during which the War Council was in control of its affairs.

AMERICAN NATIONAL RED CROSS

REVENUES

Twenty Months Ending February 28, 1919

NATIONAL HEADQUARTERS —

First War Drive Collections	$ 92,947,000.00	
Second War Drive Collections	136,852,000.00	
Membership Dues	18,930,000.00	
Donations of Surplus Funds from Chapters	1,420,000.00	
Interest	3,157,000.00	
Other Revenues	6,697,000.00	
Total Revenues — National Headquarters	$260,003,000.00	
Add — Fund Balance, June 30, 1917	3,135,000.00	$263,138,000.00

CHAPTERS —

Chapters' Proportion of War Drives	$ 53,800,000.00	
Chapters' Proportion of Membership Dues	18,440,000.00	
Chapters' Proportion of Class Fees	390,000.00	
Sales of Materials to Members for Relief Articles	20,290,000.00	
Contributions, Legacies, Gifts	9,580,000.00	
All Other Revenue	31,340,000.00	
Total Revenues — Chapters	$133,840,000.00	
Add — Balance, June 30, 1917	3,200,000.00	$137,040,000.00
Total Revenues — National Headquarters and Chapters		$400,178,000.00

AMERICAN NATIONAL RED CROSS

EXPENDITURES

Twenty Months Ending February 28, 1919

NATIONAL HEADQUARTERS —

War Relief in France	$57,207,000.00
War Relief Elsewhere Overseas . .	63,841,000.00
War Relief in United States . . .	28,978,000.00
Disaster Relief	939,000.00
Collections, Enrollments and Publications	4,660,000.00
Operation of Relief Bureaus . . .	2,727,000.00
Operation of Bureaus for Handling Relief Supplies, also, Transportation in United States of Relief Supplies	5,530,000.00
Operation of Administrative Bureaus at National and Divisional Headquarters	4,360,000.00
Other Activities	854,000.00

Total National Headquarters $169,096,000.00

CHAPTERS —

Materials Purchased for Relief Articles	$60,660,000.00
Canteen Service	2,320,000.00
Equipment of Military Hospitals, Ambulances, etc.	3,070,000.00
Home Service	8,790,000.00
Miscellaneous War Relief	480,000.00
Spanish Influenza Epidemic Relief Work	1,680,000.00
Disaster Relief	520,000.00
Public Health Nursing	380,000.00
Transportation of Materials and Supplies	290,000.00
General Operating Expenses . . .	7,490,000.00
All Other Expenditures	17,900,000.00

Total Chapters $103,580,000.00

Total Expenditures — National Headquarters
and Divisions $272,676,000.00

AMERICAN NATIONAL RED CROSS

RESOURCES

February 28, 1919

NATIONAL HEADQUARTERS —
Supplies —

In United States	$27,698,000.
Overseas	20,980,000.
Total	$48,678,000.

Cash Advances — (To Provide Working Capital)

Overseas Commissions	$ 9,509,000.
Divisions in United States	2,994,000.
Miscellaneous	331,000.
Total	$12,834,000.

Current Assets —

Cash in Banks	$19,063,000.
Cash and Securities in Hands of War Finance Committee	31,703,000.
Securities Owned	1,206,000.
Bills Receivable	3,000.
Miscellaneous Accounts Receivable	631,000.
Total	$52,606,000.
Less — Accounts Payable	3,362,000.
	$49,244,000.

Total Resources Nat. Hdqrs. (Exc. End. Fund)	$110,756,000.
Less — Amount Obligated by Appropriations but not Expended on February 28, 1919	16,714,000.
Net Resources National Headquarters (Excluding Endowment Fund)	$ 94,042,000.

CHAPTERS —

Balance February 28, 1919	33,460,000.
Total Resources (Excluding Endowment Fund)	$127,502,000.

Endowment Fund

Balance July 1, 1917	$ 1,361,000.
Add — Revenues 20 Months to February 28, 1919	1,072,000.
Total	$ 2,433,000.
Less — Income Payments to National Organization, A.R.C.	106,000.
Balance — February 28, 1919 . .	$ 2,327,000.

The following statistics may also be of interest. They represent the great volume of production and work which the American Red Cross undertook both at home and abroad : —

Red Cross members: adult, 20,000,000; children, 11,000,000	31,000,000
Red Cross workers	8,100,000
Relief articles produced by volunteer workers	371,577,000 [1]
Families of soldiers and sailors aided by Home Service in the United States	500,000
Refreshments served by canteen workers in U. S. . . .	40,000,000
Nurses enrolled for service with Army or Navy or Red Cross	23,822
Kinds of comfort articles distributed to soldiers and sailors in U. S.	2,700
Knitted articles given to soldiers and sailors in United States	10,900,000
Tons of relief supplies shipped overseas	101,000
Foreign countries in which the Red Cross operated . . .	25
Patient days in Red Cross hospitals in France	1,155,000
French hospitals given material aid	3,780

[1] Representing: Surgical dressings	306,967,000
Hospital garments.	17,462,000
Hospital supplies	14,211,000
Refugee garments	6,329,000
Articles for soldiers and sailors . . .	23,329,000
Unclassified	3,279,000
Total	371,577,000

Splints supplied for American soldiers 294,000
Gallons of nitrous oxide and oxygen furnished hospitals in
    France 4,340,000
Men served by Red Cross canteens in France 15,376,000
Refugees aided in France 1,726,000
American convalescent soldiers attending Red Cross
    movies in France 3,110,000
Soldiers carried by Red Cross ambulances in Italy . . . 148,000
Children cared for by Red Cross in Italy 155,000

INDEX

Ægean Sea, Red Cross work on islands of, 261.

Allied Prisoners' Commission, 281.

Ambulance Corps, Red Cross, 21; sections absorbed in Army Medical Corps, 141–142; sections established on Italian front, 213, 215.

Ambulance drivers, heroism of, 139–141.

Ambulance ship *Surf*, 55–56.

Ambulances, for naval establishment, 61.

American Committee for Armenian and Syrian relief, coöperation of, with Red Cross, 255; cable from, to Red Cross War Council, on conditions in Palestine, 261–262.

American Hostels for Refugees, 158.

American Library Association, 50.

American Relief Clearing House in Paris, 4.

American Society for Relief of French Orphans, 158.

Annel, story of hospital at, 138–139.

Archangel, Red Cross ship sent to, 279; relief work base at, 280.

Armenians, relief work among, in Palestine, 265.

Athens, work of Red Cross for children in, 260–261.

Austrians, defeat of, by Italian army, 215, 217–219.

Baker, Secretary, requests Red Cross to take over service at railroad stations, 39.

Baltimore, Institute for Blind in, 130.

Baltimore export warehouse, report of, 120.

Base hospitals, personnel for, supplied by Red Cross, 56–57; fifty furnished to army by Red Cross, 144; entertainment supplied at, in France, by Red Cross, 146–147.

Base Hospital Units, organization of, 81–83; amount spent on, 83; active work of, on declaration of war, 83–85; abandonment of system, 85.

Basle, care of *évacués* in, 188.

Belgian children, in Switzerland, 190.

Belgians, in France, work for, 153–156.

Belgium, appointment of special Red Cross department for, 22; German vandalism in, 193; heroic qualities of, 193–194; the Red Cross to the rescue of, 194; work in, organized as a department of French Commission, 195–196; problem of living quarters for refugees, 196–197; coördination of relief agencies for, 197–198; plight of army of, 198–199; Red Cross relief work for army, 199–201; Red Cross work supplementary only to that of Government of, 201–202; erection of barrack houses in, 202; stocks of food supplies prepared, 203; splendid work done by Queen of, 204–205; work of Countess Van Steen, 205–206; other private enterprises of relief in, 206; the *Colonies Scolaires*, 206.

Beltiu, Rumania, gruesome conditions in, 236.

Bernstorff, Count von, departure of, from Washington, 4.

Biddle, General, quoted, 225.

Blind, reëducation of the, 126–127; Institute for the, in Baltimore, 130.

Brest, base hospitals in, 57.

British Red Cross, coöperation of, with American Red Cross in Rumania, 245. *See* Great Britain.

British Relief Fund for Palestine and Syria, 262.

Brooklyn, U. S. cruiser, converted into a floating hospital, 275.

Bureau International de la Paix, 180–181.

Bureaus under Red Cross administration, 38.

Cæsar, cargo of, bought by Red Cross, 255.

California, Junior Red Cross activities in, 97, 98.

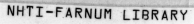